DISH & TELL

Believe,
Patricia

Always
Trust your
instincts

Dare to Dream!
Annie

Be yourself!

BOMBS
away!
Lauren
from Miami

Be a bombshell!
Sara

DISH & TELL

Life, Love, and Secrets

THE MIAMI BOMBSHELLS

Patricia San Pedro

Mercedes Soler

Annie San Roman

Tammi Leader Fuller

Lydia Sacasa

Sara Rosenberg

wm

WILLIAM MORROW

An Imprint of HarperCollinsPublishers

FIRST EDITION

Designed by Nicola Ferguson

Printed on acid-free paper

Library of Congress Cataloging-in-Publication Data

San Pedro, Patricia.
    Dish and tell : life, love, and secrets / the Miami Bombshells and Patricia San Pedro.— 1st ed.
       p. cm.
     ISBN 0-06-077771-0 (acid-free paper)
     1. Women—Florida—Miami—Biography. 2. Women in the professions—Florida—Miami—Biography. 3. Working mothers—Florida—Miami—Biography. 4. Women—Psychology. 5. Work and family. 6. Self-realization in women. I. Miami Bombshells. II. Title.

HQ1439.M45S35   2005
305.4'09759'381—dc22   2005041557

05 06 07 08 09 DIX/QWF 10 9 8 7 6 5 4 3 2 1

Daisy, my amazing mother, whose spirit has guided this book from its inception. Even though you left us way too early, you set an example for my life with your love, strength, and determination. You're always with me. For Tony, my dad whom I adore—you are, have been, and always will be the most important man in my life. Thank you for always taking care of me. *Te quiere tu cuquita. Mua!*

—*Patricia*

Emilio, my rock, and to the five Gigis in my life who make it worth living: Chelsea and Courtney (my loving *principesas*), JoJo and Rara (my fabulous sisters), and most of all—the incredible Grandy and Papa Jookie. The gifts you've bestowed on me just keep on giving and I thank you for every one of them . . . ILYMTYLM—Betcha owe me!

—*Tammi*

My family, without whom I wouldn't have these stories to tell (you made me, you made me crazy, you make me happy . . .). And especially to my Sparky, who pretends he can't tell the difference between the sane days and crazy days, and tells me he loves me every day, no matter what.

—*Sara*

To my husband, Mario, and my children: Manny, Christine, and Andres, whom I love unconditionally. To the most important women in my life: my mother, my sister, and my nieces Terry and Eli. To my *abuela,* who instilled in me the strong work ethic that helped me excel in life, and to my father, whose moral values have always guided me in the right path. *Papi,* your lively soul will forever live within me.

—*Lydia*

To the two people I love most in this world: my children, Jackie and Andres. To my parents who are always there for me, no matter what. To my *amigas,* Belen and Maria, you are the sisters I never had. And to every woman who has persisted on a journey, in spite of all the bumps on the road.

—Annie

My pillars. A few months before he died, my dad asked me to focus the passion we both shared for books into developing one of my own. I dedicate my contributions here to his memory and to all the other great loves that sustain me: my one and only, wonderful children; adoring mother; my second mother, Adriana; my loving sister Lili; and my twin, Mery, who is my best friend, my conscience, and my hero.

—Mercedes

CONTENTS

Acknowledgments

Thank you! Thank you! Thank you!

It took three years and at least three dozen incarnations to get this book finished, but it was the collaborative generosity of what seemed like three hundred friends and supporters who opened up their hearts, brilliant minds, and expertise to help us get this book to you. We call them our "Honorary Bombshells." To them, we take off our hats. They rock!

In the early days, it was BARBARA GUTIERREZ, the editor behind one of America's leading Spanish-language newspapers, *El Nuevo Herald,* who helped us shape our stories. She found our stories to be full of "golden nuggets" and convinced us we were on to something. When LIZA GROSS left the top newspaper in Puerto Rico to help run the *Miami Herald,* she packed our manuscript in her suitcase with the rest of her belongings. First week on the job, she played two roles, managing editor of the newspaper by day and book editor by night. Liza was the one who held up that proverbial mirror and made us see that we really *were* every woman, then sharpened her pencil and became our ingenious "book doctor," putting us on the track that led us here. It was ultimately JOAN LEADER, Tammi's mother, a former university professor, who inadvertently became our de facto, unofficial editor, helping us rewrite this book for the umpteenth time. Her wisdom and positive outlook were like a cup of warm chamomile tea juxtaposed against our frantic e-mail chatter. We love our Official Mom-shell Joan.

Our legal eagles, ALAN ROSENTHAL and GREG ST. JOHN (Adorno and Yoss, P.A.), lit the way for us to protect our interests, in spite of our willingness to bind our legal business in blood with the prick of a finger. We drove them nuts with naive questions, burning up what should have been thousands of dollars in billable hours, though they never charged us a dime.

We thank them profusely for their patience and their brilliance, especially Alan, who held our hands every step of the way and was on his cell with us nights, weekends, and holidays. To attorneys BONNIE SOCKEL STONE and JOHN FULLER (Tammi's beloved ex-husband), we say thanks for setting us up and helping guide us on our journey to Sixcess from the very beginning.

Kudos and thanks go out to Planning Group International, especially GASTON LEGORBURU and BILL BITTORF (Sara's terrific husband), for bringing us into the twenty-first century. Gaston is an incredible web visionary who "got" the potential of the Internet long before others could see it. They put www.miamibombshells.com on the web map with help from CAROL MONTOTO, ALLISON BISTRONG, ARIEL BELLUMIO, PATRICK MACDOUGALL, STEVEN NEDLIN, and NOAH SCHEINER. And thanks to JAYME LAM from 4thReaction.com for helping us get our original website up and running.

Special thanks go out to MITCHELL KAPLAN, from Books & Books, the most beloved bookstore in Miami. He was our guiding light and gave us hope and support from the beginning, no questions asked. CAROLINA GARCIA AGUILERA, seasoned author and friend, counseled and advised us from her huge heart. To her, and to RAQUEL ROQUE from Downtown Books, we say *muchas gracias,* as well as to our friends DICK and CAREN LOBO from Sarasota Books & Café, whose friendship and guidance have been such blessings.

We are eternally grateful to DAVE BARRY, the funniest man in the world, who inadvertently introduced us to SCOTT WAXMAN, who in turn brought us to our incredible agent, SALLY WOFFORD-GIRAND, at

Brickhouse Literary Agency. Sally believed in us from day one and brought us, on a silver platter, to HarperCollins/William Morrow, our publisher.

Mucho amor and immense gratitude goes to CLAIRE WACHTEL, the best executive editor we've ever had (OK, so we've never had one before, but we know it doesn't get any better than this!). We loved her from the moment we met her, maybe because she believed we'd fit into William Morrow as perfectly as a pair of Jimmy Choos. Thanks to our fabulous publicists: DEBBIE STIER, PAMELA SPENGLER-JAFFEE, and HEATHER GOULD for turning us into media celebrities, to KEVIN CALLAHAN for his sense of humor, daily e-mails, and support, and to RICHARD AQUAN, an art director with heart. He masterminded the awesome book jacket that jumped right off the shelf and into your hands!

Lots of love and thanks to our TV friends for believing in us and donating their time and energy to helping us document our evolution on videotape: to RICK CIKOWSKI for his countless hours and creativity in the edit room, and to NIKKI KONEFSKY, EMILY FRIAS, DALE WEST, CHRIS NICKLESS, and RAUL HERNANDEZ for their invaluable help.

Special thanks to MINDY FRUMKES BAER for being our video "voice," to OUTPOST AUDIO for bringing it to us loud and clear, and to SCOTT ALAN HAIR STUDIO for "dolling" us up for the cameras on our first TV shoot.

Nothing beats the "Diva-for-a-Day" feeling we got the day we shot the cover of this book. But it was the behind-the-camera people who were the actual stars. We bow in honor of our stellar photographer ALEXIS RODRIGUEZ-DUARTE. He captured our true essence while turning us into real bombshells. Master makeup and hair artist LAZZ RODRIGUEZ forbade us the use of fake eyelashes (though Mercedes begged, to no avail) and insisted on emphasizing our natural, everyday/every-woman look. We applaud his wisdom. He was assisted by makeup artist CATRIEL LEIRAS. And thanks also to celebrity makeup artist BEVERLY FINK. Last but not least, a round of applause to mother-daughter stylist duo TERESITA AND JESSICA MIRANDA, who coordinated our wardrobes with clothing from Dillard's and Caché at the Falls (thanks MARTHA ESTRADA). Together, this group of professionals actually helped us believe that dreams really can come true.

A big "you are marvelous" to IVON CARRILLO, who took on double duty at San Pedro Productions so Pat could concentrate on this book. A big kiss *(mua)!*

Many others also helped us in our quest to deliver *Dish & Tell.* Our accountant, STEWART LIEBLING, taught us to understand the financial lingo, and MARK STEIN, our trademark lawyer, advised us well. Special regards go to KLEVER GUERRERO, who designed the very funky Miami Bombshells book proposal cover that ultimately brought interest from six New York publishing companies, and also to JESSICA JONAP, book publicist extraordinaire, for teaching us the rules of the game, and to WENDY ROBBINS, for her tireless, tedious work in helping us get this book out. Thanks for helping us get noticed.

Melodious notes of gratitude go to our very own Latin jazz flutist (and Latin Grammy winner) NESTOR TORRES, who not only edited some of the original chapters in this book, but is also working on the Miami Bombshells theme song. Keep the music and inspiration flowing, maestro! We all love you (especially Pat).

And to all the other characters who fill up our lives, we say *thank you, gracias,* and *todah rabah* for sharing in our dream to become the Miami Bombshells. We couldn't have gotten here without you!

—*Patricia, Tammi, Sara, Lydia, Annie, and Mercedes*

And last but certainly not least, the rest of us want to express our love and appreciation to our dear friend Pat, for bringing us together, and for all the blood and sweat she has poured into this experiment. Without her, this book could not have been written and would certainly have never been published. We are indebted to her for life and pray that we'll all be together in the next one.

In the Beginning . . .

We see you, stealing a glance at these pages during your lunch break, in between errands, late at night, or in the bathroom while your kids and husbands are calling your name, and you pretend not to hear. We know all about you because we're just like you.

We're fortysomething, successful career women who are *not* perfect. We don't have adequate time for our families, yeast infections, root canals, grocery shopping, or, especially, ourselves. Because most of us are the major breadwinners in our homes, we're sleep deprived, work too hard, and don't work out enough.

We've lived through the ups and downs of womanhood just like you: from happy marriages to painful divorces, from the joys of childbirth to burying our parents, from fighting depression and raging hormones to making tough career choices, juggling daily life, and setting out on spiritual journeys. We've captured the full breadth of what it means to be a woman in the twenty-first century, and we are exhausted.

Think of us as a bunch of complicated women riddled with guilt—overworked and underappreciated—reaching out to you, our stressed-out sisters, to reassure you that it's time to take a breather, let go a little, and trust that all will be OK. None of us is flawless, though we were once under the impression that perfection was a requirement of the female species. That may be why, between us, we have seven plastic surgeries under our belts (though all our breasts are saline-free). Now we know better. Or maybe, finally, we've accepted the notion that it just doesn't matter anymore.

Consider this book authorized voyeurism. Take a peek into our lives to see how we're coping, struggling, growing, and ultimately finding contentment in the lives we've created for ourselves. All it takes is a sense of humor, courage, a willingness to let go, and a circle of other women who understand. That's what we found in one another.

A full lifetime of rambunctious living is what qualifies us to write this book. Between us, we've had our share of relationships; all of us have been married, some more than once. We've seen the other side of marriage, too (divorce, and even affairs), but no matter what the experiences, we've emerged stronger because of them.

As the Miami Bombshells, we are redefining what it means to be a bombshell. News Flash: It's more about being courageous than curvaceous. It's also knowing that beauty and sensuality is a state of mind, and that the only way to live is to grab life by the horns and squeeze the essence out of every moment.

We are overachievers who wanted it all, got it all, and eventually became entangled in the strings attached. We are women just like you, only we're willing to hang out our dirty laundry on this literary clothesline, hoping you will see just how much our species is alike, no matter how different we may appear on the outside.

We all share a collective vulnerability and hidden strength. This became evident when we began monthly meetings at one another's homes to whine and wine. We would get together, gorge on the obligatory chocolate, drink the required *vino,* kick off the power pumps, and start talking. Those sessions became the seeds for this book.

None of us knew each other at first, but we shared one common denominator: a deep-seated love for our friend Pat. We trusted her enough that when she asked us to form a "women's group," we cleared our calendars and did it with open minds. We took our time to get to know one another and, eventually, began to share intimate secrets and listen without casting judgment. It was a process we grew into slowly and carefully; but when each of us finally took that gutsy plunge, it was incredibly cathartic.

We came clean about our daily challenges, balancing our high-powered jobs, insanely accelerated schedules, and schizophrenic lives, and we divulged our most telling romantic and sexual secrets. We fell into this sisterhood when we realized we weren't alone, and that it feels much better to try and tackle life together.

After several sharing sessions, it became evident that our lives had all the components of a good Spanish-language soap opera, that is, a *novela*. That's when we decided to write this book, beginning our journey into very unfamiliar territory. The goal was to liberate ourselves from the rigors of everyday combustion and sheer fatigue through introspection and validation. Some of our stories are funny, some are full of depth and raw emotions; others are just a bit outrageous, which only proves that truth really is much stranger, and a lot more interesting, than fiction.

We wrote honestly and openly, and, inevitably, we started dropping Bombshells. There was the time we were counting up our sexual encounters and someone admitted to having been raped. BOMBSHELL! Or the time a few of us fessed up to having had affairs, living with and covering up for a bipolar lover, or getting a limp organ to perform. BOMBSHELL!

Those stories became the Bombshell stories, anonymous to protect the innocent, or more accurately, the guilty. We all have families, and many loved ones we want to protect. After reading our stories and getting to know us, you might try to figure out who wrote the unsigned Bombshell stories. But we'll never tell.

Our ethnic backgrounds add flavor and spice to our storytelling. Four of us are Cuban, the other two are American born and Jewish, which makes the guilt part pretty self-explanatory. We discovered there's very little difference between Jewish and Catholic guilt. Five of us were raised in that hot, muggy, and politically incorrect city called Miami; one grew up in Cuba, Spain, and, ultimately, Chicago. *Spanglish* is the official Miami Bombshell language and café Cubano fuels our drive. We always ask our gringa friends, why would anyone spend $3.50 on a latte when a 35-cent espresso in Little Havana can deliver an all-day buzz?

We don't want to preach, only to inspire, and at the very least, encourage you to find a circle of women with whom you can grab a glass of wine, unload your troubles, and remove your mask. A wonderful thing happens when it peels away; you begin to embrace your inner demons and start loving yourself for who you really are. Only *then* will you become a true BOMBSHELL!

Meet the Miami Bombshells

Patricia (Pat) San Pedro is a three-time Emmy Award–winning television producer turned airline spokesperson turned newspaper executive turned marketing and public relations entrepreneur. Twice divorced, she is childless and single. Pat believes in working hard . . . and playing harder, spending sixty hours a week running her business in addition to the twenty hours she expends conjuring up community projects and volunteering for charities. Still, Pat has enough energy on weekends to dance till the wee hours of the morning. Pat functions from both sides of her brain, playing the corporate executive as skillfully as the creative bohemian artist. She is a spiritual being who loves nature, animals, and people. Nobody forgets Pat once they meet her, because she makes you feel like you really matter. And to Pat, you do.

Mercedes Soler is a world-renowned senior news correspondent for Univision, the Spanish-language television network. Mercedes claims to have unexpectedly tripped over God in Machu Picchu, Peru, while reporting on a story. The effect changed her life and she has since become an aspiring shaman. She's won five Emmys for her solid reporting and skillful interviews, which include ones with more than a dozen Latin American presidents. Blessed with the gift of expression—in both English and Spanish—Mercedes speaks and writes with the same exuberance she brings to life. Mercedes is married to her one and only and they have two small children they're simply crazy about. This diva has a heart of gold and is drenched in Cuban sugarcane sweetness.

Annie San Roman, a natural blond, blue-eyed Cuban beauty, is a well-respected school psychologist who counseled violent juvenile delinquents for almost twenty years. She has now left the war zone and is working with severely emotionally disturbed adolescents. Annie is obsessed with pearls and leopard prints, and everything in her world, from furniture to underwear, is spotted. When she is not counseling or calming down parents, she is designing outrageous handbags made from authentic cigar boxes. Annie is also the football fanatic of the group; we honestly think she puts on a jockstrap at the beginning of every fall season. After twenty-four years of marriage, Annie is embarking on a new life as a single woman. She has two teenage children, a daughter and a son who is known as DJ Infamous. On most weekends, Annie is carting her son's sound equipment all over Miami, while worrying where her daughter is out partying.

Tammi Leader Fuller is an Emmy Award–winning network television producer with the power to plaster your face on the evening news if you've been bad, or help bring you national recognition if you've done something really worthwhile. Known as Tammi-in-Miami, her television production company is flourishing because many of her clients consider her one of the country's leading producers. She's worked hard to get to the top. Her two darling daughters never knew, until now, that before her TV incarnation, their workaholic mom, who divorced after fifteen years of marriage, spent a whole year teaching topless aerobics at a Caribbean Island resort. Eleven years ago, she and her mother founded a nonprofit organization to help abused and neglected children; this is, by far, Tammi's proudest accomplishment.

Lydia Sacasa is a mortgage executive who has dedicated her professional life to the successful opening and restructuring of mortgage offices for several national banks. Currently a senior vice president, Lydia can't seem to ever shut off the job. She keeps her Weight Watchers points' guide in her BlackBerry, which gets buried under her pillow at night, just in case an important message comes in. Passionate about designer handbags (real ones!) and thousand-count bed sheets, she is just as passionate about stopping at the Krispy Kreme shop when the "HOT NOW" sign is flashing. Diet or no diet, Lydia's love for life keeps her singing at the top of her lungs with gusto. Active in several nonprofit organizations, Lydia is married, for the second time, with three children, three stepchildren, and now a gorgeous little granddaughter who just turned her into the only granny Bombshell.

Sara Rosenberg is aging out of her role as the youngest person at the executive level. Having achieved career highs at a young age, introducing new products for Fortune 500 companies, she's now on her own as a consultant, specializing in marketing to women. Despite wearing the vice president corporate persona, she has always refused to conform and has been spotted at board meetings sporting blue-streaked hair to express her creativity and test the bounds of political correctness. We call her the "Smart Tart" because her personality fluctuates between the free spirit of an artist and the rigidity of a control freak. We can always count on her for her outrageous outfits and razor-sharp sense of humor. With a hard edge to those who don't know her, Sara has a soft, mushy center for people and causes close to her heart. She is married, round two, with one son and two stepsons.

one | Occupational Hazards

Work. It rules our lives, causing us to be cranky, tired, and stressed. Hard work has taken most of us to the top rung of the corporate ladder, and the money we make helps us justify our inability to balance the demands of work with a regular life, which includes time for family and friends, many of whom have dumped us. Most of us have put in our forty hours by Wednesday, and eat at least five meals a week in our cars or at our desks.

"Hooray! I'm all alone! I can do whatever I want!" Lydia shrieked with glee as we wrapped up a recent Bombshell meeting at her home one Sunday afternoon. She was jumping up and down like a small child at an amusement park. Her husband had taken the kids out of the house, and Lydia looked around like she had never really seen the place empty before. Her home was always filled with people: children, Mami, her granddaughter, or friends.

"What do you want to do?" asked Pat.

"Whatever." It didn't matter. Lydia never had time like this to herself, with no errands to run, e-mails to check, or calls to return.

Some of us look at her questioningly. "I've been working like a maniac," she explains, "twelve- to fourteen-hour days, every day. I work at home, I work on Sundays." As a mortgage banker, Lydia has work to do at all hours just to catch up on what piles up during the week.

"She works in her sleep," interjects Pat, laughing.

"Yes, I wake up at three in the morning thinking of solutions to issues in the office," says Lydia, completely unaware that Pat's comment is a joke.

"It wears me down. I want to spend more time with my children, I want to be able to see them; they're growing up too quickly. But I made my bed with designer sheets," Lydia is fond of saying, "and now I have to lie in them."

She'd like to slow down one day; we'd all like to at some point. Or maybe we wouldn't, and just fantasize about having the financial freedom to choose where we work, when we work, and why we work.

Both Sara and Pat left their cushy corporate jobs to start new businesses. Each had hoped that the life of a consultant would allow for flexible working hours and more time for themselves. But it didn't happen that way, admitted both Sara and Pat, who now grumble when working 24/7, since every hour is a billable one and a mortgage payment is always sneaking up on them.

Annie, on the other hand, is a school psychologist who works 8 A.M. to 4 P.M. We tease her that she's the one with the real banker's hours. Her stress, which is probably more real than any of ours, comes from counseling emotionally disturbed teens. But when Annie goes home, she leaves her work behind. She's the only one of the Bombshells who does.

When we got the call from our New York literary agent telling us six publishers were interested in our *Dish & Tell* book, we immediately called and made our travel reservations. All of us except Annie, who felt guilty about leaving her family. But after encouragement from a coworker and flak from the other Bombshells, twelve hours before takeoff, Annie changed her mind.

It was her first official business trip. As we boarded the plane from Miami to New York, Annie, still in disbelief, confessed, "I can't believe I'm going to New York to meet with book publishers. This is so *big time*! The farthest I've been from home, for work, is ten miles when I've gone to local school conferences to discuss the changing role of school psychologists!"

"That's our Annie," smiled Tammi. "This is why we need you. You're the only normal one of the bunch."

Tammi is anything but. Her work as a television producer takes her out of town at least eight days a month, so when she's in town, she overcompensates, driving extra carpools, rushing to pay overdue bills, waking up at 4 A.M. to answer e-mails and catch up before jumping on a plane again. We don't expect her to make every Bombshell meeting, but she calls in to almost every one.

She even dialed in from a satellite phone while shooting on location on a glacier in Alaska. Tammi has always taken her work very seriously, even when she was teaching aerobics, topless, in the Caribbean. Life's a beach!

The deadlines that came while writing this book were not easy on any of us. During the presidential elections of 2004, when the whole country was on hold awaiting the final outcome, the Bombshells were crashing to revise stories for our final manuscript. As a senior correspondent for the Spanish TV network Univision, Mercedes was really under the gun. She worked till midnight on election coverage, went home, only to be awakened by her boss at 5:30 A.M., who was sending her to Columbus, Ohio, immediately. "Ohio's become the new Florida," she told her. "Your flight leaves at 7 A.M.; you connect with your photographer at New York's La Guardia airport and arrive by 1:30 for a 5 P.M. live shot."

In the short time she had to pack, shower, and drive to the airport, Mercedes took a moment to log on to her computer, and e-mail herself the *Dish & Tell* stories she still needed to work on, so she could later access the work from the hotel business center after her seventeen-hour workday was done. Being a famous newswoman may seem glamorous, but the workload can be unbearable. Mercedes did manage to sleep all of two hours that night, and she met her deadlines, albeit with bags under her eyes.

The Miami Bombshells are six very strong women with very different perspectives on how to make work, work. All of us are striving for balance, and each has learned, in her own inimitable way, that there really is no such thing as having it all. But we may die trying.

Life's a Beach

TAMMI

Ever want to run away from it all and live on a remote tropical island, leaving bills and obligations behind?

I did it. For a whole year. Only I *worked* on the Caribbean Island of Martinique. Taught topless aerobics. For real.

I wasn't exactly hired to take my top off and dance, but the year was 1982 and I was employed at a singles resort as an entertainment organizer for six hundred wild and crazy guests every week. Need I say more?

I had been out of college a couple of years and should have felt satisfied with my life. I had just landed a great, entry-level job as an assistant TV news producer, working nights and weekends. I was paying my dues and dating a really nice guy. I was crossing my fingers, hoping that he'd propose soon, but it wasn't looking promising. So when a girlfriend asked me to join her on a wild and crazy vacation to help heal some of her wounds from a bad breakup, I felt it my civic duty to go with her. Technically, I never came back.

We had the time of our lives for an entire week. The ratio of men to women was eight to one, and I think we talked to everyone on that island with gonads. Had our way with a few of them, too, and even spent one long night on a pier with a gorgeous Asian man (whose name I can't remember), only to be awakened by local fishermen at sunrise. I didn't even feel guilty for playing the field. I was twenty-three, and though I didn't know it then, the wings I grew on this vacation would really help me soar through this new, altered course that was about to hit my life.

Martinique was a crazy place back then, run by a bunch of bikini- and Speedo-clad Europeans, whose English consisted of three words, "No problem, mon." When my friend accidentally stepped on a sea urchin and got dozens of thorns in her foot, the nurse actually told her that the acid in human urine would loosen the thorns and prevent infection. We believed her, and because my friend was in so much pain, began collecting specimens from everyone we could, soaking her foot three times a day. This place was not to be believed.

We returned home with incredible photos, and even better stories. But after a couple of weeks, just about the time my friend's foot started turning black, I began dreaming of going back there . . . for good. I made a few calls, wormed my way into an interview, and somehow, got chosen out of five hundred applicants for a job as the *professeur de danse* on my very own Fantasy Island of Martinique. Over the course of two days, I had quit my job, sublet my apartment, and packed my bags. My parents were furious, my boyfriend thought I had lost my mind, and my boss told me I'd never work in this town again, since I was leaving with no notice. I stayed up all night before I left to finish the Leonid Brezhnev obituary I was preparing, just in case, and then headed off to paradise. For $100 a week.

Culture shock. I was one of eight Americans in a sea of French people. More than a hundred of them worked for this particular village, where the only thing mandatory was the noontime poolside dance gathering. Miss it three times and you're fired. Most of the resort employees knew English but refused to speak it. They really despised Americans, thinking we're all just a bunch of classless, cultureless isolationists, always in a hurry to get nowhere. Each week brought in a new busload . . . always referred to as the BBQ (Brooklyn, Bronx, and Queens) crowd.

It was a party that never ended, ever. Sex and booze were around every corner. Even some of the supervisors would drink with us late into the night. This was clearly a place where sleeping your way to the top was *not* held against you.

The bathing suit, they say, is the great equalizer. On a tropical island, you've got nowhere to hide, and money doesn't mean a thing because at this remote beach resort, the currency isn't cash, it's beads. Therefore, it doesn't matter how many Porsches you own in Malibu. Here, if you ain't got personality, you've got nothing at all. And you only have one week to reveal your true self. Amazingly, some real relationships actually begin there, and vacationers waste no time blitzing through the crowd in search of Mr. or Ms. Right Now. It's a meat market in every sense of the word. And the display case changes every week.

My job, aside from teaching classes, was to act as a hostess in the morning, seating people in the dining room for breakfast. In the beginning, *"Combien?"* (which asks, "How many?") and *"Bon appétit"* were the extent of my knowledge of French.

It wasn't until I started feasting on some French men of my own that my vocabulary exploded. The village photographer, Jean Charles, was an excellent teacher, and Philippe helped me a lot, too. Pierre got me into shape, but it was his twin brother, Yves, who I ultimately fell in love with. I connected with them all . . . the first month.

Those were the *Flashdance* days, and aerobics was hot. My classes were packed. I always wore a leotard for my 6 p.m. class on the stage but was usually topless for my morning classes on the beach. That's not how it started though. When I would blow the whistle, inviting people to come exercise, most of the women who were on the beach were European and didn't even bring a bathing suit top with them, so they'd take my class topless. They chided me as the shy American, so, feeling a little bit pressured, I too removed mine. So began my topless aerobics career. My classes were very popular among the BBQs, as you might imagine. I remember once when one of them called me over while on his back, and, asking me to bend down to answer a question, grabbed my boob and squeezed it, then roared with laughter. It was a glamorous job.

I worked out about three hours a day, went scuba diving and waterskiing at least twice a week, played softball and beach volleyball every evening, and taught aerobics classes in between. For the first time in my life, I was proud of my rock-hard body. I helped choreograph dances for the nightly shows put on by the employees, and then we'd all party on into the night. Every single night. No exceptions (wasn't sure if I mentioned that).

Then one week, out of the blue, my younger sister Jodi came to visit. She was in her last semester of college, and I'm still not sure if she was there to give me a sanity check or if she, too, needed a hiatus from life. When she arrived, it was late, so we headed straight to the beachside disco for a nightcap. When we got there, music was blaring and three women were hanging from the rafters, sans panties, legs spread-eagle, with a limbo line of drunken guys dancing their way under them, tongues a-wagging. Welcome to the wild and crazy Caribbean. The rules *were* certainly different here.

My sister had a blast that week, and she too eventually came back to work there herself. And she was even wilder than I was on her six-month stint in Martinique. A married kindergarten teacher now, she loves to tell the story of the day her group of coworkers was bidding farewell to another busload of New Yorkers. She noticed a guy who looked pretty sad, and when she asked him what was wrong, he told her he hadn't met a single girl all week and was worried about going home with no story to tell his buddies. Everyone gets laid here, he whined. Only he hadn't.

So my sister checked her watch, decided they had enough time, and took the poor schlep back to her room for a quick roll in the hay. He left with a smile. She could have been employee of the week for that kind gesture. Back then we called it "taking one for the team." I'm willing to bet that singles vacation wasn't this guy's last.

As for me, I had the time of my life that year, but I knew deep down, I couldn't live like that forever. I realized that when I returned home for a short break and learned that Brezhnev had died four months earlier. We had no idea, because back then, TV, phones, and radios were not part of the whole singles vacation experience. I knew then that I'd had more than my fair share of fun and was ready to trade in my bathing suit for a double-breasted one. I was ready to use my brain again.

From Martinique, I moved to New York, and for an entire year, ran into former Martinique vacationers all over Manhattan. And there were lots of them when you consider six hundred a week for six months. I saw them in the strangest places in NYC, but almost all of them greeted me with the same obnoxious, "Yo, topless aerobics teacher, I don't recognize ya wit ya clothes on!"

Talk about a reality check. Fantasy Island is nothing more than a distant memory for me, but I'm not sure I ever let go of the dream to run away again.

Eventually I came back home to Miami, married the guy I initially ran away from, had two beautiful babies, and a decade and a half later, got amicably divorced. At the moment, I'm trying to find a headhunter who can place me in an island village with a charter school for my kids on the premises. This time, though, I'm setting my sights on Tahiti.

Fatal Wounds

ANNIE

Had I known what I would face when I arrived at work that day, I might have been tempted to pull the covers up over my head and just stay in bed. Fortunately, we face each day with little knowledge of the events that will occur, and I feel certain that this is a gift from our Higher Power. It was the Friday before Mother's Day, and as the alarm rang at 5:45, I looked anxiously toward the weekend, hoping it would play out as a low-key, restful few days with my family.

As I walked into the front office of the alternative school that is so much a part of my life, I immediately felt a sense of deep concern. I heard loud screaming that did not sound normal. I followed the noises and raced quickly toward the gathering crowds. The scene I encountered shook me to the core. At the center of the crowd lay one of my students, who had apparently been stabbed, bleeding profusely. The pool of blood was growing rapidly around her. Looking back on the chaos, I do not know how I managed to take immediate control of the situation and do what I needed to do. I knelt down next to the young girl as she desperately pleaded for help, and her eyes filled with tears as she grabbed my hand. I could feel the difficulty she seemed to be having with each breath she took. From my crouched position next to her, I wiped the tears as they rolled down her cheeks.

Out of the corner of my eye, I could see the security guards canvassing the area, searching for the alleged aggressor. My mind began to wonder how this could have happened. Was it an isolated incident, part of a gang fight, a stabbing or a gunshot wound? The person responsible for inflicting this horror was apprehended moments later, after being positively identified by several who had witnessed the attack. The attacker was another one of my students.

As we waited for the ambulance to arrive, I held this child's hand, praying she would not see the fear on my face. I forced myself to remain stoic and calm. I did not want to increase her fear by allowing her to witness the pain I felt for her. She kept asking, "Am I going to die?" A thousand thoughts raced through my head as I searched for the right words to reassure her. All I could say was, "Hang in there, baby, help is on the way." I truly meant the baby part.

These children have become part of my own family. I have worked with these troubled youngsters for more than a decade and each day presents new challenges for all of us. But this was a new one for me. I could feel this little girl's entire body trembling in my hands. Her skin was cold, but I kept talking to her in an attempt to keep her awake. I was afraid that if she lost consciousness, she might never regain it.

The ambulance finally arrived, and I stood by helplessly as they gingerly placed her on the stretcher. I wished I could go with her but I knew I had to take care of business now. As the siren faded out in the distance, I had to place the call to her family and tell them their daughter had been stabbed. The alleged weapon, a kitchen knife, had been found nearby. My knees were shaking as I walked into the building. I could hardly stand up. I was drained and overcome with sadness. I did not know how I would muster the strength to make this call.

I picked up the phone, took a deep breath, and began to dial. I found myself groping for the right words. "Good morning, this is the psychologist at your daughter's school. I'm sorry to have to tell you this, but your child is hurt and on her way to the hospital." The mother immediately began to sob, and her anguished cries resonated for several seconds. Then there was complete silence. I, too, was quiet as I offered a silent prayer.

I reached deeply into my memory bank to retrieve the many years of counseling and psychological preparation that could help me comfort this poor parent, whose foundation I had just rocked. All I really wanted to do was reach through the phone to embrace this devastated mother. Instead, I gave her the necessary information about her daughter and the name of the hospital where she was taken. I wished her well and we hung up. My composure had held on when it had to, but I then broke down in tears. I cried for the student, for the parents, for the school, and for all those parents who have ever received one of these phone calls. I cried for my own children and prayed that I could protect them every single day of their lives.

Despite her multiple injuries, the young girl miraculously recovered. She was very lucky. When she came to see me months later, she was smiling, and although her visible scars had faded, I could tell how deeply her wounds really went. I later heard that she had completed high school at another location and was enrolled in a community college.

Sometimes people wonder why I do what I do. But I love my job as the school psychologist. In the alternative school, I work with students who have failed in their neighborhood schools due to problems, which may include truancy, failing grades, weapon possession, or assault on peers or staff members.

I know it's difficult for others to understand, but the rewards really do outweigh the challenges. I love working with these kids and trying to understand what makes them tick. I get a charge from digging deep to help them find their real potential. I have learned to measure success in small units, but I do believe my work still makes a difference in the life of a young person. I have also gained a different perspective on life.

It makes me sad to see the number of young people who have been neglected or abused. They often develop a thick armor to protect themselves from the hard hand they have been dealt. Getting through to the real person who lies underneath the bravado is what I hope to achieve in my quest to teach these kids positive strategies for survival.

When I told my "soul sisters" about the stabbing, Mercedes was moved to tears. "Stories like this make me feel as if I want to put my children back into their cribs and keep them locked up and insulated for life." Pat's only comment? "And you wonder why I never had kids."

A lot of my kids have so much baggage that I often wonder how they even get out of bed every day. Many of them don't have parents, so they find themselves being raised by extended family members or in foster care units. Sometimes, they don't learn the basic social skills needed to survive in our society, so they learn to cope with the limited nurturing they've received.

Unfortunately, they consider their learned behavior to be "normal" and so it becomes their only means of survival within their own peer groups. My school provides these young adults a safe harbor and an opportunity for them to find themselves.

For some we are often their last chance, offering them a nurturing environment with sympathetic teachers and counselors willing to look beyond their inappropriate behavior and help them to find their true potential. Unlike mainstream schools, we are able to focus one-on-one with our students due to the high percentage of counselors available.

It scares me to hear a fifteen-year-old girl talk about suicide. To be so young and to see no future, only dead ends, has to be so incredibly frightening. I can almost understand their wanting to end it all. It might even be easier than having to face the difficult realities ahead of them. How do you give hope to these kids? All you can do is accept them for who they are and help them find a way to cope each day, one day at a time. I try intervention, counseling, and training to rebuild an injured psyche and hope I can lead these children on a more positive road. That's what we try to provide in a day-by-day program. Teaching them to value themselves as "good people" and helping them to be self-confident are our primary goals.

I'm often afraid to open my newspaper. I've seen too many of our students make the headlines, and it's not usually for winning essay contests or doing the "right thing." They may not be from our school but each of them represents a lost child. The other morning the paper had an article about another teen losing her life in a school-related incident. Stories like this remind me of how rough and dangerous the world can be.

Unfortunately we cannot control all our kids' moves; we can only hope that something we said or did will help them make the right choices. Every once in a while, an old student will come by to say hello, to let me know that he or she is traveling on a forward path. (I don't usually hear from those who haven't found that path.)

These short visits from former students give me the validation and encouragement I need to keep going during the rough times. Maybe I am really making a difference.

Throughout the years I have tried to leave it all at school when I walk out the door, but it's not easy. I often find myself thinking of these kids while I am at home with my own children, hoping that something I said to them during the day will keep them from making the wrong decision that night. I also keep my fingers crossed.

Reality

SARA

There's just never been an option for me: I was always going to work. I was going to be good at it, at least as good as—or better—than men. When babysitting was not enough, I went to work in the clothing store owned by the woman whose children I baby-sat, thereby watching over *all* of her most valued possessions. I was thirteen.

My generation of women fought to achieve our definition of success—having it all—without ever thinking about whether we even *wanted* it. Our well-meaning mothers, married in their early twenties (or earlier), college educated at a "finishing school," looked into the faces of their beautiful baby girls and told them they wouldn't have to live the same life. "You can be anything, do anything," our mothers promised, believing it as they said it, and signed us girls up for basketball teams, at a time when "tomboy" was no longer considered disparaging.

So maybe I was brought up a feminist, but I prefer to think of myself more as a pragmatist. I believe that whoever gets to the door first should open it. I don't think it's necessary for a man to stand when I get up from the dinner table, and I especially dislike the "parting of the Red Sea" that occurs when a woman is standing in the back of an elevator full of polite men.

I believe in meritocracy and was brought up with a strong sense of fair play. You should earn what you get and get what you earn, and we should all be evaluated on our merits. But I'm not an idiot, and I know that in reality, the world just hasn't come that far. As women, we may think we can do anything, but has somebody told that to the men who still run most of the companies?

In the male-dominated world of corporate senior executives, I've seen how a man who frequently goes to lunch with male colleagues ends up with a strong social network, but a woman who lunches with male colleagues is considered the office tramp. I've watched a father who leaves work to care for a sick child praised as a devoted family man, while a woman who does that is criticized for not being serious about her job.

Personally, my career has suffered because male counterparts with results-oriented, get-down-to-business attitudes are character-ized as effective and efficient leaders, while I am labeled as aggres-sive, and other, less flattering terms.

It doesn't help that I excel at what I do, or that I am insightful in ways that force others to think differently. I am outspoken and have never backed down from a debate when I believed something was best for the business. I challenge freely, and I suppose that makes me threatening to people who don't share the same views. Why should I walk on eggshells to protect fragile egos when I'm being paid for my opinion and expertise?

Often, I show up at a Miami Bombshell meeting frustrated by something that has happened at work that day. Only a few of the

Bombshells understand the corporate environment, and they commiserate with me. Pat, whose exodus from that world is the model to which I aspire, smiles and sighs, and I can tell she is thinking what a good decision she made to get out.

Annie doesn't understand it at all. "This is very alien to me. I've been working in the school system for so many years. . . . I've never experienced that kind of stress."

"But haven't you seen some of the inequalities?" I ask.

"Yes, I guess it has its share of corporate world hassles and 'good old boy' alliances, but when you are in a school setting like me, you see it less often. I can't tell you how frustrating it is when you give your job your all and you get the same pay increase as a coworker who does a fraction of what you do."

While we talk about the inequities, we hardly ever talk about giving up what we've worked so hard to achieve. It's ironic that as women we are stereotyped to chatter, but when it comes to certain subjects, the conversation happens only inside our heads. Sometimes we start to talk, but stop ourselves, fearful that speaking these words—"I wish I could just retire, or that my husband made enough money so I didn't have to work. I know I shouldn't, but I can't help hoping for Prince Charming to come and rescue me"—will separate us from the sisterhood. Maybe we'd be branded as traitors to the generation of women who have fought to get us where we are today. Not to mention some of the men who would say, "See? We were right all along."

The people at the top are much more likely to have testicles. In Fortune 500 corporations, not even two in ten officers are women, and only a handful are CEOs. That shines a bright spotlight on those women in the CEO spots but leaves no room or tolerance for failure. In a way, these few represent the success of all womankind, an added pressure they don't need, or deserve. Male CEOs fall on their faces all the time, then show up with a million-dollar signing bonus at some other Fortune 500 company.

Women are still a minority in senior management, and minorities tend to be misunderstood and undervalued. Once, when I called a business client to try and convince him to test-market a new product, I ended up with an invitation to join him in Las Vegas. Another time, as I tried to close a deal with one of the biggest television producers in Hollywood, we made plans for a final meeting to sign the papers. This producer actually asked me to wear the same skirt at the next meeting because he really *liked* the way it looked on me. I really wasn't bothered by this inequality until one night, years later, at a memorable executive dinner in London when the male CEO of a sister company looked at me as if I were a criminal and asked me how I could leave my child at home "whilst" I traveled to Europe for business.

I find it ironic that some of the smartest businesspeople I have ever met are also the most clueless when it comes to women and the contributions they make to the workforce. If the reality is that some men still think with areas outside their brain, then I'll use that to my benefit. In fact, I'll use everything at my disposal, as long as it is within the boundaries of ethics and good taste. Any man would. If the fact that I'm an attractive woman gets my phone calls returned, so be it. I won't wear a short skirt to distract a prospect; I would never lead on a man to think there could ever be a chance with me.

"It's a double burden," says Mercedes one night while we're on the subject. "You think you're competing for the job because you're smart, but you're immediately labeled too pretty, too coiffed, too well dressed to be smart." Or in the worst-case scenario, the attractive girl gets the job because she's not bright, and no threat. She becomes the flower arrangement in a grand decoration for somebody who can't see intelligent women in a capacity of leadership.

So I'll continue to think with my head as opposed to the head of *his* sex organ, and that gives me the advantage. A full house beats a straight every time.

Women should *earn* their spots at the top level. I've seen too many women elevated to senior executive positions they had no business venturing into. The CEO would boast of the diversity in the organization, and then fire the woman a year later because she should never have been put there in the first place. That diminishes my credibility as a woman because she represents all of us—unfairly.

I had a boss once who shared the same passion and fiery temper as myself. We debated frequently, and he respected disagreement. He was a great coach and helped me ascend the company ladder; we became friends as well as colleagues.

"Are you sure you want to have the top job?" he would ask. "It's not the same. You have to leave your friends behind."

"Why? Why does it have to be that way?"

"Because you have to be the leader. You can't go out drinking as a group anymore. People have to see you as the boss."

"So why can't the boss have a little fun?" I countered.

"You can, just not with the people who report to you," he said.

I thought he was wrong, and I told him so. That wasn't the only thing we disagreed on. As our business hit difficult times, we each had a different vision for a turnaround. Unfortunately, his included promoting someone else into the job I wanted.

"Lucy, you have some 'splaining to do," I joked as I walked into his office. I was in no mood for humor, but I couldn't confront him head-on.

"What are you talking about?"

"How could you put him into the job instead of me?"

"He has the global perspective. And the CEO wanted him there."

"This job was made for me; I've practically been doing it for the last year."

"I know, but the timing was just not right."

As I argued, the anger boiled over, and my voice began to rise. His responses elevated with mine, and before long, we were shouting at each other.

"You can't come in here and yell at me," he said.

"You're yelling at me!" I shrieked back.

"That's different," he said.

"Why? Because when a woman yells she's hysterical, but when a man does it he's being firm?"

"No," he said emphatically, and gave me a hard look. "Because I'm your boss."

Well, at least the rules were clear.

This is what I ask of the world, then: give all us equal opportunities, men and women alike. Give me equal pay for equal work. Don't ask me how I can be a good mother and do a good job at the same time. And for God's sake, when the elevator doors open and you're standing in front of them, take the first step.

Riding Solo

PATRICIA

I've been thinking about doing this for years. Sure, it's risky. But others have done it and survived. Even thrived. I take a deep breath . . . and jump right in.

I brace myself as best I can. Should I keep my eyes open, or shut them tight? I decide that it's best to see what's in front of me. If I know which way the wind is blowing, I can shift so that I'm moving with the flow, instead of against it.

In the beginning . . . it's a breeze. Wow, this isn't so difficult, I think to myself. I'm amazed at how quickly I get the hang of it. I can do this! My confidence grows.

And then I see the drop. I wasn't expecting it, even though I knew it was a possibility. But now I'm not afraid anymore. So I support myself as gravity takes over and I descend what seems to be fifty, one hundred, two hundred feet! I lose my breath but not my determination. I will not panic! I am a grown-up. I can handle this.

After my stomach catches up to the rest of my body . . . the ride smooths itself out, but only for a moment because then I'm thrown for another loop. Literally. Oh my God. I'm not going to make it! What was I thinking? I was so comfortable before, so secure before I jumped. How could I be so stupid? But I survive. Again.

And so begins my second year of being out on my own and riding solo for the first time in my life.

No more steady paychecks. So long good insurance benefits. *Adios* paid vacation days. Good-bye six-figure salary.

I am now a full-fledged passenger on the turbulent roller-coaster ride called self-employment.

Maybe I should have done this with someone else, taken on a partner. It's always good to have someone to rely on, to hold on to. Especially when it gets rough. Problem is, I can't really think of who would want to go on this ride with me. Or for that matter, someone I could totally rely on. So I hold steady and take the journey, solo.

I'm often asked how it's going. My answer seems to depend on the week. I've gone from "Great. I should have done this earlier" to "It's just a little slow, the economy you know, but things will pick up."

I was a corporate call girl for nearly thirty years. When my bosses called, I was there, ready to do the job, faster and better than anyone else.

I started young. My first job was at Capitol Records promoting rock 'n' roll stars like Paul McCartney and Wings. I had the coolest job of all my friends in college and the biggest record collection. Eventually I moved on to TV and radio. I went from entry-level positions to hosting an afternoon movie on TV called *Dialing for Dollars,* where I even had my very own fan club. I then moved on to a local NBC TV station where I was producing Emmy Award–winning hour-long documentaries, musical programs, and public service campaigns. That's where I met my Bombshell friend Tammi, back in 1985.

After a few years at the station, I began thinking about starting my own company. But financially I wasn't ready, and in hindsight,

I realize I didn't have the experience back then to make it work. In the midst of my internal debate, American Airlines called, looking for someone to head up their corporate communications efforts in Florida, Latin America, and the Caribbean. I took the job and became the head PR person for seventy-five American Airlines cities, from Miami down to the tip of South America. I encountered lots of turbulence in my six years at American, but it was the most incredible ride of my life.

Eventually though, my brain started to fly in other directions . . . I really thought this time I was ready to fly solo. That's when the local newspaper called and offered me the position of vice president; I couldn't refuse. So I put my solo career on hold, again.

In the beginning, it was all I had dreamed of—lots of money, a huge corner office right on Biscayne Bay with dolphins and manatees swimming outside my window, and a wonderful staff. I thought I was in paradise.

The honeymoon lasted for a few years until the corporate downsizing began. I understood it wasn't their fault; they had to answer to their shareholders. I was ordered to cut back here, make more money there, and then go back and cut here again. I had no choice but to double, then triple my workload, and to bring in more money, then cut expenses again. The day they told me to fire the single mom who ran one of my areas was the same day I was told I couldn't take the day off to bury my thirteen-year-old dog. My in-box was piling higher and higher, and it became impossible to handle the two hundred plus e-mails that came in on a daily basis. I attended board meeting after board meeting, and just kept swimming against the current.

And lucky for them, the corporate slave always came through. I reduced my staff, once, twice, three times, and increased their profits, once, twice, three, and four times. I sat for hours in those pry-your-eyelids-open type of meetings as I'd dream of starting my business and taking real time off to hike in Colorado, pamper myself at the Mandarin Oriental Spa on Biscayne Bay, or attend spiritual re-treats in Peru and Sedona to reconnect with my soul. I wanted con-trol of my own schedule. If my ideas were able to generate millions of dollars for our corporate conglomerate, why couldn't I do the same for myself?

For the first time, the itch to ride solo was just too strong. The hardest part was giving up the big bucks, but I went with my gut and gave my notice. My friends at the paper understood completely and on my last day of work we celebrated in style . . . even taking a champagne-laden limousine to the airport as I headed to Mexico, and then Hawaii, to celebrate my freedom!

After fifteen years of internal debate, I had finally found the courage to make my decision, three months before 9/11. Amazingly enough, I did very well in the beginning, even though the economy was going down the toilet. My first client became the newspaper I had just left. Their business gave me the financial foundation to build on. The second client I signed up was a huge, multinational company based in Latin America that needed help setting up their U.S. headquarters in South Florida. I became their public relations, marketing, and networking guru.

The day I got that first hefty monthly retainer check, I only wished my *mami* had lived to see her little girl all grown up and running her own business. My dad was so proud to see me making it on my own. I knew it because when he fills with pride for me, his eyes water and his neck turns red. I love him so.

In a few short months, I had become the CEO of my own com-pany, making more money on my own than I ever did as an execu-tive in corporate America. I quietly wondered why it took me so long to get here, but still counted my blessings.

I worked like crazy but also enjoyed life in a way I never had done before. I took time for myself and for projects that were near and dear to me. It was during that initial time away from the paper that I decided to bring a group of women together: five friends who, just like me, were "victims" of their own success and finding it impossible and exhausting to be the perfect corporate executive, mom, wife, daughter, and granddaughter. I decided the time to stop trying was now and that we needed to get together on a regular basis, to vent, dish, support, and nurture one another. That group became the Miami Bombshells.

Back then, Tammi was the only one of the group who had fled the corporate rat race and was achieving success on her own. As we all sat and bitched, questioning why we were working so hard to make money for others, Tammi seemed so happy in her work, running her own television production company. She was the one who had really pushed me hard to take the plunge the summer before I finally left the paper, calling me often from Colorado, where she was vacationing for an entire month with her family. "We're off to go hiking again today, and then to a pops concert and a campfire tonight. It's cold here," she'd brag, as I was sweating out the summer in South Florida, working six days a week. "You could be here too, you know—it's all about choices." I think it was those calls that made me see that the only one who could control my destiny was me. And for Tammi's tough love, I will always be grateful.

My dear old friend Lydia wasn't sure I had done the right thing. Not one to take risks, she feared the financial implications of my leaving the corporate world and told me so. As I sat around the table one day with the Bombshells talking about my predicament, Lydia confessed. "I would like to take the plunge myself but I'm afraid," she said. "I have always excelled in what I've done profesionally but I know that going on my own could open up the chance for failure."

"Or success," I scolded her. "Or even greater success!"

"Yes, you're right Pat," she said. "I'm a worrier, you know that."

"Yes, we *all* know that already, and we just met!" laughed Sara.

Annie just kept shaking her head. "I don't get it," she said. "Sitting at this table, as a school psychologist, I'm the one with the most degrees, yet I make the least amount of money . . . so it's hard for me understand how you can walk away from a six-figure salary. I'd gladly give up my leopard-print outfits to wear a three-piece suit."

"Be careful what you wish for," I told her. "You may become school superintendent one day and then you'll be screaming for your leopard prints again!"

Those initial months away from the boardroom were when I learned to control my time and think about life. The rushing, running, and reacting had stopped.

The money was rolling in. My clients were happy. Life was good. I couldn't believe it was so easy. This ride isn't so bad after all.

I decided it was time to make one of my dreams come true by buying a little summer home in Sedona, Arizona. My business brain justified the expense as a great investment and my soul was ecstatic over this home, which is set near imposing red rocks I am convinced are healing in nature.

And just as I was getting used to the amazing high, the earth dropped out from under me and I plummeted. My multinational client's business started to go to hell because of economics in Latin America and the monthly retainer went *adios*. Then my newspaper trimmed its marketing budget, and although I kept their business, my fee was cut by two-thirds. I thought about returning that sapphire bracelet and ring that I bought on a business trip to Aruba but crossed my fingers that work would soon pick up again.

My confidence, which had grown and developed over the past few months, started to shrivel up and hide. I stopped eating out at restaurants and started cooking at home, which is not the way I like to live my life.

And then, out of the blue, a new client showed up. It was the largest newspaper in the Caribbean. I signed them up, but unfortunately, it was just a six-month contract. Then came another huge client, an HMO, but that too was a short-order deal . . . three months and the money dried up.

As I approached the end of both projects I was developing a knot in the pit of my stomach. How was I going to pay the bills? Sleepless nights. Four bank accounts that dwindled down to one. I'm forty-seven years old; how was I ever going to retire? I didn't see a light at the end of this very long and winding tunnel.

But I was able to hold on with a few new clients I brought in over the traditionally slow summer months, including the Latin Grammy Awards. Still not enough to pay that new mortgage payment in Sedona, so I decided to rent it out for a while.

Whose idea was it for me to start my own company anyway? I was exhausted and broke again. And now I had a second mortgage payment. UGH! I wanted to get off this stupid ride.

And then, once again, out of the blue, my little guardian angels reappeared and brought me several new clients who paid big monthly retainers.

I told the Bombshells about my new clients at another one of our Bombshell meetings, where Sara dropped her news. She too was going out on her own and starting a company that markets to women.

One month later, Sara sent me this e-mail: "I had to get up at 7 A.M. to do a presentation for an 11 A.M. meeting on a *Sunday*. Tell me again why I went into business for myself? Promise me it gets easier . . . ," she begged. To which I responded, "Sorry to say it doesn't get easier. The more clients you get . . . the busier you'll be. It's more exhausting than anything I've done before. I practically work 24/7. *But* it's worth it. I don't ever want to sit in an executive board room again listening to how many people I need to fire because the shareholders aren't making enough millions!"

I constantly remind myself, and Sara, that there's nothing like being on my own. The trade-offs are scary. No more 401(k) preparing me for a nice retirement. No way to know how I'm paying next month's bills. There's no way to budget because you never know what will drop in or off your radar screen the following month. The payoff, though, is that there's nothing like being free of those corporate chains. Nothing can compare to making your own schedule and living the life you want to live, even if it has to be within a more limited budget.

Up . . . down. Down . . . up. Round and round. Up and down.

You need a strong stomach for this kind of solo ride. It's certainly not for everyone. But I think I've got the hang of it now. And I know I'm OK, as long as I keep the Pepto in my pocket and the angels by my side.

A Public Life

MERCEDES

Fame is one of those ephemeral man-made concepts I have yet to comprehend. I'm the first one to pick up a gossip magazine at the checkout counter. But, as much as I may become fascinated by, say, Andy Garcia's life, I don't understand why anyone would think the life of a TV correspondent like myself is anything more than ordinary.

It still blows my mind that people want to take a picture with me, ask for an autograph, or run up to hug me as if I were some long-lost relative. Those are the peculiarities of this interesting job of mine.

The funniest story I can remember happened in an airport hangar in Tikal, a teeny-weeny town outside Guatemala City. I was told we were bumped off our overbooked flight and I was furious—we had to get back to the States to file a story, but nobody seemed to care about our problems . . . we were in the middle of the jungle.

Inside, behind a rickety desk, was a happy Indian teenage girl ready to serve grumpy passengers like me. As I started to plead with her to find me a return flight, her eyes popped open in disbelief and her jaw dropped. I had barely finished begging, when she screeched in delight. *"Ay ay ay!* You're that girl from the TV."

No way, I thought. We're in the rain forest. This is a third world country. How in the world could she be up-to-date on Spanish TV from the States? But I used it to my advantage. After a few photographs and the type of attention normally bestowed on a real celebrity, she found us the seats on the flight we needed, probably bumping someone else off. We would leave on schedule. It may sound brutal, but that's the way things work, and I've either benefited or paid the price for my quasi fame long enough to accept it.

I probably shouldn't have been surprised. Earlier in the trip, as we drove to the luxurious Camino Real Hotel in the middle of the jungle I saw women knee-deep in river water washing their clothes. When I peered inside their huts I noticed no furniture except hammocks nailed to tree trunks. But, upon closer examination, I caught myself gasping in the realization that there were satellite dishes perched on those thatched roof huts. I was astounded to learn that television has become as pervasive an intrusion on our most ancient and disconnected civilizations as it is on our own.

That realization would finally sink into my head several years later. It was with great excitement that I headed to the hospital on August 8, 1996, to give birth to my firstborn. I was happy but terrified. As I reached the maternity unit I was informed that the hospital had reserved the best birthing suite for me. It was another special celebrity perk that I had not asked for but couldn't possibly refuse. They were ready to treat me like a queen, simply because I am on TV.

The labor was intense. It started at 6 A.M. and twelve hours later I was in such wretched pain that I literally asked my husband to kill me when he asked if there was some way he could help. The baby was stuck in the birth canal. She had positioned herself sunny-side up, and with every push I managed to deliver, her little legs would lodge themselves in my back, making it feel as if someone was hacking away with a machete. The doctor kept maneuvering inside of me to turn her around. But it didn't work.

Finally, I gave up. I announced I couldn't go on, couldn't stand the pain, and refused to keep pushing on the grounds that I was being lied to and the baby was not really moving. The doctor had a mirror brought in so I could peek for myself. When I saw a sliver of black hair peeking from between my legs, I regained the strength to finish the job.

Those last minutes of pushing, I felt like I was in a trance. My husband later confessed he had never seen me more focused. As if I had a choice. I pushed and pushed and then finally, miraculously, a little baby girl slipped out of my body and into my life.

As I saw her, I broke into uncontrollable sobs. When the doctor put her on my chest I cradled her in my arms and kissed her incessantly as if enveloped in a bubble of love where there was only room for the two of us.

And then a screeching voice burst my bubble. "She's a *Primer Impacto* baby," someone yelled out loud. That's the name of the show where I've worked for over a decade. I incredulously lifted my gaze from my baby only to find a crowd of spectators applauding my delivery. Word had gotten out that I was about to give birth, and the room had filled up with hospital staff. My delivery turned into a celebrity sighting!

To my horror, there were over a dozen people watching one of the most intimate and sublime moments of my life. I hadn't even noticed. I had been too busy, too tired, too focused. It never occurred to my husband to restrict entrance to the room because who would've expected such a blatant violation of privacy.

So there, with my legs in the stirrups and my genitalia fully exposed, while the doctor stitched up my bleeding episiotomy, I again embraced my so-called fame and did what my TV job had trained me to do. Right on cue with the last clap, I composed myself, feigned appreciation, and as if ready for a close-up, I just looked up, and I smiled. Tape at eleven.

Kicking the Corporate Habit

LYDIA

I am an immigrant. My parents, sister, and I fled Cuba forty-four years ago to escape Communism and came with only the bare necessities. My sister and I watched our parents struggle to start from scratch in a strange land . . . their education and corporate experience in Cuba was worthless in Miami. Here, if we wanted to have food on the table, they were forced to take jobs for which they were totally overqualified.

As a kid, I dreamed of reaching for the clouds and grabbing every star I could, just to deposit them at my parents' feet. I wanted to make them proud. And I did.

Most people would call mine a corporate success story. I sit in the corner office at the top of my field, bringing home a hefty six-figure salary. I make no excuses, as I have earned every cent, but now, thirty years later, all I think about is why I am still doing this. I've had my fill of power, glamorous boardrooms, designer suits, briefcases, and enough meals in fancy restaurants to last a lifetime. I feel very blessed, but at this point in my life, I dream of walking away from it all and finally enjoying a personal life. Then I wake up.

As much as I fantasize about gardening, traveling, and quiet, home-cooked family dinners, I've spun myself into a golden web and can't find my way out. I also love what I do! People say that loving something passionately makes you good at it. I am hooked on mortgage banking. I actually get high on business deals. I thrive on the challenges, and stress gets my blood pumping. My job keeps me spinning in my Salvatore Ferragamos.

Maybe mortgage banking doesn't sound as sexy as being an actress or a rock star, but to me, the highs and lows of the financing process, watching anxious people spend every cent they've saved to buy a new house, gets my juices flowing. The contract and interest rate lock-in deadlines leave me breathless.

I hold the key to a new life for people who want a fresh beginning for themselves and their families. It's a stimulating game that never gets old. Combine that with a hefty salary, and you've got a recipe for instant gratification.

Early on, it became very clear that if I wanted to excel in my profession, I would have to work harder than my peers. In order to succeed I felt I needed to become a workaholic. I climbed the ladder from an assistant VP, to VP, and all the way up to Senior VP, ASAP! But to enter that highly competitive men's club, I had to juggle not only the job but also the duties that came along with being a mom, wife, daughter, and sister.

My workday always continues into the evenings. My workweeks morph into the weekends. My family, the ones I love most, share in my wealth, but not in my presence.

A few weeks ago, I was away on a business trip, and when I returned home Wednesday night, I saw a reminder from my son Andy's Catholic school that his saint project was due on Thursday of the following week. This gave me exactly one week to maneuver the details. I had become proficient at juggling and wasn't a bit worried.

My son had to prepare an oral presentation about St. Andrew (his chosen saint for the project), and he had to dress up as that saint. And there was an extra credit project option, too. The teacher asked the kids to make a papier-mâché doll of their holy chosen one. No problem. Tomorrow we'll start working on it; I thought we had six days to finish this enormous project that was assigned to the fourth-grade students, but executed by their parents. It's funny how that happens.

Thursday morning, I went to the office and attended meetings all day while trying to catch up on the three hundred e-mails that were waiting for me. That night I had to take my daughter to buy an outfit for her Catholic confirmation, taking place thirty-six hours later. I had also planned a postconfirmation lunch for thirty-five invited guests.

We didn't get to the mall until 8:00 P.M. but found my daughter's outfit just as they were locking the place up. No energy left to work on the saint project, but I figured I'd work on it Friday.

Friday was Halloween and work consumed my time during the day, while the evening was spent trick or treating with my husband and Andy until 10:30 P.M. From there we all ran to the airport to pick up my stepdaughter who was flying in from Seattle. We stayed up chatting till 3:00 A.M.

Saturday flew by with the confirmation at the church, the lunch, and then a business dinner for my husband's company. Sunday, I spent quality time with my stepdaughter since she was returning to Seattle on Monday morning. There went the weekend.

Monday took me to Ft. Lauderdale for my weekly executive meeting. After a day filled with conflict and a three-hour round-trip commute, I sped home to take my daughter to a tutoring class, since my husband was caught up in the office. By the time we got home we had just enough time to make dinner and fall into bed, completely exhausted.

Tuesday was a whirlwind. I had one crisis after another at work. Conference calls, closings, meetings, e-mails, more meetings. By the time I made it home it was 9 P.M. and I still had to answer several dozen e-mails. After dinner, I collapsed again.

When Wednesday finally arrived, it hit me: we were twenty-four hours away from the time the saints were to come marching in, and I had not done a single thing. I was in a meeting at my office, but all I could think of was St. Andrew and pray he would help me. *Maybe little Andy can call in sick to school tomorrow,* I thought, before thinking about the message that would send. I decided to take control.

I left the office early, at 6 P.M. Stuck in the Miami rush hour traffic, I was counting the minutes to get to the closest party store. The saint costume I was so desperately looking for was nowhere to be found. I went to four different stores but had no luck. At about

8:30 P.M., I settled for a fabric store and bought material to make the outfit myself. I was desperate.

From there, I found an open shoe store and bought sandals that looked "saintly." The costume was miraculously coming together, except . . . I don't know how to sew!

So I put on my Martha Stewart domestic goddess hat and started working. It was almost 10:00 P.M. and time was running out, so I took a scissors, draped the fabric over my son's head, and then cut a hole in the middle.

I had bought enough fabric to cover every inch of his cute little body. I cut the hem and tied a rope around his waist. Then I draped the other color material across his chest and voilà! It wasn't Christian Dior, but it could pass for St. Anyone.

Thursday morning came, and all dressed up by 7:30 A.M. sharp, we were at Andy's school. I was feeling awfully good about myself as corporate executive and master juggler, who could defy the odds and do it all. But when I parked the car, I saw them: the *other* children.

They were wearing designer saint outfits that were out of this world. Beautifully woven, customized outfits made of the finest fabrics. They looked heavenly and I detested them all. And they were all carrying their extracredit papier-mâché dolls, which my son and I never got to. As I sat in the classroom, I couldn't believe my ears. These alien children gave major dissertations on their saints. It was pathetically obvious that their stay-at-home moms had written each and every oral project in that room.

My son's brief essay was great—simple, sweet, and honest because he wrote it all by himself. He didn't even look at his cards once. He knew exactly what he was talking about, while the others kids were trying to pronounce words they had never heard before. My little saint looked fabulous in the messy little *"monk*'s" outfit created by his *mommy*. And he got an A, too, just as I would have if the teacher had given me a grade for *my* effort on this project.

Weeks like that really make me take a second look at my life. Do I really want to be the "corporate executive" and spend the rest of my life in the rat race, barely able to squeeze in time for my family? Twelve- to fourteen-hour workdays—thinking, eating, and sleeping work—is not my idea of a fulfilled life, even though "Corporate" expects it to be. I'm tired of getting home at the end of the night only to read and answer e-mails from my bed. Both my husband and I would like to spend more time together instead of just saying friendly good mornings and good nights. But where is the trade-off?

All the hard work and long hours have paid off financially. But that's part of the problem. I am spoiled rotten, live in a great neighborhood, and have a housekeeper who irons my pajamas. I can satisfy almost any craving that crosses my path, from food to travel to clothing, without having to count my pennies.

My Bombshell friends are constantly giving me a hard time about my expensive purse fetish. They can't understand this passion of mine. But, then, I'm not the only one in the group who wears designer labels. Sara once told me, "I let you take all the heat, Lydia, but my shoe collection rivals Carrie Bradshaw's." It feels good to know I am not alone.

My kids attend private school and those expenses will grow as they do. How can I deprive them of that? And then there's my two-year-old granddaughter, the little angel born to my son (whom I had in my teenage years). Only cashmere is soft enough for her skin.

From time to time, I struggle with the idea of calling it quits. Especially when my ten-year-old son begs me to stay home more. One night I asked him if he wanted me to quit my job, reminding him I wouldn't be able to buy him as much as I do now and that we'd have to cut back a lot. He asked if he could sleep on it; the next morning as I was rushing to get to work, he admitted he didn't want to give up all the goodies, only that he still would like to see more of me. His solution? Work part-time.

But you can't do what I do from nine to one. I know the minute I decide to step off the corporate treadmill, I'll probably be fine with a simpler life. But I don't know how my teenage daughter, who also has a purse addiction, and my ten-year-old son, who thinks everyone travels to Europe for summer vacation, will be able to cope if I cut back. And then there's my mother; nothing makes me happier than showering her with gifts and taking her on elaborate cruises, which would have to stop if I quit.

At the end of the day, when I finally let myself pass out on my bed, I resume my dreams about kicking the corporate habit. But when the alarm rings at 5:30 A.M., I will get up and do it all over again, and again, and again, until I can break my addiction, if ever!

Mental Masturbation

BOMBSHELL

I never thought I would ever have sex for money. But that's kind of what I did, in an abstract sort of way. It's not that I needed the cash. In fact, by most standards, I would be considered upper middle class. I live in a wonderful home and drive a luxury car. My salary gives me the freedom to acquire most of what my heart desires in the way of fashion, products, and services. It's a good life. In fact, having grown up poor, I dare say it's a great life. I'm proud of my achievements and my successes. I'm proud of having earned what I've worked so hard for. But, as with anything in life, it has all come with a hefty price tag.

I realize now that making money can be very costly. The price I've paid for wealth and success has been extracted from me in ex-cruciatingly long hours at the office apart from my family and the support group that keeps me balanced. I have to admit that no one put a gun to my head. In fact, I've done most of it willingly and with a great sense of duty. I've truly enjoyed my career, the creative process that it involves, the exciting places it's taken me to, and the amazing people I've met. But all those things have also robbed me of my freedom. They have stolen my time, the time that I need and want to pursue other interests that make me happy. They have chained me to my job. And as time passes I feel more and more enslaved, almost like an indentured servant who can never repay as much as she has borrowed.

It was that feeling of lost time that caused me to rebel. I started to loathe going to work and hated putting in the time. That's when I began to plan my escape. To do so I needed to make the same amount of money I was already making but on my own terms. The only way I knew how to do that was by getting by on what had never failed me. Ingenuity.

After the Miami Bombshells was formed, long before we decided to write a book, we agreed that helping women empower themselves would be our first mission. After one of our late-night meetings, having had a few extra glasses of red wine and the obligatory chocolate, we took a detour from the "dishing and telling" and delved into the world of erotica. Though we may have been a little tipsy, we took ourselves quite seriously. For the next few months we plunged into the research and development of a great new product. We were certain we could come up with a way to help women give themselves pleasure and sexual fulfillment.

We would design a dildo to beat anything available on the market. It would be better simply because it would be designed by women for women. We would not only make them more pleasurable, but we would *shape* them with women in mind, none of that male-dominated lascivious cockamamie pornographic stuff that only men can get off on. We would build a vibrator to suit the needs of women! Or . . . something like that.

We brainstormed for weeks and were inspired by everything, including a bitten strawberry that bore an uncanny resemblance to a clitoris. We developed all kinds of things with sexy innuendoes, including the name of the corporation we were determined to launch. *Sixcess,* we pronounced ourselves. It rhymed with sex and success, and there were six of us in the group. We created the Remote Cun-trol (although my male-designed laptop insisted that word was a misspelling). It was a combination TV remote control/vibrator, de-signed to get that male partner interested in something other than channel-surfing all night long. We came up with *Sexsentials,* a bag of goodies full of accessories that could be turned into sex toys. It in-cluded beads for penis massaging, scarves for passionate tie-up situ-ations, scarf broaches that could double as cock rings, lubricating perfumed oils, a little bottle of honey for late-night licking, and then someone asked brilliantly, "How about a menthol throat lozenge?"

I had never heard of that. One of the girls seemed to know all about it. "Oh yeah, you put as much menthol in your breath as possible and then have oral sex. It's incredible, the ultimate aphro-disiac."

Filled with wonder, I knew immediately I had to give it a try. And so I went home with thoughts of perfect sex preparedness and a little menthol candy dangling at the end of my new entrepreneurial carrot stick.

But, as usual, by the time I got back, I was exhausted. And then the whole thing just slipped my mind. Until my child got really sick, with a very high fever. It spiked dangerously high for a couple of hours and the usual home remedies weren't working. Out of desper-ation, I called my husband. He was dining at a chi-chi new hot spot with a colleague when I gave him the bad news. "We may need to rush to the emergency room. I can't break the fever," I said. He was back in a flash, but not before first following his friend's recommen-dation and stopping at the drugstore to pick up something new.

As soon as my husband walked in the door, I dug into the brown paper bag to find a fever-reducing gel pad that sticks comfortably to a child's forehead and cools it down to reduce fever. My poor child fought it for a bit, but eventually gave in. And it really worked! The fever came down, and the miraculous product that brought my little one back to health was . . . a patch of menthol!

It had the texture of Jell-O smoothed over a soft cloth. When applied to dry skin it adhered to it and cooled it down with a refreshing feeling. Well, faster that you can say "orgasm," my business mind had made the connection. Menthol, masturbation, sex product, SIXCESS! I was breathless. This was it!

I needed fieldwork, research; I had to test this out! I took the box and read it. Nothing, no list of ingredients, but no warning signs either. So I decided to take the plunge. I cut a sheet into about four sections and took one about an inch in length and half an inch in width and went to the bathroom. I opened the lips to my vulva and inserted the patch, placing it not in my vagina but right on my clitoris. The effect was immediate. It was a tingly, cool, oh-it's-so-good kind of a feeling that sent me plunging into desperate desire. Luckily I had a willing partner salivating at the mere sight of me.

But, like any good researcher, I wanted to take my time. How long would that delicious prelude, that solo foreplay, hold? It kept me rocking and swaying in that soft heaving motion that can only be placated by deep and repetitive penetration. Ten minutes, twenty minutes, thirty minutes, I guess I could have held it longer. But, as it was, I waited long enough.

My oozing vagina was aching to be rubbed, to be stroked, my clitoris was swollen to the point of bursting, my breasts were aroused, and my pelvis was erect in a begging position. I was in heat, exuding sex. I needed lovemaking now. And when I got it, I exploded. My vagina convulsed over and over in electrical thrusts of ecstasy as I lay on my back, basking in the warmth of it all. I couldn't wait to tell the girls. I had found the perfect sex toy. We were going to be rich!

I went to our next meeting armed with a box of fever-relieving gels. I hugged the girls, told them the fabulous news, and took out my samples. I cut up a piece for each and ordered them straight to the bathroom to test them out. We were about to conduct group research. One by one they went with curious faces, conniving expressions, as if in some clandestine cult ready to commit grave sin. And out they came with smiles. They liked it, they felt it, and they were impressed.

The first Bombshell came out wobbling like a penguin, hardly able to walk or hold the feeling between her legs. "This is really amazing." She said. She sat on a stool, and then got up and walked and generally kept on moving because that's exactly the feeling the gel gives you, a need to rock the hips. Bombshell number two came out next, with a big grin and a happy strut. The two-gelled girl-friends joked and even did a little dance. It was a celebration. Then out came two more. They also had big smiles on their faces. "Oh baby, I love this," pronounced one of them. The last Bombshell never could figure out what all the fuss was about. "Maybe this strip is damaged, let me try another one." Nope, didn't do it for her. But five out of six isn't bad. So we decided to move forward.

We would investigate the product; its ingredients, its patent holders. We would negotiate with them to market the gel as an alternative sex product, or maybe develop our own. We would go into mass production, corner the sex toy market with something that held no phallic symbols, only pure pleasure. Just imagine, we could wear them to work, during the day, to a party, to dinner, any ole time we wanted to be aroused without the inconvenience of touching ourselves in public. It was a sexual panacea, a real women's liberation! We went home with fantasies . . . of the *sixcessful* kind.

And so this is how I, a well-to-do professional lusting for freedom from a too-demanding career, ended up experimenting with children's medicine to buy my way out of the rat race.

Though we eventually gave up on the idea of marketing sex toys for a living, I still think the patches can and should be marketed to women. They only cost a couple of dollars, and to this day, praise the goddesses, they're some of the most exciting sexual stimulants I've ever tried.

two

Family Matters

I t's all relative. Family *does* matter, and whether the fruits that grow on your family tree are rotten or delicious, they never go away. All of our Miami Bombshell families are deeply rooted in tradition, whether they're Cuban, American, Catholic, or Jewish.

We grew up with moms and dads and siblings and grandparents, and our family dynamics have shaped us. Mercedes is a twin, Pat and Annie are only children, and there's not a brother among us, only sisters. Sara's the only Bombshell who grew up with divorced parents. Lydia's grandmother was the love of her life, Sara's grandmother was her role model, and Annie's favorite role is that of daddy's little girl.

Sara, who loves to feed the other Bombshells (as does Tammi, maybe it's a Jewish mother thing?), showed up to a meeting one afternoon with minihamburgers. Each had a sliced pickle and some onion. And then out of her bag came a bottle of Heinz ketchup.

"You just proved my theory," said Tammi. Sara looked around, bewildered. "Did you grow up using Heinz in your house?"

"Yes, always."

"What about Hunt's?"

"Eww. Never."

"That's my theory: if your parents' brand was Heinz, then Hunt's will always be out of the question. Same goes for mayo; those who ate Hellmann's think Miracle Whip is disgusting."

"That's true!" Sara exclaimed. "I hate when I find Miracle Whip in tuna, it's gross."

Life is very simple according to Tammi: we live our lives as our parents did, perpetuating their habits, good and bad, and only open our minds to change when we absolutely have to.

Annie, who lives and dies by the color-coded charts she designs to keep her family organized, learned to live that way from her mom. Lydia's father was the obsessive-compulsive one, and now she feels compelled to lay out her groceries in a straight line on the conveyor belt. She knows it's crazy, but she can't help herself.

We used to think our lifestyles were patterned more through nature than nurture. But, in reality, children learn what they live, whether they like it or not.

While some of our mothers stayed home to care for us, not one of us Miami Bombshells has made that an option for ourselves. Sure, we feel guilty about not being there for our children, and worse when it comes to some of the choices we've made about who should care for them when we're working. But we can't imagine living any other way.

Mercedes says her ambitions for a well-paid exciting career were breast-fed to her by her own professional mother, a Ph.D. in Pedagogy and Social Work, who at one time managed all of the government-sponsored homes for all the elderly in Cuba. She literally had to beg her mom to retire at age seventy-two to care for her new infant; since then Mima Chela has lovingly helped raise the children. Mercedes can't imagine how Tammi has raised her girls with twenty-two nannies who she's hired and fired over the past fifteen years. "How could you be so desperate as to hire anyone who claims she can cook and clean, without even conducting a criminal background check?" she asks her, horrified. "You could have a murderer living in your own house." It's one of the rare moments we've ever seen Tammi speechless.

Lydia, who also has had more than her fair share of babysitters, throws her two cents in, as she crosses her chest with a Hail Mary, "I just count my blessings that my children have never been in an accident with all the drivers I've hired to chauffeur them from schools, to soccer games, and to dance practice."

That's when Pat, Lydia's old parochial schoolmate, belts out a very loud "Amen!" What does she know? Pat's never had, or even wanted, kids. The rest of us Miami Bombshells can't even imagine life without ours. Today's families are a mixed bag. Add exes and steps to the mix, and they take on lives of their own.

As we begin to reach midlife, we find ourselves sandwiched between our aging parents, who require more of us than ever, and our growing children, who need us even more. Unfortunately, our busy schedules don't often allow us enough time to adequately care for either, not to mention ourselves.

But sometimes, it's a family member, with friends, who comes to our rescue when we've given all that we have to others and really just need time for ourselves. Sara's husband, Bill, took care of all of the Bombshells when he planned an elaborate birthday surprise for Sara. Working with Tammi and Pat, he arranged for a limo to take all of us to the Bal Harbour Shoppes for a day of luxury. The limo was packed with champagne on ice and a chocolate birthday cake for celebrating.

Pat, who wanted Sara to dress up for the occasion, sent out a fake invitation, saying we would be having a special guest, so "you might want to dress a little nicer than usual."

When the limo pulled up to the house, Pat suggested Sara go to the door. Sara hesitated for a moment, a bit intimidated by who could be in the limo; after all, Pat does know her share of celebrities, and we were expecting a "special guest." But when Sara opened the door, and the driver handed her the birthday card that explained the surprise, her husband and son jumped out of the limo, and she burst into tears.

Tammi high-fived Bill. "I don't think she had any idea."

The six of us lunched, then shopped till we dropped, trying on clothes, makeup, and jewelry. But we left with so much more than what fit in our little Saks Fifth Avenue bags. We recharged, climbed back into our stretch with our Bombshell sisters, sipped our champagne, and headed home to another reality—family matters.

Nanny Nightmares

TAMMI

When my maternity leave ran out and the time came to hire a nanny to care for my precious new baby, I did extensive background checks on every single applicant, with a little help from my friends at the FBI. Here it is now, sixteen years later, as I'm rescuing Dolores, nanny number twenty-two, after her arrest for shoplifting; I'm horrified to find myself asking her tentatively, "Can you stay till Friday?"

Whatever happened to my maternal instinct? I think it's fallen into the nanny abyss . . . it's a hostage crisis that's taken me to infinity and beyond.

I should know better. I've overlooked mistakes in judgment that should have me committed. I justified some pretty bizarre behavior over the years, trying to convince myself (and my children) to open up our minds to "cultural diversity." But these days, I meet a lot of seemingly intelligent, working moms like me, who are as pathetic and desperate as I am in the day-care department. We are so overwhelmed by the daily demands of kids and work that unimportant nuisances, like dinner and homework, suck us dry. Yes, we are fortunate to be able to afford someone in the house to help us, but most of us can't figure out how to keep them there. That's why we'll tolerate almost anything.

I'm not kidding when I say Dolores was number twenty-two.

During my daughter's first two years, we went through three nannies. All were terrific, except that they weighed more than eight hundred pounds collectively, and feeding them almost wiped out my 401(K).

But the real nanny nightmare began the morning Francesca (number four) was taken away by ambulance (we're still not quite sure why) after cooking her usual breakfast of hot dogs sautéed in butter. She had stayed a month as had Belinda from Mexico, who left one Friday with no notice and a $300 phone bill. Next came Elinna. She was from Honduras and couldn't wait to vacation with us in Colorado that summer, till she blacked out on the mountain. We thought she died, and a month later, I nearly did when I got that $2,000 bill from the hospital. She, too, was gone by the time I ultimately paid it off.

When my eighty-five-year-old grandmother decided to stop driving, we put her rickety old car in the name of nanny number who knows what. Her name was Vera, and we thought she was here to stay. Vera was to be the first babysitter we would allow to drive our precious cargo. She had already been with us six months and a week, to be exact, but she split twenty-four hours after we put the car's title in her name. She apologized, but explained she was now free to start school, since her transportation problem had been solved. She never even said thanks.

Linda came next, a miserable woman from the Virgin Islands. I found myself kissing her feet, because I was traveling a lot on business and shuddered to think about what I'd do if she left me stranded. But the day my daughter's teacher tracked me down in Alabama to tell me my three-year-old had wet her pants and Linda refused to bring her dry clothes, "just to teach her a lesson," I sent Linda packing. That's when my mom moved in for a few days.

Elizabeth (from Peru) and I were pregnant together, and when the baby came, so did number twelve (or was it thirteen?). Her name was Maria. A sweet little thing from Colombia, she had a big thing for the college kid across the street. His parents were as unhappy as I was when they ran off together. I heard she was deported later that year. Bummer. I probably would've rehired her.

Then came Fiona from England. We liked her, but *she* dumped us to go live on a sailboat. Fiona was followed by Tanya, the local pot dealer (and we wondered why she had visitors 24/7?), who slipped out in the middle of the night during our family trip to Disney World. We didn't even call the police when we awoke to find her missing. We were hoping she'd been kidnapped!

But when Betty Boops came into our life and stayed, we were ecstatic. She lived with us till she earned enough money to build a house in Jamaica. When her son almost lost his foot in an accident, we brought him here, and he lived with us for months following surgery. That's what you do for people you love. And we love our Betty.

She held our hands and our hearts through divorce, and far too many deaths over those six difficult years, taking care of all of us as if we were her own. She's actually the only nanny the girls even remember . . . we cried, but understood, when it was time for her to go back to Jamaica.

So many nannies followed, I can hardly remember their names. So I started writing them down. More than half a dozen helpers came and went the following year; the girls and I chuckle now when we look at the list: Kelly, who routinely kicked the dog; Suzanne, who physically pushed me when I asked her to leave (she snuck out to the beach in the middle of the day and got home after the kids did!); another one (whose name I've already forgotten) who broke, then hid, the pieces of a cherished family heirloom, and then claimed *no comprende* when I asked her where it went.

Bombshell Lydia's had quite a few bad seeds herself. She came home once at midnight to find her young kids had taken over the house. That's when her first grader proudly announced that Maria had been sleeping since the little hand was on the nine. Lydia fired her and hired Rosa, who insisted on cable and a phone, plus her own personal towels. Rosita came around Christmastime, in time to help with their family Christmas party. But when the party started, Rosa got all dolled up, drunk, and danced all night. When the party was over, she went straight to her room. Rosa lasted a week and a half.

Why are we so successful in business and such losers when it comes to running our households?

OK, my family isn't exactly the Cleavers, but we're hardly the Manson family, either. Our life isn't very normal because I travel too much, often on a moment's notice, and my children have essentially been "raised by the village." But they're good kids, and I can't figure out why we're having so much trouble finding a helper who's compatible with us.

I often wonder if I shouldn't just quit my job, sell the house, and scale down our lives a bit. Maybe Dolores's arrest was a sign. I'm always searching for them. So I called a family meeting.

When I told the girls of Dolores's brush with the law, they were unfazed. "I told you she was a loser," was my eight-year-old's response. "It's a miracle she wasn't arrested for bad driving." I was horrified. My baby had spent an hour a day being chauffeured by an accused criminal. I secretly said a prayer of thanks that my precious little girls had survived nanny number twenty-two relatively unharmed. Shame on me for ignoring their complaints about Dolores's driving. I had merely blamed it on her old car.

I apologized profusely to my daughters. For not being perfect like their friends' moms, who prepared home-cooked meals on real plates every night. For serving E-Z Mac in plastic bowls in front of the TV more nights than I care to recall. For forgetting to remember to buy customized birthday presents for all their friends (though I eventually learned to keep a reserve of unisex Blockbuster Video gift cards in the closet). For sending out blank birthday invitations (thank heaven for return address labels . . . those soccer moms are still laughing at me). For having to sign report cards via fax from some remote city somewhere. For clothes shopping on the Internet because there is never time to run to the mall. And for not being the mom they deserved. Fighting back tears was tough, but I was holding my own. After all, I was the perpetrator, not the victim here.

My oldest one started to giggle. "Mom, don't you *get it*? We've got the greatest life of all. I have more frequent-flier miles than most grown-ups. I'm spending my childhood doing really cool stuff that none of our friends get to do. We're the only ones I know allowed to sleep at our grandparents' house on *school* nights. We get to do special things like feed the rhinos at the zoo while other kids have to catch a glimpse from far away. How many kids do you know who went hot air ballooning on their eighth birthday, huh, Mom? None of my *friends'* moms play slumber party with their kids, with dinner and a movie on trays in bed." My youngest chirped in, "Yeah, that's why all my friends ask if *you're* gonna be home when I invite them over. You might not be here every day, Mom, but when you're home, you're *really home*. We like it that you're not normal. Those 'normal' moms are so boring."

Annie laughs when I tell her this, because she considers herself one of those normal moms. Overworked, her budget never had room for a nanny, so Annie's always been the housekeeper, the babysitter, and the cook. Still, she regrets dragging her kids out of the house at dawn so she could go to work, counseling other kids— juvenile delinquents—in order to make a living. But she was home after school with her son and daughter every single day, a gift I now wish I could have given to my children.

Now that my girls are becoming teenagers, they try to convince me they've outgrown the nanny thing. After the last one, they ask the inevitable, with hope in their voices, "Don't you think you could find a college student to come after school and help us with our homework and take us to Burger King on the nights you're working? And when you're away for work, can't we stay with Daddy, or Grandy? We'll help clean the house, Mom. We're big girls now."

So I give in, and though it hasn't been easy, my girls and I have our house, and our life back. It's no picnic teaching kids in their teens to make their beds and clean their bathrooms after they've had someone cleaning up behind them for most of their lives. But they're learning. Turns out, firing the nanny was the best thing I ever did for my daughters.

More often than not, it's takeout food eaten on paper plates. Those are the nights I miss some of those nannies whose culinary talents would have made Martha Stewart proud. I wish *I* could cook, but I can't even find the time to get to the grocery store. I just read that by 4 P.M. on any given day, 75 percent of working moms have no idea what's for dinner. And that statistic assuages my guilt.

Sometimes, the logistics of life seem so much more complicated when there's no safety net. But as I think back on all the times I left my kids in the hands of strangers, some who lie and steal, I could kick myself, but prefer to thank my lucky stars we survived unscathed. And *that* is why I believe in miracles.

Birth of an Angel

MERCEDES

The phone rang in the middle of the night. It could've been 2, 3, or 4 A.M. I don't remember. It was the call I had been dreading for days. My mother was on the line sobbing. "The baby is dead," she screeched. My heart stopped and I started gasping for air in that familiar asthma attack trigger that I'd known all my life. But I managed to control myself as I told her I'd be right over. Without my saying a word, my husband knew what the call meant. I was furious. *"Coño!"* I screamed. "Damn!" I pounded the bed with my fist. I refused to cry. I jumped out of bed and threw on some clothes. Though my husband was already dressed and ready to go with me, I methodically took time to make the bed as if needing those extra moments of doing a normal household chore would compose me further.

The Children's Hospital was only a block away. And although driving would've been faster, I insisted on walking. Outside, the night was dark, very still and chilly for Miami. As I approached the hospital I began to shiver. The white lights behind the automatic doors and the antiseptic smell of the building pierced my senses. The elevator ride slowed what had become frantic running through a maze of nondescript corridors. I felt myself desperately sinking into hopelessness. We found the neonatal intensive care unit. As we rushed through the doors a nurse tried to stop us. "I'm the baby's aunt," I said, and they quietly moved away. She directed us to another set of doors where we met up with our family tragedy.

We searched through a low-lit pavilion with long hanging curtains that separated half a dozen bed units. I did a quick scan of them, but all were empty. Finally, behind one of the curtains I heard the soft weeping; I knew it was my twin sister, Mery. I pulled the drape and found her sitting on a rocking chair, talking to her dead baby. My brother-in-law, a lifelong bodybuilder with the look of a Mr. Olympia, seemed shrunken, on his knees next to them. I knelt on the floor, too, next to the baby's face. I could hear my husband embracing my brother-in-law, and I heard them weep. Mery and I just stared into each other's eyes, unable to speak, only able to communicate through our own language, with tears rolling down our faces and an indescribable grief in our hearts.

It's true what they say about twins. When one suffers, the other one bleeds from despair. I had always been a willing participant in Mery's life cycles, the good and the bad. But this we couldn't share. This pain she had to suffer alone. I couldn't really know what it was like to lose a child. I wasn't a mother yet. And, even if I had been, it's too personal an experience to possibly explain in all of its enormity. All I could do was try to calm her, even if I could barely calm myself.

After weeks of praying for Rebecca outside the neonatal unit's glass window, this was the first time I had been allowed to see her up close. She was nestled inside a cascade of her mother's long, curly black hair, finally protected in the motherly cradle the incubator had so denied them. She had been born prematurely, and her organs weren't fully developed. She had been put on a respirator with heavy doses of drugs. But all the efforts to save her were in vain.

She was twenty-four days old and tiny, never having weighed more than three pounds. She looked just like my sister, same pretty little nose, same black hair. She was wearing a white cotton T-shirt that contrasted sharply with the yellow of her skin. Her whole body was wrinkled, full of tubes and needle marks. Her eyes and lips were semiopened, her minute fingers firmly curled around her mother's hand.

I leaned over and kissed her forehead. It was a prolonged kiss in which her baby down hair gently tickled my nose as I breathed on her. She no longer had the delicious smell of a newborn. She smelled like alcohol and iodine. She already felt a bit rigid and cold. I realized Mery must've been sitting there for about half an hour.

As I lingered on the only kiss I would ever give my niece, my sister instinctively brushed me aside to protect the soft spot on her baby's head. "Be careful," she murmured. I moved back, feeling my throat lock in the pain of contained crying. Mery was in denial. She was not ready to let her baby go.

She began talking to her tiny preemie. "Don't be afraid my baby, Mommy's here, my angel, Mommy will always be with you, Mommy will love you forever. Mommy and Daddy will be with you again one day, you'll see. And then we will never be separated again. You are my love. You are the love of my life. You were so brave, so perfect. We're so proud of you. I'm sorry. I'm so sorry, my baby. How can I let you go? Oh God, why did you give her to me, only to take her away," became her weepy lament.

The nurse had been watching, engulfed in our nightmare. She

now moved in to ask for my help. It was time for Mery to release her baby. It fell to me to beg my beloved sister to give up the daughter she adored, the little angel she had stayed on absolute bed rest for over five weeks to save, the infant whose life was so precious to her that when her placenta previa turned into unstoppable hemorrhaging at twenty-four weeks of gestation, she refused an emergency C-section to give the baby more time to live . . . if only within her uterus. And now, after all her heroic unselfish effort, after she finally had that child in her bosom, I had to plead with Mery to give her daughter up forever.

I forced her to get up from the rocking chair, raise her arms, and give her to the nurse. She kissed and hugged her a thousand times. She tried negotiating with God. "Please take me, let her live, give her back. Why did you give her to me only to take her back?" She pleaded with the little strength she had left. The nurse just turned around and left with little Rebecca. It was more than Mery could take. She fell into her husband's arms, and then we all hugged and cried as we stumbled out into the hallway.

My twin sister, my soul mate, the woman I had loved and protected since childhood was now a child again for me to console. Only, I had no words. I could find no meaning, no lesson, no reason. There was only wretchedness. In this broken state she was made to sign documents and was grilled about hospital procedures.

By the time we made our way out, it was daybreak. We took her to our home where the family had started gathering. I eventually slipped away, unbeknownst to others, in an effort to make it to her home before she did. I was quick to remove all signs of the tragedy from her household.

I dumped dozens of tiny frozen bags of breast milk from her freezer. Mery, in her unwavering drive to save her daughter, had been extracting immunity-rich breast milk for almost a month to try to nurture her sick infant. But someone from the hospital staff had fed the baby formula. We still don't know why.

That day was a blur. The men went out to make funeral arrangements, and we women were left to deal with the sorrow. We ordered the hospital bed and monitors she had used during her bed rest removed from the house, put away all baby items, and helped Mery face the daunting job of telling her five-year-old son and two-year-old daughter that the baby sister they had been visiting at the hospital was not coming home.

At the viewing, Mery requested an open casket. Our tiny Rebecca was lying in a small white box dressed in the pink outfit and bonnet her mother had chosen to take her home in. She didn't look like a doll. She looked like a dead baby. I could only bear to look at her once.

My sister's crying and mourning had been so severe that she was hoarse and physically and emotionally spent. But it wasn't over yet. There was still the funeral. We all stood hanging on to each other under the green tarp tent. A priest said prayers and the little box was lowered into the ground. The family ushered Mery away. I decided to remain, alone, for her, for us, until the last shovel of soil entombed the little casket.

As I stood there alone with the gravediggers, the grief overcame me and I fell to my knees with such a thump that it made them bleed. I realized this was a precious moment. I too decided to talk to my baby niece myself. I asked her to be strong, to look for and find God and our dead relatives so they would love her and guide her as we would have done here on earth.

I told her she was not alone, and I especially asked her to help her mother and give her the same spiritual strength and unconditional love that she had been shown when she brought her into this world.

Rebecca María Flores died on the twenty-fourth of January. She had been a New Year's Day baby. Mery has never again attended a New Year's Eve celebration.

It's been a decade since Rebecca's death. My sister had two more beautiful boys after her. But never again the other little girl she so longed for. Although the depression and anguish has diminished for her with time, she once told me that the loss of a child is like the loss of a limb—just because you have another, it doesn't mean you don't sorely need the one that's gone. And just as some people claim to still feel their limbs years after they've lost them, so too my sister still feels her little girl, deep within her, as an angel who protects her from above.

Flying the Coop

LYDIA

It wasn't until I navigated my way through his cluttered room on tiptoe that reality set in. Boxes were all over the place, but by tomorrow at this time, his room would be empty. Manny, my firstborn child was going off to college, and I *just* wasn't ready. Over the years, I had heard so many parents counting the days until their children would move out. But I was never one of them, and I didn't know how I was ever going to cope with his leaving.

I tried to imagine opening the door to his room and finding nothing. I was already missing the mess he always made, and sorry for all the times I had yelled about it. I'm pretty anal and get a little frantic when things are out of place. But to Manny that never mattered. His room continued to be in a perpetual state of disarray, and today I realized how much I was going to miss it, along with the strawberry ice cream that is always in our freezer. Just to feel better, I continued to buy it even after he was gone. I dreaded thinking about dinnertime and not having Manny around questioning the daily menu, followed by the usual "is that all?" To Manny, who had a hole in his stomach, there was never enough food on the table.

How was I going to survive without him? Why couldn't I stop myself from thinking that this was all about me? I needed to get a grip and help my son experience the excitement of entering a new and exciting stage in his life. But I knew it would not be easy.

As we began loading up the cars for the trip up to Gainesville, it was torture to see my son's whole life packed into a handful of boxes. I tried to console myself with the thought that we were merely entering another chapter in our lives, but I knew in my heart that my baby was leaving for good. And while I was sure he would always be nearby, this rite of passage was the biggest one yet.

We hit the road in a caravan. Manny drove his car with a friend while my husband, infant daughter Christine, and I followed. It was the longest five-and-a-half-hour drive of my life, as my son's entire childhood flashed before me.

I remembered how in the 1970s, I used to hold his little hand while driving. Now he drove his own car toward a brand-new adventure and, as always, I was following behind him, making sure he'd get where he was going in a way I saw fit. On that trip, though, Manny never looked back.

After we got him settled into his off-campus apartment, helped him unpack, and took him out to dinner, I was satisfied with his new setup. Only then could I think about saying good-bye. But I still wasn't ready. I wondered to myself if I ever would be.

It was a tearful drive home, and I spoke to Manny at least ten times, reminding him to do all the little things I was afraid he still couldn't do for himself. But he tolerated my neurosis and assured me he'd be fine.

Ultimately, I survived, and while I experienced a lot of sleepless nights missing my son, I was actually starting to enjoy not having to worry about his curfew or waiting up for him anymore. We were ecstatic when he surprised us with a visit a month after school began, but then panicked at the thought of him driving that long stretch back to Gainesville, alone. I was glad he hadn't told me he was coming in the first place, sparing me the worry.

It was great to have him visit, but even when he was home, we hardly saw him. He spent most of his time in and out of the house, hanging out with his friends. The curfew I had so adamantly set had been tossed out the window and there was nothing I could do. My teenager had returned home as a man, and I wasn't sure if I liked it.

My son did exceptionally well in college, graduating on the dean's list, making me a very proud mom. Manny worked for one year, then went on to get his master's at the University of Miami. My baby has had great success professionally and personally—with a wife and a beautiful baby of his own now. He has made me a grandma, and the love I have for his daughter rocks my world. But I never stop worrying about *my* baby . . . my firstborn.

I gave Manny his wings and he flew, but lucky for me, his roots are firmly planted, and I shudder to think of the day *his* baby flies the coop. I only hope I'm there to see him let *her* go.

Daisy

PATRICIA

I sat by her as she took her last breaths. When there was no one around, I whispered in her ear, "It's OK Mami, you can leave, I'll be fine. Please rest. I love you." And then I told her to follow the light when she was ready. I gave my mom permission to die before I really knew how important it was for me to do that.

An hour or so later, my mother left us. She was surrounded by her family and friends as she exhaled that long, deep last breath of life. My mom died one day before Three Kings Day, a traditional Hispanic holiday similar to Christmas. It was also one day before the thirtieth anniversary of our arrival in Miami, after fleeing Cuba to escape Communism. My mom, who was only fifty-nine, passed away on a beautiful South Florida day, in the serenity of her own bed, tucked into her sheets and favorite comforter, surrounded by mementos of her life and countless pictures of her, my dad, and me.

My grandmother's explosive wailing as she realized her only daughter had died is the only thing that broke the silence and tore at the sadness and sacredness of the moment. I remember that my dad and I kept telling her to calm down because we thought my mom's spirit might still be lingering and she would hear. We didn't want that to be the last sound she heard on this earth. But my grandmother was inconsolable.

Numbness took me over and I shifted into automatic pilot. I don't remember if I cried but I do know that I kept holding her hand. I wanted to ingrain in my memory the feel of her skin and the scent of her body. As I looked at her hands and her nails I realized that I have exactly those same hands. Knowing that these were my last moments near my mom made me ache in ways I didn't think possible. I didn't want to let her go. I felt like I was drowning and gasping for air. I thought my heart was going to implode.

I went out to the living room with my dad to tell my cousins and friends who had gathered that she was gone. My cousin, who was very close to my mom, became hysterical . . . her husband desperately tried to comfort her. I remained calm through it all until my boyfriend arrived. He showed up as I was taking a moment by myself in the home office. His sweetness knocked down my stoic wall and threw me into the reality of the moment. I was overcome with sorrow.

He hugged me with love. His arms held me up. After more than a decade, I can still hear Nick's exact words, "I'm so sorry, baby." I could let loose with him and cry to my heart's content. Then I looked out the window and saw the undertaker arrive. That's when panic struck.

I rushed back to my mother's side, desperately wishing the moment away, but I knew I didn't have much time left with her. I kissed her repeatedly and told her that I loved her. Clutching her hand again, I told her not to worry because I would take care of my dad and grandmother. Though I wish the moment would have lasted longer, I had no time to linger; the undertakers started circling like vultures gripping that horrid body bag! Have they no heart? Can't they hide that thing in front of the family? It was more than I could take. I would not watch that "standard operating procedure," she was *Mami* . . . not a corpse. My heart could not take the sight of the woman who raised me and adored me with her entire existence being packaged up like a bundle of trash. I had said my good-bye so I escaped to the backyard.

You might think I was already a woman at age thirty-four. I had lived on my own for years and was self-sufficient, but Mami was always available if I needed her. My dad is amazing, and I thank God for him every day, but what daughter doesn't need her mom, even more so, as the years go by?

She was my crutch, my security blanket, always there to listen to my problems. She would cook for me, guide me with my business decisions, advise me on my love life, whether I wanted her to or not, and help me climb out of stupid holes I dug for myself. She understood and accepted me unconditionally. She was my best friend. When she died, I felt alone; I could no longer be Mami's little girl. Her death left a deep hole in my life.

At her funeral, my friend Tammi embraced me and asked how I was *really* coping, all alone with no siblings to help share the enormity of my loss.

Tammi only had one daughter then and her marriage was already in trouble, but on that day, through my tears, I told her, almost begged her to give her little girl, Chelsea, a brother or sister. I told her she should be spared what I was going through, dealing with the death of a parent, alone.

She listened and swears she has my mom, Daisy, to thank for her precious little Courtney who was born several years later. That's just one gift my mom left scattered on this planet.

I do believe in the afterlife and that we go on and our soul never dies. But I miss my mom in my physical life. I miss talking to her. Sometimes . . . I still find myself reaching for the phone to call her.

So I pray. And sometimes I ask for signs.

On what would have been my mom's birthday a few years ago, I woke up and talked to her, knowing deep inside that her spirit is always with me. I asked her to give me a sign to show me that she was OK. I thought and thought and then I said, "Mami, please show me daisies today so I know you're still with me." Her name was Daisy.

Then I was off to work where my day filled up with the usual meetings, deadlines, and headaches. I totally forgot about my request. At the end of the day I went for a much needed soothing massage. My masseuse's daughter Celeste was spending a day off from school with her mom. When she came over to give me a hug, I noticed that she was wearing little overalls filled with daisies. I was moved to tears. Up until that moment, I had forgotten my morning talk with my mother.

As I walked out the door, after the massage, this little girl handed me a drawing she had made just for me. It still hangs on my refrigerator. It was a beautiful field of daisies. The smile on my face expressed the gratitude that my choked-up voice could not release.

From there I drove, as if on a cloud, to a strip mall to pick up a watch I was having repaired. I kept thinking of my mom and asking myself if the daisies were a coincidence. As I arrived at the mall, I noticed that all the parking spots were taken except one. I turned into it, and there, in front of my eyes, was an art gallery. And in the window was a huge wall-sized mural of . . . DAISIES!

I never made it into the jewelry store. I was too overwhelmed, so I drove home.

Annie was deeply moved by my mom's story. She too is an only child who is extremely close to her parents. As it turns out, Annie's dad worked with my mom in Cuba more than thirty years ago. We discovered this connection for the first time when I bought my house, next to hers, in Coral Gables. "Pat, I can't even imagine what it would be like to lose one of my parents . . . I'm so close to both of them," cried Annie. "I'm not sure if I could hold up. I've warned my kids that the day I lose either Mami or Papi, I'm going to be a mess." Ironic how Annie and I are now such close friends and neighbors, and our parents knew each other before we were even born.

Death hasn't become easier for me. I've lost family members, friends, and too many pets I cherished. The profound sense of loss makes the grieving process very difficult. I realize that my anguish is a selfish emotion, though, and I'm doing my best to look at death from a higher and more spiritual perspective. I believe that when someone dies, they've completed their mission on this earth. The grieving and deep mourning that follows isn't really for the dearly departed, as much as it is for ourselves, and the loss that we feel.

Life has shown me that those who love us remain with us in this lifetime and throughout other ones. I believe we are one village and we always return to those we love.

Postscript:

Thirteen years after my mom's passing, I went to see the channeler John Edward. I had read his book, *Crossing Over,* and was riveted by his tales of communication with those who have died. My friend Mercedes told me he was coming to town, and she was going with her twin sister, Mery, who had lost a baby ten years prior. I jumped on the bandwagon, still being the ever-present skeptic, but always willing to give things a chance. We arrived early, at least we thought so, until we saw two thousand people waiting to get in. I couldn't believe it.

Standing in line, I learned that folks had traveled from New York, and other parts of the country, just to see this man who might communicate with their loved ones who had died. It was an amazing feeling to be surrounded by so much love and hope.

We took our seats and waited in anticipation. When John Edward walked onstage, the crowd jumped to their feet and roared. It concerned me; *he's not a rock star,* I thought. He's not the pope or the Dalai Lama, but there was a definite feeling of reverence in the audience. It was sweet, but also a little creepy. Whatever. I'll give him a chance.

The session started with a monologue where Edward explained what he calls "the process." He said that he too was a skeptic at first, but after several years he could not deny the fact that he was able to communicate with spirits. After thirty minutes or so, he opened up the floor to questions.

A lady stood up to speak. We could all see her on the big-screen TV as the camera focused in on her. Mery jumped when she saw who was in the audience behind the woman asking the question. It was the wife and son of someone we both knew who had recently passed. "Oh my God . . . that's Tom Fraioli's family," Mery said. "I can't believe they're here." In a sea of two thousand people, it was amazing to spot someone we knew. During intermission, before Edward started the channeling portion of the evening, Mery visited Tom's family. It turns out that Kitty, Tom's wife, had dragged her stepson, Jay, to the event.

Tom had passed away less than two months before and life was still very difficult for both of them. Jay decided to appease his stepmom and accompany her to the session, but he was somewhat wary. It's not that he didn't believe that readings take place, but he was skeptical of those who don't have the gift of channeling but take advantage of people's emotional states to capitalize on making money.

When Mery returned to her seat, John Edward came back onstage. As two thousand people sat there, waiting in silence, Edward paced the stage, back and forth, until he finally looked toward the back of the room and said: "You, the woman in the red dress . . . and the man in the blue tie, you've lost a father figure recently?" He was speaking to Kitty and Jay. We freaked!

Jay stood up. "Yes," he said. Edward continued: "Tom, Thomas" . . . Jay's voice cracked in acknowledgment and tears rolled down our eyes. Oh my God. "What is this thing Tom had with food?" Edward asked. Jay laughed and responded, "That was his life." Mery and I just looked at each other in disbelief. This was real. We knew these people. It wasn't a setup. Oh my God!

Edward then asked who Picky . . . or Pinky . . . was. Kitty stood up and yelped. "Oh, my God . . . Mr. Pinky, that's our cat! Tom was crazy about Mr. Pinky." The audience was stunned. We later found out that Mr. Pinky was Tom's favorite cat who is a little neurologically impaired—making him all the more special. Every night he would crawl into bed and into Tom's arms to fall asleep against his chest.

For one hour, John Edward communicated with loved ones who had passed, but obviously still remain with us. He talked to a young couple who had lost their two-year-old son, asking them if he drowned. They said no. He insisted he saw water. The parents finally acknowledged he died from fluid in the lungs. The boy's message was for the parents not to despair. There was nothing they could have done. It was meant to be and he was still with them. The baby's spirit thanked his family for whatever it was they were doing to keep his memory alive.

From there he went to an elderly lady. Edward laughed as he hesitantly communicated a message from her dead husband who was telling her he didn't like her new hair. Turns out he used to brush her brown hair every night. After he died, she dyed it blonde! Edward then blushed as he said, "I'm only the messenger here."

After about twenty spirits came through for their loved ones, it was time to go. We were stunned, amazed, and totally uplifted by this incredible evening. Even though our loved ones hadn't visited us, it didn't matter.

It confirmed for us that they're still here. As John Edward explained, we can speak with them directly; we don't need a channeler to communicate with our loved ones who died. We just need to be aware and open to signs.

Tammi and Sara looked at each other in disbelief as I told this story at a Bombshell meeting. Sara stayed quiet. Tammi, as usual, didn't—"Oh Pat, puh-leese . . . it had to be a setup." I simply ignored her and continued my story.

One week after the John Edward experience, I was in Boston celebrating my forty-eighth birthday. I woke up in the morning and I prayed to my mom: "Would you mind showing me a daisy today?"

Feeling guilty, after having asked this before and receiving it, I immediately told her it would be OK if she didn't want to. But deep down, I wanted yet another reconfirmation of what my heart already knew but my skeptical brain still questioned.

The day passed and no daisies appeared. As before, I forgot about my request. The following day, I took a train to New York City. As I picked up a USA Today newspaper . . . I saw a picture on the front page. It was a man, standing in front of a shop. The sign hanging from the store read: "Daisy Flower Shoppe" . . . and had a picture of two daisies.

Thanks Mami. I promise I won't ask for any more signs. I know you're here and I love you very much. We'll talk later.

Nana Banana

SARA

The phone rings shortly after eleven. Who is calling here so late? I'm just on the edge of sleep, when you know you're on your way, but still waiting for it to envelop you. This state is so tenuous, so tentative . . . even the smallest sound can pull you out.

"Hi, Sara, sorry to bother you so late, but I've got some bad news. Nana died a little while ago."

Dad sounds so unruffled. Just a few weeks ago, he and I had had a discussion about Nana's impending death, when his brother-in-law passed away suddenly of unknown causes. When that call came, and I heard the sound of my father's voice, I knew instinctively something was wrong; I immediately thought of Nana. When he delivered the tragic news about my uncle, we talked a little bit about death. He was convinced Nana was ready to go. She practically said so when we went to visit her on her ninetieth birthday.

I ask how my aunt Andie is doing. She lives in the same city as Nana and had to take care of the day-to-day responsibilities. Aunt Andie buried her husband three weeks ago. Dad says she's doing all right, and that he, my stepmother, and youngest sister will be flying to Buffalo as soon as they can get flights. I ask about the funeral. It'll be the day after tomorrow, or worst case, day after that. I tell him I'll book a flight in the morning, and we say goodnight, almost too calmly.

I have no hope of going back to sleep. I can't believe I actually imagined I could receive news like that and roll over, push away the thoughts until the morning.

My husband tries to comfort me, but I don't even know how to comfort myself. Sometimes we just have to feel it.

"Did I tell my father that I love him?" I ask and get out of bed.

Nana's world centered around a hospital bed and a feeding tube. Her memory was nearly gone. She was nothing like the grandmother I remembered from our summers together. She'd been quite a character. While most grandparents doted on their grandkids and bragged about them, Nana made it clear *we* were the lucky ones. "You'll miss me when I'm gone," she'd promise.

She would have me tweeze the sharp, black hairs from her wrinkled chin. And I'd worry about inheriting her beard, which still terrifies me every time I tweeze a hair from my chin, barely forty years old.

Before she became so frail, Nana came down to visit my father and they'd always jump in the car and head for Miami. Ten years ago, Nana stayed with us for a week.

She was very demanding. Dinner had to be a formal affair—one she dressed for, wig and all—even at the kitchen table. One Friday evening, I phoned home from work to discuss the dinner plans.

"How about we just go out and have some Italian food?" I suggested. I was exhausted from a week of work. Let someone else cook.

"No, I don't feel like going out," she replied.

"Ok, I'll pick something up," I tried.

"No, I'm in the mood for something homemade," she countered.

"How about if I make some pasta?" I tried again. Boiling water, sauce in the microwave. I could handle that.

"No, I have a taste for something specific. I want veal cutlet."

She wanted veal cutlet, which required a trip to the store, battering, breading, frying. Ugh. Veal cutlet.

But I made it. Because she was Nana. And I couldn't say no to her. She *loved* it, complimented me on the food, thanked me for satisfying her craving, said it was one of the best meals she'd ever had. She was so content she went to bed early.

We were all on Nana's schedule that week. She'd been up at 6:15 every morning, eating her banana and drinking her Kava no-acid coffeelike drink. But the next morning, we were up and Nana wasn't. It was 7:30, and she was still in her room. We waited a little while, and then had breakfast.

It was 8:30 now. We listened for sounds at the door, made weak knocking sounds, with no response. By 9:00, I was worried. Could my home-cooked meal have killed her? Was my veal cutlet Nana's last supper? We snuck into her room and put a mirror up to her nose. It fogged. She breathed, and so did we.

For her ninetieth birthday, Nana's kids threw her a big party. Family and friends came in from all over, and it was a big celebration. She was aware of most of it, but toward the end of the day, she started drifting away. She began talking about a trip she was going to take. I was working in London at the time, and she imagined I was going to take her there. It was obvious to all around that her health would never have allowed for such a strenuous trip, but I had other ideas.

I bought a small tape recorder and had the flight attendants and all my London friends talk to Nana on my next trip over. I gave her a play-by-play of the flight, and of the lovely country hotel where I was staying. I had always intended to complete the tape with tours of the best sights—Big Ben, Tower of London—but my job ended and I never got back there.

I figured I could finish the tape reading excerpts from my tourist guidebook. She wouldn't know the difference. But I never did finish it. Maybe it was because Nana would never tolerate anything less than total honesty. Maybe it was because I never made it a priority. Or maybe it was because I wanted to believe there was no rush; she'd be there when it was finished.

Grandparents are our link with the past, but by the time we are old enough to appreciate them, they've grown older, too.

Tell them you love them. Finish what you start for them. Cook them their favorite meal. Take them to London before they're too old to make the trip. We are the lucky ones. Tell them *that*.

The Tooth Fairy's Gone AWOL

TAMMI

When we were kids, we *lived* for special occasions . . . crispy autumn days at the pumpkin patch, decorating Easter eggs my grandma used to insist were for Passover. But for me, those mysterious visits from the Tooth Fairy took the cake. I'd lose a tooth, put it under my pillow, and lo and behold, every single time, a quarter would be waiting for me as I wiped the sand from my eyes. Those mornings were among the most treasured of my whole life, and my mom seemed to revel in them, too. So now that *I'm* a parent, why do all those *irregularly scheduled* rites of passage seem like such a hassle to me? Sometimes I wonder if the balancing act I'm trying to perform each and every day is pushing the scales (and me) right over the edge . . . when did the fun part of raising children get lost in the shuffle?

I really liked the Tooth Fairy thing in the early days of parenthood, but, just like those Barney songs and annual ballet and hiphop dance recitals (which cost $500 between those ugly costumes and $15 tickets for every single branch on the family tree), after a while, it all seemed to get old. There are a lot of teeth in a kid's mouth, and most of them eventually fall out. But the Tooth Fairy obligation never seemed to go away.

When Chelsea, my oldest, lost her first tooth at six, she was chomping on a piece of popcorn at the movies with a friend. Back then, it killed me that I wasn't there to see it. As a working mom, there were so many milestones I'd missed. But when Chelsea lost that first baby tooth, I ran right home and we celebrated for days. It was so important back then. It was one way to compensate for working so much, and missing so many of the big moments in her life. The Berlin Wall was crumbling the day my daughter took her first steps, and I didn't get home until she was almost running. That's why Chelsea's Tooth Fairy was way more generous than *mine* had ever been. She left a twenty-dollar bill, probably to overcompensate for her guilt.

The payout dropped to five dollars for Chelsea's next few teeth, and by the time we got to the incisors, she was lucky to find a buck or two under her pillow. Eventually, my oldest passed her fascination for the Tooth Fairy on to her little sister, Courtney, who, by the time it was her turn, was happy with a few quarters. A few times, the Tooth Fairy even fell asleep, forgetting to make a deposit under the pillow. The excitement may have worn off, but I'd always awaken at 3 A.M. in a panic, and never actually missed one completely.

Until the time I was in New York on a business trip. The girls' dad had already moved out, and Chelsea had lost yet another tooth. The trusted nanny du jour was trying in vain to understand the Tooth Fairy deal long distance, but English was not her first language, and although the Spanish dictionary I carry translated "pillow" as *almohada,* this babysitter thought I was asking her to put money under the almonds in the cupboard. When you come from the hills of Central America, secretly hiding money under your kid's pillow in exchange for nothing doesn't make much sense.

But back then, the Tooth Fairy gig was definitely not up. Guilt over not being there once again got the best of me. So I threw on some sweats and ran downstairs to the hotel's business center. It cost me five bucks, but I sent my daughter an IOU from the Tooth Fairy via fax. Chelsea was just happy to know she hadn't been forgotten, and when I got home, she proudly showed me the fax, asking when I thought the Tooth Fairy would come back to pay up. I was just glad she'd reminded me.

My girls are teenagers now, but they milked the Tooth Fairy game as long as they could. Courtney was already ten when she lost two teeth in one day, and when she awoke to find the teeth and no money, she marched into my room, furious, demanding to know what had gone wrong. I knew she couldn't *really* still believe, so I fessed up: "The Tooth Fairy had two glasses of wine last night and passed out." I gave her an extra buck that morning and told her the Tooth Fairy had gone AWOL. She didn't understand what that meant, but I was too tired to explain.

Maybe I'm not the mom I had or the one I sometimes wish I could be. But I love my girls more than anything in the whole world, and they know that. They also know I'm not perfect, and that we're making memories every day, even if our holiday displays remain in storage year after year. I only hope that when they look back on their childhood years, they remember all the laughter more clearly than the times I wasn't there.

Crash Course

ANNIE

My teenage daughter has completely remodeled my shiny little car by rear-ending a brand-new Mercedes Benz. She says the brakes gave out; at least she has good taste in selecting automobiles with which to merge.

My vehicle no longer has headlights, a smooth hood, or a tight bumper. That makes two of us. My car now sits patiently at the body shop waiting to have the nips and tucks that I wish I could afford.

I have not yet recovered from the nightmarish phone call that every parent fears. It was a rainy evening and my daughter and son had taken a short drive to rent a movie, an innocuous trip, I thought. And then the phone rang and I heard my son's voice. He was calm as he explained that they had been in an accident. At first, I thought he was kidding and then I heard my daughter sobbing in the background.

I began to panic silently as the beads of perspiration began to form under my arms. "Oh God, are you guys all right, is anyone hurt?" as I began the parental interrogation. My son assured me they were both fine but begged me to hurry. All of a sudden, my independent teenagers needed their mom.

My husband was at the mall (where cell phones don't work) and although he's much better at all types of emergencies than I, obviously I would have to go this one alone. I sat paralyzed for about sixty seconds and then picked up the phone and called my Bombshell friend and next-door neighbor, Pat. By the time I hung up the phone, she was outside my house with the engine running.

As I buckled my seat belt, I thought about some statistics I had read recently: most automobile accidents occur during the sun-setting hours. Why, oh why, didn't I ask my kids to wait until the sun went down? I knew I was thinking irrationally but I couldn't help myself. The drive seemed eternal despite the close proximity to the video store.

The accident was easy to spot as we pulled up to the red and blue lights reflecting off my wrinkled Saab. I saw my shivering kids standing in the rain and then my crunched-up vehicle; my heart broke for both. When I saw that my children were okay, I began to sob. Was I crying for them or my car? I wondered.

People have often said that as parents we worry about our children until we know they are fine. Then we can take the time and energy to be furious about their indiscretions, whether real or perceived. My daughter took one look at me, threw her arms around my neck, and began to cry. I calmed her down and then I wanted to kill her. All I could envision was my insurance premiums climbing ever higher into the stratosphere, or even worse, maybe they would cancel our coverage altogether. I know I should have been more grateful that they weren't hurt, and I really was, but why was I focusing on the monetary aspect of this ordeal?

The police officer was brusque, almost to the point of rudeness, as he wrote out the ticket. Although my daughter had a valid license and a current insurance card, she looks so young, maybe he thought she was an underage driver on a learner's permit.

The driver of the other car was now marching toward me. I was the mother of the criminal who had just banged up her car. She was irate as she declared how inconvenienced she was by this accident. I had news for her; it wasn't exactly on my agenda either. But I politely apologized and made a futile effort to explain that accidents do happen.

My daughter cautioned me sternly to have the car towed, as she was sure a brake malfunction had caused the accident. However, I trusted my gut that said the accident was human (i.e., daughter) error, rather than mechanical failure, and got behind the wheel. My good friend Pat was in front of me all the way home as my trusty little car held its place on the slick streets.

My car spent twenty-seven days at the Car Spa getting rejuvenated while I was mass-producing worry lines on my face. My daughter quickly overcame her fear of driving and has now suggested that a car of her own would definitely make my life easier. Yeah, right! Her kindness is overwhelming, but she did volunteer to get a part-time job to pay for the additional insurance.

At a dinner with the other Bombshells, when I shared my concerns about having a teenage driver out on the streets, Tammi practically jumped out of her seat. "I can so relate," she reminded us. "I live about twenty-five minutes from where my girls go to school. They have to take I-95 twice a day. It's awful. Imagine this—last June, while Chelsea was on a learner's permit, a friend of hers was killed in an automobile accident on I-95 on a rainy evening. I've been a wreck ever since worrying about my girls on that treacherous highway!"

(Tammi said both she and Chelsea were so devastated by the young friend's untimely death that she has since sold her home and bought a new one only minutes away from the school, sans highway driving. Chelsea has her license now and she drives back and forth to school twice a day, picks up milk and orange juice for her mom, and sometimes drives Courtney, her younger sister, to dance class, all within just a few miles, still without highway driving. Both mother and child are sleeping better these nights.)

"I don't even want to think about when my little girl starts to drive," frowned Mercedes. "Somebody once said, it takes about six weeks to get back to normal after you've had a baby. I don't think there is such as thing as 'normal' once you're a mother. You will always worry."

Every day I implore St. Christopher, the patron saint of travel, to keep my daughter safe. And I'm bracing myself for the day my son is old enough to drive. It's just around the corner and I'm already fastening my seat belt for that bumpy ride.

Abuela

LYDIA

One afternoon, as the Bombshells were enjoying a delicious Sunday brunch at the beautiful Coral Gables Biltmore Hotel, Pat's cell phone rang. It was Pat's 100-year-old grandmother, Mimi. It was only a reminder, she told Pat, to go to the drugstore and pick up her prescriptions. Within the next twenty minutes, Mimi called five more times, each time setting a new reminder of another errand Pat needed to run for her. This quickly turned the topic of our conversation to grandmothers, and before I knew it, the six of us were all competing to see whose grandma would win the grand prize.

Tammi's grandmother, also called Mimi, named her grandkids

"the five delicious flavors," but Tammi boasted about how she was definitely the cherry in her family. "She always called me her number one, and I know it wasn't just because I was the oldest," Tammi bragged. "I was so blessed to have her around until I was forty. She was my very best friend."

After listening to the stories about the bonds these grown women shared with their grandmothers, I swear I could almost smell my grandmother's cooking . . . the *bistec empanizado, arroz blanco,* and *platanos maduros fritos* (breaded steak, white rice and fried sweet plantains), which still stops me dead in my tracks, longing for just one more day with my *abuela*. To most of us Cubans, our *abuela* is almost as important as our mother and, in some cases, even more so. Now it was my turn to sing her praises. But Sara wouldn't let me. "My grandmother was the epitome of style," she said. "She even wore her colorful cardigans, pencil-thin skirts, and Ferragamos to her chemotherapy treatments."

"Well, my grandmother is about to turn a hundred and one and she's amazing . . . she refuses to leave the house without makeup, is still sharp, reads the entire newspaper every day and is ready to go out to dinner, travel, or party at a moment's notice," states Pat.

"Now we know where you get it from," laughs Sara. Tammi was still rambling on about Mimi's chicken fricassee and how she was the best cook ever.

What is it about food and grandmas? As I walk down Little Havana where most restaurants are preparing the traditional Cuban dishes, the smell of certain foods still brings back great memories of the endless energy of an overweight, four-foot ten-inch woman. At fifty-one, she left Cuba and migrated to the United States with my mother (her only child), my father, my sister, and me.

Leaving my grandfather behind to take care of his ailing mother, my grandmother committed the rest of her life to taking care of the four of us. Looking back today, I realize just how much she gave up for us and how very important we were to her.

As an immigrant in a foreign country, my *abuela* was a survivor.

She took English classes and cooking classes and did everything she could to be independent. That meant riding the bus, since she did not drive, and finding a job to help support our family.

Abuela became an expert on the Miami transit system. She would take my sister and me on the bus to ballet classes and shopping all over town. Everything we did depended on public transportation unless my father was off from work on the weekend. My mother did not drive.

Struggling with her English always made going to the grocery store's butcher shop an event. As a child, my taste in food was anything but typical. I liked lamb, liver, rice with squid, and other foods not usually found on a restaurant children's menu. My grandmother would actually have to imitate a sheep when she needed to order lamb at the butcher. It was the only way to order what she wanted.

So we would stand at the counter as *Abuela* chanted *"B-a-a-a . . . b-a-a-a-a"* until the butcher would *"B-a-a-a . . . b-a-a-a"* back to her. For a five-year-old girl, it was embarrassing as hell. But, for *Abuela,* it became a ritual that would create laughter and joy for all who stood in line with us. I have to admit that deep down it also made me giggle. Thinking about it today simply warms my heart.

As hard as she tried, months went by but her English was just not progressing. She eventually understood some words, but never quite got it, even after attending endless nights of school. Limited communication did not stop *Abuela,* however. She challenged herself by religiously attending her cooking classes.

On the bus rides to the class, she would study her books to learn the art of decorating cucumbers, stuffed tomatoes, and other beautiful food preparations. On the bus ride back, she would carry the treasures of the night's lessons. Every night was a new treat as we sampled the masterpieces she had created. I remember looking forward to each new edible creation. *Abuela* may not have mastered the English language, but she definitely learned the mastery of cooking. Martha Stewart has nothing on my *Abuela*!

We lived on Miami Beach, what is now referred to as South Beach. It wasn't hot, sophisticated, and chic back then when the population consisted mainly of retired elderly people. My grandmother would take us walking along the beach, stopping on occasion to see *el baile de los viejos* (the old folks' dance). The dances were held in a hall located right on the beach. What a setting for these retirees; warm weather with the vast ocean and palm trees swaying to the rhythm of their music. The moves looked like a distant cousin of square dancing, where the youngest person on the dance floor was eighty years old. You would have thought old band music would have been more appropriate, but the radiating energies of these old folks was even surprising to me as a child. Talk about having fun; we used to stand there for hours and just enjoy the hilarious outfits and hairdos, not to mention the nifty dance moves.

Abuela never seemed to get tired; she was our family's Superwoman. Every day she would get up at five in the morning to leave everything ready before my sister and I went to school. She would then take the bus to work, where she spent all day at a children's clothing factory. If her cooking was awesome, the clothes she made were over the top. At the end of a long hard day, she'd jump back on the bus and get off at the grocery store. This tireless woman would then walk one mile to our house, grocery bags in hand, just to prepare supper, pick up, wash the dishes, and then sew our clothes. She would also bring some additional *piezas* (clothing sections) home to sew to make a bit more money. *Abuela*'s Singer sewing machine was more powerful than the Batmobile.

Abuela was an amazing seamstress. Parties, a high school dance, the prom . . . on the spur of the moment, *Abuela* would design a dress, pants, blouse, anything I wanted. One year she even made the cheerleading skirts for my sister's entire squad. *Abuela* never bought a pattern in her life. All of her patterns were self-made out of newspaper or brown paper grocery bags. Apparently, that's another trait exclusive to our grandmas, as I learned the night Tammi told us lovingly about the dozens of baby booties and afghans her Mimi knitted for all of her friends' newborns over the years.

I am a grandmother now and wish I could give my granddaughter gifts with a personal touch but, instead, I order the baby gifts from the Pottery Barn Kids catalog.

As I think back I wish that I had half of my *Abuela*'s energy. I don't know if it was the Cuban coffee that kept her going, but she was definitely nonstop. *Abuela* only paused when she tuned us out to tune in to her favorite *novelas* (Spanish soap operas). Through it all, she smiled and never complained.

Regardless of the sacrifices she made and all those long, laborious days, my *abuela* made a point of saving money to buy beautiful jewelry for my sister and me. She was a regular at the very upscale Mayor's Jewelers, where she was known for putting things on layaway until she could pay them off, dollar by dollar. And always by the time our birthdays or Christmas came around, *Abuela* would have sparkling heartfelt gifts just for us. For our fifteenth birthday, the Cuban's version of a Sweet Sixteen, *Abuela* bought us each diamond rings! Thirty years later, I still wear that beautiful ring and cherish it with all my heart.

When I became a parent, at age seventeen, *Abuela* retired to take care of my son while I worked and went to school. Even then, she continued to lavish her love and attention on both my sister and me.

Years passed. My son had just turned seven. We were at my parents' house ready to enjoy another great family dinner. The warm and sweet smell of my grandmother's cooking filled the house. After dinner I went to freshen up in the bathroom and found my grandmother lying on the floor. As I helped her to get up, she nearly fainted. "I don't know what's wrong with me," she said. I immediately alerted my parents and called her doctor, who told me we had to take her to the hospital.

I was not prepared for the commotion of the ER. My parents' worried faces did not offer me any comfort. My nerves were shattered and my prayers intensified by the second. The doctor finally came out and advised us that *Abuela* had suffered a massive heart attack and the outlook was not positive. As practicing Catholics, we immediately contacted a priest to come and give her the last rites. We were preparing ourselves for the worst.

But Superwoman pulled through. In fact, she seemed to come back stronger than ever. Our *abuela* wasn't giving in to a massive heart attack, and she almost didn't skip a beat. Months later *Abuela* was right where she left off, cooking, cleaning, and washing. We begged her not to do so much but there was no way to stop her. It brought her joy.

One night, three years after her initial heart attack, we all looked at each other as she served dinner. I will never forget it. The dish was *carne con papas* (beef stew), but it was floating in an ocean of grease. *Abuela,* the great cook, had overdone it on the olive oil. We thought it was just one of those things, but it kept happening and with greater frequency.

Little by little, her cooking started to decline. As months passed, other signs of a worsening condition appeared. She would put two and sometimes three pairs of underwear on with as many dresses on top of them. We would get home and *Abuela* would be wandering in the street. In desperation my mother took her to a psychiatrist, which only made matters worse. He prescribed drugs, which not only accelerated her condition but also gave her a bleeding ulcer.

Eventually, *Abuela* became bedridden. She could not talk or feed herself. My family was devastated. We hired at-home care, but eventually we realized it wasn't enough. The hardest decision my mother ever made was to place her in a home away from all she loved and in the hands of strangers. It was there that she was finally diagnosed with that most dreaded disease, Alzheimer's.

My *abuela* passed away, from complications related to Alzheimer's, on October 1, 1990. She was two days away from turning eighty. My *abuela*, our backbone, was gone. Though I was thirty-three years old, I was not prepared to let her go. The void was immense. Our only solace was in knowing that she was out of her pain. We know she still watches over us and guides us from above. Her strength and determination will live on in our hearts.

To this day, I smell *Abuela*'s cooking. But it's not just a smell. It's a penetrating essence that touches my soul and makes me think of the good times we had with her. It's a smell that takes me back in time and always makes me smile.

Years after my grandmother's passing, I volunteered my time on the local Alzheimer's Association Board. I wanted to do my part to help beat the disease that stole my *abuela* from me. While I can't bring her back, I know she'd be proud to see that I have reached out to others who are plagued by what, for now, remains an incurable disease. And as she looks down upon me, I pray that she is as proud of me as I was of her.

Confessions of a Stepmom

SARA

One of the topics we talk about most at our Bombshell meetings is our children. Sometimes it's how wonderful they are, the play she is appearing in, the adorable thing he said. But those are the easy things to talk about, and that's not what we go to meetings to discuss. We are there to air the thoughts and frustrations that are bottled up inside of us, to say that which should not be said.

And we do go on, about weight problems and sleeping issues and homework troubles. But as the girls speak, I am thinking one thought: if you think parenting is difficult, try being a stepparent. It is undoubtedly the hardest job in the world.

When I voice my feelings to the group, they don't really understand. Only Lydia has been in the same boat: she is stepmother to three children from her husband's first marriage.

"I've never had any problems," says Lydia. "For me, being a stepmom has been a joy. I have a very special relationship with my step-daughter, Julie. She's become a true friend and we share almost everything."

"Have they ever lived with you?" I ask, and the reply is "No, they never lived in Miami full-time. They spend vacations with us."

"Vacations are different," I say. "They're easy compared to the day-to-day stuff. Rules are relaxed on vacation; there's no home-work or chores to do." I'm feeling alone on this particular subject when it comes to the Bombshells.

And I'm the only one in the group to also *have* a stepmom, so I see the situation from both perspectives. "Maybe you shouldn't base your relationship with your stepkids on the one you have with your stepmother," says Tammi. "Why do you assume they feel the same way about having a stepmother that you do? It's a completely differ-ent situation." I know she's right, but it's impossible for me to sepa-rate the experiences.

And it's not like there is a particular incident that causes me to feel this way; the fact is there are hardly any "incidents." It's more that I feel like an intruder in their lives and a stranger in my own house when they're around. Sometimes I think the only thing hold-ing our relationship together is the marriage certificate.

"Why don't you just tell them how you feel?" asks Pat. It's such a simple question, and I'm tempted to make a sarcastic comment about how she doesn't have any children of her own, but I know she's absolutely right about this. If I want the relationship to change, I need to do something about it. And it needs to start with talking to them.

But how to speak to two teenage boys, ages fourteen and sixteen, whose idea of communicating is one-word answers and grunts? That's where the pen comes in. "Write them a letter," suggests Mercedes, who has been writing to her children since before they were born. "Just write down how you feel and let that be the first step."

Dear Kids,

I'm writing to tell you that I really do love you, something I
need you to know. It may not seem that way sometimes, like
when I make you eat healthy food, or tell you to pick up your
underwear from the bathroom floor, do your homework, or
ask you if you've brushed your teeth, or any of the numerous
nagging activities in which I partake.

In this way, I don't treat you any differently than I treat
my blood son, the one I pushed out through the birth canal,
but then again, you weren't born to me and didn't start out
with the innate predisposition to love me unconditionally.

It's important to say "I love you" in writing given the fact
that over the past five years I've only said it to your faces a
few times. This is not because I haven't felt it, it's because I
never wanted to put you in a position to have to say it back.
And I suppose I never wanted to find out if you would. And
the reason I'm not very physically affectionate with you—
even though my son and I hug and kiss all the time—is
because I never wanted to take anything that wasn't
voluntarily offered. I don't come into your room every night
before you go to sleep because I don't want to bother you.
You don't seem to need or want the goodnight ritual I am
accustomed to with my son. And the few times I have gone
in, and pressed my lips upon your foreheads, it seemed to
me like something you hoped would be over quickly.

I know it must seem that your dad and I are a unit now, a
package deal. We like to be together, which means we do a
lot of activities with you kids as a family. And because we
don't see you all the time, when we are together, we like us to
be *together*.

But you probably want some time with your father alone,
or one-on-one. In a two-parent/two-kid household without

any "steps," one kid might spend time with one parent while the others do the same. That doesn't happen very often with us, since the "other" kid doesn't generally want to get left with the stepmonster. I don't think that's a reflection on me; I perceive it as not wanting to give up time with Dad.

The nagging is well intentioned, really. I see you guys growing into adolescence, developing your talents and strong personalities, and want to make sure you have every opportunity in life to be successful. And yes, that means proper manners at the dinner table and learning how to be a good houseguest, in addition to good grooming and social skills. I want you to become healthy, prosperous adults, and I just don't see that unlimited PlayStation gets you any closer to that goal.

And in spite of my constant reminders, the two of you have been nothing but respectful toward me throughout our relationship. I've braced—in vain—for the shouts of "You're not the boss of me" or "you're *not* my mother," but you've never even raised your voices. I've told you I would never try to replace your mother, explained that sometimes in public it's easier to let strangers assume I'm your mom, but that's only out of convenience.

On the other hand, I've never really defined what I am to you. I came onto the scene, unbidden, and you had no choice in the matter. As if two parents telling you what to do aren't sufficient, you got a third authority figure, and if that wasn't bad enough, she was always kissing and hugging your father. It's enough to make you sick.

So here's what I hope to be to you: someone to inspire you to try new things, develop your passions, and enjoy life. Someone to guide you to make good decisions, and take risks. Someone to come to if you ever get into trouble, who will rescue you regardless of the situation. And someone to give you a goodnight kiss when you want one, or deliver a hug when you need one.

Don't be frightened by the stepmonster: she may look tough on the outside, but inside she's all heart. And the truth is, she's much more afraid of you than you are of her.

Love you two, really I do. And you should consider this letter an invitation to love me back.

Sara

three | # Who Am I?

I t would be difficult to find six women more different than the Miami Bomb-shells. Some of us think Pat's brain must have been baking under the South Beach sun when she decided to put us into one another's lives. We are all full-time professionals who then become overtime mothers, wives, sisters, and friends.

Most of us travel the globe for work. Trying to coordinate schedules for our Miami Bombshell meetings was ridiculous. We communicated from Alaska to Tokyo to Santiago, Chile to Colorado, through insanely expensive hotel phones, e-mails at Internet cafés, and cell phone conference calls. We might have even considered Pat's idea of smoke signals if that would've helped us keep in touch.

Since we started meeting each one of us has been soaring professionally higher than we had ever imagined, but we have also been going through some major midlife crises, many hitting us without warning. Through the really tough times, though we're not sure how, our Bombshell buddies became our very best friends, and in those friendships we found the freedom to be ourselves.

And being ourselves means eating. Every one of us loves food.

It's just who we are. We either diet too much or don't exercise enough. Mercedes does neither. Lydia is happiest when she's eating, until the heartburn kicks in, which is usually followed by guilt, and then the Weight Watchers Points Program, which she scores in her BlackBerry.

Annie's also a Weight Watchers lifer, and Sara's forever in The Zone, spending a fortune to have gourmet, low-carb meals delivered on the weeks she's not cheating. Tammi, too, is either eating no salt, sugar, dairy, or candy, but never all at the same time.

Four Miami Bombshells have their self-esteem tightly wound to the numbers on the scales none will even put in their bathrooms, which only escalates their envy of skinny-minny Mercedes, who can down half a tray of Godiva-covered macadamia nuts at every single meeting with no consequences. That alone makes her our diva.

Since losing twenty pounds last year, Pat only eats fist-sized portions of healthy foods (along with chocolate) and she's become obsessed with not looking her age, making the rest of us worry that her next boyfriend will be younger than some of our children.

Food may bring us together, but our cultures have clashed enough times to give us whiplash. Cuban moms Mercedes, Lydia, and Annie find it reprehensible that the *Americanas* can pack their kids up and send them away to camp all summer, exposing them to dangers, strangers, and probably very bad influences. These Latin *mamis* would never take their eyes off their kids. They live, eat, and sleep every minute of their lives physically attached to their children, and still consider chaperoning a positive rite of passage in every young adult's life. If not for that Latin protection shield, how else to remain Daddy's little girl?

Tammi and Sara have never been able to grasp the concept of Cuban Time, which is generally an hour later than Eastern Standard Time. They are always punctual, and having scheduled every moment of the day, they easily get frustrated when their Cuban Bombshell friends arrive at meetings religiously tardy. Case in point:

Bombshell Meeting, May 2003

Sara and Tammi prepare lunch in Tam's kitchen, as they wait for the Cubans who are all half an hour late (again). They don't *comprende* the Hispanic tardiness thing and are seething (yet again). Outside, Mercedes, who had warned the *gringas* she would be half an hour late, pulls up just as Annie and Pat are taking their time, getting out of Pat's car.

Lydia is still missing in action, presumably getting her nails done. It is always a given that she will arrive forty-five minutes late and won't even pretend to make excuses.

But as Tammi's Cuban boyfriend opens the door for the three latecomers, Sara starts complaining. Mercedes turns to the beau and makes an obnoxious comment in Spanish that the gringas don't understand: *"Oye, ya estoy harta de estas reuniones"* (I'm getting really sick of these meetings). The two laugh while Sara and Tammi scowl. As all sit down at the dining room table to get the meeting rolling, Sara's face begins to turn red, really red, as her mounting rage becomes apparent.

Fifteen minutes later, the boyfriend brings out lunch, and the doorbell rings (again). Lydia saunters into the room with a big smile, sharing her inimitable good cheer. As she sits down, Sara explodes, justifiably, at everyone's lack of respect for time and says she's sick of always having to wait for the others. The Cubans look to Pat to take on the role of mediator. "The reason we started this group was to get away from the corporate America mentality, Sarita; this isn't a board meeting," says Pat. Mercedes is getting very offended, and her voice is getting louder. "My parents didn't take me out of Castro's Cuba to come here and endure someone else's tyranny." Tammi jumps in to try and make the others see how rude they've been. But it is getting late, and there is food on the table; eventually, everyone gets distracted by the salmon and salsa. Annie, who usually won't enter into conflict, turns away to answer her "I'm a Barbie Girl" singing cell phone, as Lydia, perfectly coiffed and accessorized, flashes a conspiratorial smile at Pat, her best friend, who's tolerated her tardiness for thirty-five years now. *Ay caramba.*

But the many things we *do* have in common seem to compensate for our differences and excesses. After all, we're a perfect match. We're Hispanic and Jewish, so it's a given that we will overaccessorize, shop till we drop, and obsess over fashion. Tammi has brainwashed her children into believing all designer goods are, well, bad, while Lydia and her daughter share dozens of designer purses that she proudly displays whenever we get together. Neither one is better or worse. Neither is right or wrong. We are who we are. And we're getting too old to change that. We're now only hoping to gain enough wisdom to admit it and make the most of it.

Forever Fat

SARA

"You're a better actress," the drama teacher quipped without skipping a beat, "but she'll look better in the costume." My puzzled look told her I wasn't getting her point.

"Well . . . you've put on a bit of weight lately, and the role calls for a lithe, slim, fairylike woman." Looking back, I swear I remember her taking pleasure in this conversation.

I looked down at my seventeen-year-old waistline protruding over my pants and tried to recall the way it used to look. Fighting back tears, I saw for the very first time that beauty was more important than brains. It all seemed so unfair.

But that teacher *was* right about my weight. My breasts, once small and firm, had become fleshy and round, and my stomach jutted out under them. I tried to convince myself I was still growing as I raided my mother's closet for pants that didn't carve deep lines into my skin and shirts that wouldn't burst the buttons that barely contained my bosom. I was a teenager, way past puberty, so I couldn't blame my increasing girth on hormones. Metabolism, my former ally, had turned on me, and my regular diet of french fries, cheese steaks, and pizza was making me fat. How unjust.

My body absorbed the extra weight simply by becoming a bigger version of itself. Rather than developing problem areas, like a pear-shaped woman would, I inflated all over, making it tough for me to see how large I had really become. My mirror was no help, and actually assisted me in my denial. How could I have missed what was so obvious to everyone else?

Teenage humiliation is a powerful motivating force. Without a second thought, I put myself on a one-thousand-calorie-a-day diet and began exercising feverishly at home. Only athletes used real weights back then, but I found an article in a woman's magazine that recommended repeatedly raising and lowering canned foods over your head to build muscle and destroy fat. Canned tomatoes worked well for the pecs, and smaller Green Giant peas got my biceps and triceps burning. The harder I pushed, the better it felt.

The weight began to come off slowly, the way it was supposed to, but it wasn't fast enough for me. I wanted immediate results; I craved instant relief from the embarrassment, so I reduced my daily caloric intake to eight hundred. I literally began starving myself. But I didn't care: I wore my hunger pangs like battle scars. Each time the acid in my stomach would gurgle, I would revel in the fact that I was melting the excess fat into oblivion.

With a sharp knife I carved low-calorie foods into as many pieces as possible; with surgical precision I could make a single apple cover an entire dinner plate. I'd slice potatoes paper-thin and then bake them in the oven to approximate something between french fries and potato chips. My average lunch had gone from a sub sandwich to a small can of tuna (calories: 90). It was barely enough to satisfy a five-pound housecat, but eating those tiny portions made me feel in control. When the diet alone didn't seem sufficient, I studied activity charts to determine how best to burn more calories, then went out and exercised for hours at a time. I felt terrific.

Every meal was a small success, each "no thank you" a reinforcement of my mission. Each day, as my ribs became more visible, I began to feel more accomplished. My yardstick was not a scale—I didn't own one—but my hip bones told me I was winning my battle, and I walked with my hands in my pockets so I could feel them, every day protruding a bit more.

The more my friends told me how good I looked, the more focused I became on achieving beauty through hunger.

Because I didn't have a scale, I didn't have a goal, and I had no concept of when I would be finished with the diet and move on to maintaining my weight. My parents, though, thought otherwise. Convinced I was thin enough (there was no such thing to me), they took me out to celebrate my high school graduation and forced me to order a big dinner. I ate it all, if only to satisfy them, but the food made me feel guilty and ashamed, like I had committed a crime I could never take back.

I panicked, terrified that like an alcoholic, once I had tasted what was forbidden, I would never be able to return to my minced meals and empty stomach.

Instinctively, I concluded I needed to give back the food somehow, so that it would not leave me with anything approaching satisfaction. I excused myself from the table, went to the bathroom, stuck my finger down my throat, and threw up the meal. Just like that.

Purging is as easy as it sounds, once you have the process down. Rule number one: Scope out the bathroom to make sure you're alone. If not, you can claim illness if somebody asks, but it's better not to have to worry about strangers. For me, a single finger—the pointer—touched strategically down my throat three times in succession could bring up what I had eaten, though it took a few tries to get it all up. A cold paper towel would quickly erase the red eyes and tearing that accompany vomiting, and a short gargle would eliminate the taste of bile. I didn't do it every day, but it was so easy I used it as an option when I needed it. I realized the cat food diet wasn't filling me up anymore, and the days of binging and purging grew more frequent. What was worse, the guilt I had felt when forced to eat was subsiding since I had found a solution; the system was working and I didn't see anything wrong with it.

Nobody seemed worried about me, so it never occurred to me to worry about myself. For all the binging, I was never caught by anyone. Not even my best friends knew what I was doing. By the end of the summer, I could wear the Sergio Valente jeans I had made my goal. Size 26—and cut small; all I wanted to do was fit into them. "Fit" being a loose term to describe lying on the bed, struggling with the zipper until my fingers were red and raw, and doing deep knee bends in order to be able to walk without looking like I had no joints.

At the end of the summer, my grandmother took me shopping for clothes to take to college. I was beginning a new chapter in my life and was not going to ever let my body get in the way of my success again. When I put on the first outfit and emerged from the dressing room to stand in front of the full-length mirror, I gasped out loud. Turning sideways, I saw that I had shrunk to a sliver of a person, and the shock literally took my breath away.

The clothes were a size 2 and fit perfectly, but they were far from flattering. They showed off disproportionately skinny hips and legs, bony neck and shoulders, and a face that my grandmother would later describe as gaunt.

She said nothing; for once, the mirror said it well enough for everyone to understand. It finally became clear that it was time to start eating and stop vomiting until I looked human again.

I never did get my money's worth from those Sergio Valente jeans. I squeezed into them one night and wore them to a club, only to have to ask my date to take me home because the waistline was pressing into my stomach and making me feel nauseated. I gave them away so they wouldn't remind me of my very first battle of the bulge. I could not have known then how many more were to come.

You can take the fat out of the girl, but you can't take the girl out of the fat. When I see myself in the mirror, I will always be overweight. I will forever notice the imperfections: the cellulite, the love handles, and the arms that jiggle. At age thirty, some friends and I decided to train for a sprint distance triathlon. It was a quarter-mile swim, twelve-mile bike, and 5K run. We hired a coach and set about "two-a-days": a workout in the morning and evening. My body responded well and became muscular and strong, but I didn't acknowledge it at the time. It's only now when I look at photographs of myself crossing the finish line that I marvel at how shapely and lean my body was; I remember distinctly that at the time, I simply wasn't satisfied.

As I approached my fortieth birthday, I told my husband the perfect gift was "two twenty-year-old breasts." What I wanted more than anything was a breast reduction operation. Years of gaining and losing weight—not to mention three pregnancies—had taken me from a 34B to a 38D, and I wasn't carrying them well. Though I had settled into a size 8, my breasts hadn't decreased in size. I struggled with bra straps digging into my shoulders, frequently squeezed into bras that were too small, and slumped over with their weight.

"You're crazy!" said Tammi. "You don't need it." With a petite set herself, she couldn't imagine why I'd waste my money to go smaller. "Aren't there other things you want to do instead?" Tammi is a big supporter of cosmetic—OK, plastic—surgery, which she considers a tool to make up for not taking care of herself. She figures she can neglect sleep for three years and then tell a doctor "Do for me what I couldn't do for myself."

"Yeah, well, while I'm under I figure I might as well have liposuction on my saddlebags."

"I can understand that," said Tammi, who had gone through a similar liposuction procedure several years before to put her body back into the right proportion. "You can borrow my girdles."

Now that it's far behind me, I can say that the results were worth it. The breast reduction operation brought with it a bonus: in order to make them smaller, the doctors had to make them higher—and firmer. My new breasts immediately made me a couple pounds lighter, but they also created a torso where I hardly had one before. I have to be careful what I wear, since it is not uncommon for a nipple to peek out; they are, as I say, freakishly high (in surgery they are actually cut out and moved up on your chest). But alas, with time, they too will fall. For now, they are small, cute, and perky.

Even my fellow Bombshells agreed after I lifted my shirt at a meeting to show them my resized and shaped breasts. Some of them felt the urge to look away, I know, but they couldn't. They just stared at them, perfectly round, high on my chest, with ugly red scars.

The liposuction—well, that paled in comparison to the breast surgery. The results turned out fine, but I just couldn't keep my eyes off my new chest.

During the first few weeks of recovery from both of the surgeries, I had tremendous remorse. "I never would have had the operation if I had known how difficult it would be," I told the Bombshells just after the surgery. The whole ordeal was thorny for me; not painful, really, but extremely uncomfortable. I slept sitting up for a month; or rather, I drifted in and out of a fitful sleep. A doctor friend of mine once said most people forget there are two parts to the phrase "cosmetic surgery." The "surgery" is hard on the body, and it takes a good while to feel normal again. But by far the most difficult adjustment I had to make was the fact that I had become "one of those women": I am someone who has had plastic surgery. A new self-awareness set in. Am I really that vain?

I suppose I realized I will never be perfect, even with the help of a thousand cosmetic surgeons. I came to understand the price of beauty, and it rose well beyond currency.

Then a miraculous perceptual shift occurred on my actual fortieth birthday: I went from trying to compete with people in their twenties and thirties, to looking great "for my age." I relaxed the standards, absolutely, and with that came a freedom I had not felt before.

The years provided perspective, which allowed me to realize I have nice proportions—curves in the right places, muscular shoulders and legs—though I am also aware of just as many trouble spots. Gravity has had an effect on my behind, which reaches toward the ground like a flower angles itself toward the sun.

And there are days when I just can't see myself as I really am. I am forever dressing to camouflage a body that is overweight. And when people at work thrust birthday cake in my face with a laugh and say "you don't have to worry about your weight," I smile, and think, "if you *only* knew."

After two decades of being at war with myself over something as ridiculous as food, I try not to let it keep me from loving myself, because what I look like doesn't compare in importance to who I am inside.

So with a shrug of disappointment, I move past the strapless dresses and reach for the sheath.

And the chocolate.

Grammy Night

PATRICIA

The phone woke me from a deep sleep. We had partied late into the evening in anticipation of the big show, the Latin Grammy Awards. I was still in a daze. We had gone to bed close to 4 A.M.

It was 7:00 A.M., September 11, 2001. I didn't understand the voice on the other end of the line. I was groggy and still half-asleep. "We're at war," she said. "The Twin Towers are down."

"Who is this?" I asked. I was alone in bed and while I sat up to rouse myself I discovered a note on the bedside: "I've gone to a Buddhist meeting in Santa Monica. Be back around 11. Love, Nestor."

"Huh?" I said, as I turned my attention back to the phone. It was Nestor's sister. "Pat, it's Deborah . . . we're at war. Terrorists flew planes into the Twin Towers." Twin Towers? For a moment, I couldn't remember where they were. Chicago? New York? She started to cry, "Pat . . . Sergio is there . . . Oh my God, he was one of the first firefighters to go in." My head began to spin. "Pat, wake up. Put on the news," she barked.

I searched for the remote control and clicked on the TV. My old friend and former coworker Katie Couric was saying something about New York, but the visuals behind her didn't make any sense. It looked like a combat zone. As I slowly gained consciousness, I began to wish I hadn't.

That's how I woke up on the morning that was supposed to be one of the most exciting nights of our lives. We had come to Los Angeles where we were hopeful that my boyfriend of ten years, Nestor Torres, a world-renowned recording artist, would win his first Latin Grammy Award.

The months leading up to the awards show after Nestor got nominated took on a life of their own. Everything I did revolved around the awards ceremony. My Bombshell friend Mercedes had introduced me to a not-yet-famous (still affordable) fashion designer, Tony de Leon, a young talented Panamanian designer who resides in Coral Gables. I had to be an adequate arm piece for Nestor. And sure, this was my chance to wear a dress that would stop traffic, even in LA. At least that's what Tony promised. I had never hired a designer to create something for me. But this was the Latin Grammys and I had a feeling that Nestor would win. So I told Tony to make the most spectacular Grammy dress ever.

Tony called his creation *El Desnudo,* which, in Spanish, means The Nude. My ultraconservative Bombshell friends, Annie and Lydia, called it the Diva Dress. They were a bit shocked that I would wear something so revealing. "Oh my Lord," said Lydia.

"*Hay,* Patricia, what will your papi say?" worried Annie.

I reassured them that it was all an illusion . . . and that I was covered in just the "right" spots. They didn't buy it. Bombshell Tammi, however, thought it was the greatest dress she'd ever seen. "I hate you," she cried. "My body wouldn't fit in that Twiggy dress. But if I had your figure, baby . . . I'd be there!"

For months the dress became the focus of my life. I was working out like a maniac getting my body in shape for this very revealing gown. I went to the gym every day with my friend Max who took it upon himself to mold me into shape, although I wasn't convinced my body could pull it off. I ate (or not) for the dress. I dreamed about the dress. I obsessed with this dress. I did everything but sleep with the dress. For a few fleeting moments, the dress made me happy. I was being pampered, designed for, and admired. A girl could get used to this.

Three months later, the dress was hanging in my hotel closet in Los Angeles, waiting for the big moment where it would shine in all its splendor at the Latin Grammy Awards show. Traditionally, the night before the Grammys, the Recording Academy honors all the nominees and pays tribute to the Person of the Year at a huge red-carpet gala in lavish Hollywood style. This year was no different. The honoree was Spanish heartthrob Julio Iglesias.

That afternoon, on September 10, after having my hair, makeup, and nails done . . . something very strange happened. I changed my mind about the dress.

I decided to wear my Grammy dress to the tribute dinner instead of the Latin Grammy Awards show. Whatever came over me to make that switch, I'll never know. In hindsight, I wonder if it was some kind of unfathomable premonition or just a spooky coincidence.

Even at the gala, the dress was a hit. The lights focused on us as we made our way down the red carpet. The paparazzi went crazy. Every still photographer took our picture. Every video photographer asked me to model for the camera. All the reporters interviewed me wanting to know about the dress. It was surreal.

Two men even came up to me and said, "Jennifer Lopez, eat your heart out!"

Hey, sometimes it's all about the dress, the makeup, and the hair, and this was one of those nights. Now I know how Cinderella felt. I wasn't Patricita from Miami tonight; I was a Hollywood glamour girl. Or so I pretended. All because of Tony's dress.

How quickly it all seemed ridiculous when I heard about the attacks. I placed calls to my family and to all my friends in Miami and New York, to make sure everyone was OK. One of my calls was to Tony, who immediately screamed in his typical dramatic and flamboyant style, "Patty . . . the dress! You won't be able to wear my dress!" I guess he was as much in shock as the rest of us.

Sometimes you have to cling to the small things when the big picture becomes so incomprehensible. In the midst of this massive human tragedy, my Tony was thrilled to hear that I had, in fact, worn his creation the night before and that it was a head turner, as he had promised.

When I got off the phone with Tony, I was overcome with panic. I still hadn't been able to reach Nestor. His cell phone was on voice mail. We were in Los Angeles and I was alone in the hotel room. If New York got hit, wouldn't LA be the next logical target? I was a wreck until he walked through the door. I told him about the phone call from his sister and then about Sergio.

Sergio was a dear friend of the family, a firefighter in New York City, and he was missing. We hugged as we talked about Sergio and the horrendous images we were watching on TV. We held on tightly to each other.

We received the call in our room at the same time the networks made the announcement: "The Latin Grammys scheduled for this evening have been postponed," reported Peter Jennings on ABC. Of course, they had to be postponed. No one even cared about that anymore. What had been so important for the past few months became entirely inconsequential.

We strolled aimlessly through the hotel lobby only to find our friends, all stranded musicians, looking like zombies. Makeshift television sets had been set up in the lobby of the Beverly Hilton. Everyone was transfixed by what they were watching. It's true that misery loves company. It felt better to be surrounded than all alone.

Celia Cruz, Jon Secada, Julio Iglesias, Emilio Estefan, Carlos Ponce, Paul Rodriguez, and countless others—everyone was there. We hugged, talked, sat, and watched the news unfold, in utter disbelief. I missed my dad, my animals, and my Bombshell friends. I craved our wonderful meetings where we drink and chat and indulge ourselves with fine chocolates. I wondered if we'd ever meet again.

That afternoon Nestor and I had lunch with friends in the hotel restaurant. I was famished. I ate as if I hadn't eaten in months. I didn't care about my weight anymore. Vanity had lost its seat at my table. I was scared, sad, and still in disbelief over the events of the day.

I didn't know if I'd be around the next day, so I ate. Somehow it made me feel alive and safe. I gorged on the buffet, eating everything in sight.

I made up for all those low-fat meals I had forced myself to eat for months, for the sake of that silly dress. I can't believe I wore "the dress" to the tribute dinner. The strangeness of that decision kept nagging at me.

After a few hours we returned to our room as the phone rang. It was Antonio Banderas. His wife, Melanie Griffith, and he were opening up their home that night to a few friends who were stuck in hotels. He said it was the least they could do.

We had been to Antonio and Melanie's home the year before. Antonio had wanted to share the music he was composing for his upcoming children's CD and spy movie. They are lovely people and since we didn't really want to be alone, we accepted their gracious invitation.

That night we drove up to the gate, rang the bell, and announced ourselves. It was a clear and chilly night. The cool air made me feel alive. The smell of the trees filled my soul. My senses were on fire. We had no idea what tomorrow would bring, but right then we were alive and together.

As we walked up the steps into their incredible Spanish mansion, we held each other close. We were escorted into the family room, where the television set was on, but no one bothered to watch. I guess everyone wanted to escape the enormity of the tragedy, if only for a little while. We left the news behind and moved outdoors. The stars were shining brightly. We were in another reality, light years away from what was happening on the other side of the country.

We sipped champagne on the terrace overlooking the Hollywood power-couple's garden. We drank, not in the usual bubbly celebratory style, but mostly to numb our minds. We said silent prayers for the dead and their families. Our minds kept going back to Sergio. Still no word. Our country was under attack. How do you behave at a time like this? We were all, still, in a state of shock.

Paul Rodriguez tried to crack a few jokes to lighten the mood. Edward J. Olmos and his kids joined us at the buffet table. I was famished again. Someone asked for music, a request that was followed by an awkward silence. None of us were sure if music was appropriate on such a tragic day. But then Cuban pianist Chucho Valdez walked over to the piano and broke the ice. Alejandro Sanz plucked at his guitar, so Nestor jumped in on flute and Antonio picked up his guitar. They played soft melodic tunes, old Cuban standards, and sweet improvisations in an attempt to heal our hearts.

Nothing mattered that evening except humanity. All we cared about was peace. So much had changed in just a matter of hours. There was no such thing as celebrity among us. I sat next to Antonio on the couch. Melanie sat at his feet on the floor. The Olmos kids surrounded us.

We talked, sharing in the pain of the moment and trying to find comfort in the warmth of other living human beings.

Taking an American Airlines plane back to Miami five days later was one of the most frightening rides of my life. I checked out every single person as they boarded the plane. I was convinced I could spot a terrorist at a glance. I was petrified and thought libation was the only way to de-stress, so I insisted on upgrading to first class, wanting to drink to my heart's content. I had to calm my brain somehow. But the reminders were all around us, from the two-hour line through security, where no one complained, to the first-class cloth napkins with plastic eating utensils. Plastic? Even the simplest of things now took on a totally different meaning.

The awards were handed out in a simple ceremony at the Conga Room in Los Angeles, two months after September 11. I wore some funky pants and a top that Tony made for me. It didn't really matter anymore. Nestor won his Latin Grammy, and we celebrated at a restaurant on Sunset Boulevard in low-key style.

On the other coast, three thousand miles away, they were still searching for firefighter Sergio Gabriel Villanueva. He was assigned to Ladder 132 Brooklyn on September 11, 2001. The firehouse got the call at approximately 8:56 A.M., ten minutes after the first tower was hit. It is assumed that Sergio arrived at the scene at around 9:11 A.M., nine minutes after the second tower was hit. He presumably was sent in to help evacuate the South Tower before it fell. No one from his company was ever recovered. Sergio had just turned thirty-three on the Fourth of July.

Nestor played "Over the Rainbow" at Sergio's funeral service one year later. It was his attempt, once again, to heal grieving hearts with his music. In the twelve months that had passed since September 11, I often wondered why sometimes it takes the world to stop spinning on its axis for us to realize our priorities in life.

It's not about the awards, the work, the fame, or any of the other million and one trappings we distract ourselves with on a daily basis. And it's definitely not about a fabulous dress that stops traffic. It's all about the person who lives inside the dress, the soul no one can see, but everyone can feel.

Of course, I've always known that, but sometimes I get sidetracked. I pray I don't need other reminders to keep me on course.

————

In loving memory of my beautiful beloved friend, brother, soul mate, and outrageous designer, Tony de Leon, who moved into heaven on May 25, 2004, and is creating a scandalous ruckus with his fabulous nude and crystal angel tunics!

Mambo Jumble

ANNIE

I'm sitting in a doctor's office waiting for them to call my name. I'm listening to the elderly people around me as they share their life stories with perfect strangers. They've turned this twelve-by-twelve-foot room into their very own living room, where at any moment, I expect someone to enter with steaming espresso for all.

One elderly lady is proudly declaring that she has been a widow since 1973 and has not been with another man since that time. As she says this, I'm thinking, *Lady, you may need to get yourself a sledgehammer or a high-powered drill if you're planning to ever have sex again.* A completely inappropriate thought, but it surfaced in my brain. You figure, in a place like Miami, with its fill of Latin lovers who would bed any breathing woman within five seconds, she would have found someone to service her needs.

Another woman is preaching about the immorality of homosexuality and all I can think of is the poor altar boys who have been betrayed by their role models in long black robes. The discussion starts to become heated and a round of the rosary is about to begin, when my name is called and I breathe a sign of relief as I follow the receptionist into the office.

Protocol in a Cuban doctor's waiting room allows for conversation and the exchange of intimate personal information. Had I been waiting to see an American doctor, I would have expected people to be sitting quietly reading magazines or speaking softly to the person next to them. Basically, everyone would be minding their own business. This juxtaposition is the story of my life.

I live simultaneously in two different worlds. Welcome to Miami! This magical city, which I call home, is the new mecca of the mythical melting pot. I was born in Havana, Cuba, in 1958. Three years later, my parents and I fled our homeland seeking political asylum. Our departure was supposed to be temporary, but after forty-one years, I now call Miami my home.

I can best describe my life as a combination platter of Cuban *café con leche,* burgers, and fries. Although the Cuban culture in Miami is very potent, lots of Americana filters in each day. And while I speak better English than Spanish, and am naturally blond and blue eyed, I am in no way totally apple pie.

Navigating my way through different cultures isn't always easy. There are very specific groups of rules by which we live. I've learned that 6:00 P.M. on a Cuban wedding invitation really means the bride walks in an hour later. When I got married, I printed up two sets of invitations. The one in Spanish noted commencement of ceremonies as 6 P.M. The set in English had the correct time on it. I walked down the aisle at 7:00 and everyone arrived on time. Really!

When I shared this information at the Bombshell meeting, three women nodded in confirmation. Sara and Tammi, our *gringa* buddies, absolutely did not believe that I had done that. They had thought that the term "Cuban Time" was only a joke. The joke is really on anyone who doesn't understand that this is the way we live our lives.

I've also learned that when invited to a child's birthday party given by an American family, one is expected to drop the child off and pick him up promptly at the designated time. This scheduled drop-off and pickup is very different from a Cuban party. Most children's parties given by Cuban families include all the adults in the families and their friends. The activities usually include a domino game, lots of beer, and good *chisme* (gossip). You can bet that once the fun gets started, no one ever wants to leave. It took me some time to become acclimated to dropping my precious cargo off at the home of people I hardly knew, and leaving them there for a specified period of time.

Cuban funerals are another peculiar affair. They become social gatherings, sans liquor, where everyone catches up with old acquaintances, often in a slightly raucous tone. Many Cuban funeral homes are found next door to Cuban restaurants where guests can sneak out at some point and grab a plate of *frijoles negros and platanos maduros* (black beans and fried plantains) and a strong cup of café Cubano. In fact, silence and serenity is a rare occurrence in any Cuban event, including this last rite of life. The viewing can go on for up to twenty-four hours, followed by a mass the next day and then the burial the day after that.

The American funeral services I have attended have all been quick and to the point. Utmost decorum is usually observed. Just another cultural difference.

I always felt blessed that throughout my teenage years my parents followed the American way. This meant I was allowed to date without a chaperone—a guard dog of sorts, a Cuban tradition. So here's what I did with that freedom: I sneaked into discos with my friend's old Cuban passport, my attempt at a fake ID. Being blond and sometimes a little ditzy as a teenager, I never realized that if I used a friend's old passport, that same friend shouldn't be with me at the entrance to the disco. The bouncer was brighter than I imagined, recognizing my friend as the true owner. But like a true *chiquita,* I flirted with him until I was admitted. I was able to drink and party to my heart's content. Despite my parents' leniency, my Catholic guilt almost kept that chastity belt on until marriage.

It is uncomfortable for me to fill out applications that ask for ethnic classification. I often want to check "other" because I'm White and Hispanic. Yes, we can be both. And we can be Asian and Hispanic or African and Hispanic. I don't think it really matters. If we are ever going to exist peacefully in this world, we need to think outside that little box.

The older I get, the more I yearn to learn about my Cuban roots and absorb all I can from my parents. I love to hear their stores about the "old times" in Havana. I often feel that I missed out on a magical era that has forever been lost in time. It is a struggle to maintain my heritage, but it is very important to me. My children speak broken Spanish, but they love Cuban food. My daughter can dance salsa, but she can also hip-hop.

We celebrate both American and Cuban holidays. We enjoy *Noche Buena,* which is a big Christmas Eve dinner, but we also look forward to Thanksgiving. The way I see it is, we have double the pleasure, double the fun. What's wrong with that? *Nada.*

Split Ends

MERCEDES

I am the product of a beauty culture where any look short of perfection, that is, slightly shy of a long, leggy model, is considered grotesque. I must admit I've always had enough sense of self-worth not to buy much into the beauty myth. But, let's face it, under most standards, I've always been considered beautiful.

And a natural beauty at that; no implanted breasts or buttocks, no silicone, no bleached teeth or hair, not even lighter shades of colored contacts or acrylic nails, no liposuction, no tummy tucks. No, it's all me. Never had to diet, even after two babies, never had to chase the "look." If anything, I've always been "in." That's probably why it's been so difficult to accept that I've been losing my hair. I suppose I ignored it because at thirty-two I never imagined hair loss was even possible. I don't even remember when it was that I started bending over my sink to blow-dry my hair. I now realize I must've done it subconsciously to catch all that excess hair blowing off my scalp and penetrating every inch of my surroundings. I have one of those compulsively neat personalities that can't stand seeing things out of place much less thrown about on the floor, even if it's just hair.

Mind you, however, I'm not completely obsessive; if I started bending over to pick up hair it's because there was way too much of it strewn about in plain view to actually bother me. My hair started to trickle down my shoulders. It became such a nuisance it would tickle me annoyingly all day long; down my arms, onto my computer keyboard, in and over my blouses, it would fly into my mouth and make me gag or even make its way inside my food. I couldn't get away from it. It became a constant pest.

Since I didn't seem able to avoid it, I became fixated by it and started counting every strand that fell out. Every day became a hopeless race to count less hair than the day before. I started keeping a maddening daily tab and made weekly comparisons as I tried any and all lotions and potions that promised regrowth. I ached desperately to stop the loss.

In the morning before making my bed I'd hunt for hairs lost during slumber. I changed all my sheets to white so that I could better spot the black strands. Every day I'd find dozens of them dying a premature death, shedding earlier than a regular hair cycle.

The count would easily reach fifty and sixty, forcing me to change my routines. Instead of shampooing every morning as I'd done since I was a teenager, I started doing so every other day.

Washing my hair became a devastating ritual. During my showers I had to reach down and collect the wet clumps of fur balls gathered on the drain or the water would begin to pool. When I was finished, I would place the ball of hair on my counter and painfully separate each string to count each one individually. I'd reach well over one hundred before depositing the lost hair in the garbage alongside my self-esteem. I feared that flushing it down the toilet would eventually clog it.

My anxiety increased with every hair count. I was only thirty-five years old and at the height of my television career when I first accepted the loss. As an on-camera reporter, where appearance is unfortunately as important as substance, the wrong look could literally get me fired. Journalism was my life's work, my passion. I had been in broadcasting since age eighteen, first in radio and then on television. I had won five Emmys before age thirty and been nominated over a dozen times. Losing my job on top of my hair would certainly finish me off emotionally. I became a wreck.

I started having nightmares, shortness of breath, and loss of concentration. Everywhere I went I instinctively looked at other women's heads to compare them to the one I constantly inspected in the mirror. I could always find my kindred spirits. They were the ones using the same disguises, the hats, and scarves and headbands just like me. They were the ones pulling hair from almost ear level to brush it over and around to the other side.

Like them, I let my hair grow longer so I could more easily drape it across the crown of my head and over the sides. When anyone looked at me a little too long I was convinced that they were staring at my baldness. Society is certainly more apt to applaud a fake pair of breasts than a few hair plugs. And I didn't seem able to escape the beauty cult.

My only instinct was to hide in my own shame. I stopped attending social events and tried to keep my distance from people. I asked my camera people to shoot me in medium or preferably wide shots, claiming I looked better that way. My reporter's instinct kicked in and I hit the Web to research my condition. I eventually found out that anxiety causes hair loss. Of course I was anxious! It was a catch-22.

After about a year of trying any and all elixirs that promised long voluminous hair, I came to accept the fact that I wasn't going through some ordinary seasonal molting. The thinning was progressing. Right there, starting at the top of my forehead, a thin spot the size of an egg carved its way to the back of my head. It was impossible to miss and difficult to cover regardless of which way I combed.

I found myself staring at the heads of full-mane beauties with a sense of loss. I made myself sick with the idea of becoming a cue ball and was terrified with the thought that less hair would make me less of a woman. Those thoughts, these days, don't seem to perturb a man. They, unlike us women who always strive to be perfect, went out and made baldness cool.

I consulted a hair implant surgeon who told me that for a mere eight to ten thousand dollars he'd pull out thin rows of hair from the bottom-back of my scalp and implant them in the front with such precision that no one would ever notice. He showed me before and after pictures. Then he leaned over for me to inspect his own head where he claimed to have undergone the procedure himself. It looked pretty good.

But as I began to entertain the option and started the process of signing some papers before leaving his office, his secretary recognized me from my on-air work. "Aren't you the girl from the TV?" I've heard that query in the most inopportune times, but this was the worst. It broke me inside. I was mortified.

I couldn't bear the thought of word getting out that I, a TV personality, and a woman, was considering hair replacement. The tabloids would scalp me alive! They'd have a field day and my terrible secret would finally become fodder for ridicule.

That's the baggage you constantly carry when you become well known. You're expected to always be perfect. I knew right then that vanity had the best of me. I hated it. But I couldn't control it.

One day as my makeup artist at the TV station was getting me ready for a publicity shoot he began to tease my hair into what I considered an old-fashioned beehive. When I complained, he emphatically informed me that he was just trying to help, because there was a hole in my head and the lights would glare right on it. He then gently suggested that I try Rogaine. I was so insulted that I brushed him aside, fixed my own hair, and refused to speak to him for months.

Of course, it wasn't his fault. He just brought me face-to-face with reality. That encounter gave me the strength to see another doctor. This dermatologist ordered a biopsy. The result was devastating; alopecia. Translation: female pattern baldness. There is no cure. I had been holding my breath until then, and the absolute knowing was like a heavy blow that left me bruised and disheartened. I saw my career and my image falling into a black hole. The bad news was that one in twenty women also suffer this hell. The good news was that I hadn't yet developed subcutaneous scarring, meaning Rogaine could work on me as it does in only 17 percent of women with my condition.

Almost two years after noticing the first signs I finally gave in and started using the dreaded medication. And of course, it's my bald husband who always treks out to buy me the new bottles. After about five years of using it, I'm still too hung up on the misery in my own head to risk being spotted at the store trying to buy my own supply.

The side effects I experienced were not fun. As Rogaine penetrated my scalp it felt like a bottle opener being screwed into a burning blister. It took about six months for that discomfort to actually abate.

The dryness in my mouth, however, doesn't really dissipate, and the lowering of my blood pressure, which my doctor attributed to the medicine, continues to make me tired and sleepy when I should be full of energy. Yet I count myself lucky that I can even respond to the medicine and happily accept the side effects.

The alternative is unthinkable. Although I've only experienced moderate regrowth, I've come to accept the fact that I will never have the same full head of hair of my youth.

But I'll never stop exploring new options. The most obvious one, of course, is wearing a wig. That would probably be the final blow to an on-camera journalism career. But, then again, it wouldn't be the absolute end of the world. After years of fretting, I've come to the conclusion that I'm very lucky to be otherwise healthy and overall very happy with my life. In fact, in my line of work I see so much pain and despair that I know my fears are much too self-centered.

That's why I've decided to bare my soul and come out of the hair-club-for-women closet. I know I can't let my appearance diminish my sense of self-worth. I know there's no such thing as perfection, and looks are only temporary.

I've finally pledged to embrace my baldness. I've even toyed with the idea of some day shaving my head altogether. I know that with or without hair I will still be loved, I will still be worthy, I will still be as good a person as I can possibly be. I will still be a mother, a wife, a sister, and a friend and I will still be whole. And damn it, I will still be a successful journalist, on or off camera, because ultimately I am more than my hair.

Designer Kids

TAMMI

Sometimes, I just can't help myself.

Sitting in another faraway airport after another long business trip, I am feeling that weird, powerful force again . . . it's sucking me out of my chair and thrusting me in the direction of another tacky gift shop. So, once again, I find myself picking through crap, searching for more peace offerings for my kids who don't need or even want any more of this garbage that will disappear in a day or two anyway.

This trip, my eighth in four months, went a day longer than scheduled, as it often does, and consequently, the guilt is overwhelming, making me believe that somehow these overpriced trinkets will ease the blow of another homecoming full of apologies.

And so, I look around, seeing nothing interesting in that Jamaican airport tourist trap, but still, I buy my daughters more puka shell anklets and beaded headbands they won't wear. And then I feel worse.

When it comes to overindulgence and my kids, I speak from

many sides of my mouth. I'm not proud of that. I'm a single mom and I work way too hard to give my children the best in life, but I'm just not sure how much is too much, and I'm afraid they don't either.

I grew up in the suburban world of the upper middle class and was lucky enough to be sent to summer camp as a kid. My parents killed themselves to give my sisters and me all the things they couldn't have growing up. Just because he could, my dad ultimately bought himself a Rolls-Royce when the accounting practice he built all by himself started to flourish. When I was a child, credit cards were taboo in my house—my parents used to tell us they were for poor people who didn't have money in their wallets. Our life was very rich, but we weren't spoiled. We were grateful, and all three of us started working when we were fifteen because that's what was expected of us.

When I married a nice Jewish lawyer, I had money in the bank and always worked full-time, so money was never an issue. When we got divorced after fifteen years of marriage, my career was in full swing, so I kicked it up a notch in order to keep the house and my daughters in private school. After the stability of their life blew up, I became obsessed with maintaining our lifestyle to help ease some of their pain. But learning when to say no when it comes to my kids is something I still struggle with every day.

And I am not alone. Wretched excess is one of those subjects that comes up at almost every Bombshell gathering. One night, as the six Bombshells dined on scrumptious stone crabs at Joe's on South Beach, we learned that each of us has our own ideas about where that proverbial line should be drawn, and how and where it should be crossed. We all make our own money, but two Cuban moms in the group (and now their daughters) worship Louis Vuitton as if he'd won a Nobel Prize. I don't get that.

Lydia's never been skimpy when it comes to indulging herself. On any given day, if I added up the cost of her suit, shoes, jewelry, and fancy purse, I could probably furnish my entire bedroom for less. Her fourteen-year-old daughter, Christine, has inherited her passion, and at last count, had ten designer purses in her closet. Not one of them is a fake.

Though most of my daughters' friends at their swanky private school (many driving new Escalades and BMWs) carry handbags and wallets screaming with labels, in our house, there has always been one cardinal rule: no designer anything, anywhere. But I *have* been known to cave when it comes to other stuff, for no apparent reason.

My boyfriend Emilio, a Cuban immigrant who is more frugal than anyone I've ever met, thinks *I'm* way over the top. He criticizes me for not being disciplined enough, because he says I don't practice what I preach. His teenage son is grateful to have anything that hasn't been handed down, twice. But my daughters always seem to need more and want more, too, and I give in more than I should, even if I am considered the Bombshell cheapskate.

Chelsea is sixteen and Courtney's twelve, and they have become so obsessed with clothes that their wardrobes now double mine. They wear almost the same size, which means they've got four times more to wear than I do. But it's never enough. Both request cash for their birthdays and special occasions and save every penny for shopping sprees.

I buy them the basics and splurge on them a little too often, especially on days after I return from a business trip, when I am unusually generous.

I try to tell myself they are not spoiled. After all, they make their beds every day, scrub their own bathrooms, and even clean up after dinner. That might not sound like much, but for ten years, my two little princesses had live-in nannies who did everything but wipe their tushies for them, so they have come a long way, or so I tell myself. I don't give them an allowance.

Chelsea babysits and tutors neighborhood kids twice a week to earn her spending money. Courtney has been known to sell her clothes to her big sister (the price goes up on weekends!), or she will occasionally wash the car or swing a well-negotiated transaction to make a quick buck. She even brokered a deal with her cousin to sell an iPod he'd won to her own dad, and she walked away with a $15 commission! (Maybe I *am* doing something right . . .)

I've tried so hard to teach them the value of money, while also stressing the importance of giving it away to those who really need it. They've sold their Pokémon cards and lemonade in the park, raising money to help abused children through a nonprofit group our family has created. Both girls work extremely hard all year on that project, inviting their friends to participate, feeling such pride in their contributions. Teaching them to give back is one of the greatest gifts I've given my daughters, and they do really seem to "get" how lucky they are, especially when I explain that in their plastic world of private school and summer camp, we are merely salmon swimming upstream.

I've never believed that sixteen-year-old kids should have their own cars, but know it will help alleviate some of my driving duties, so I'm considering it. I told my oldest daughter, Chelsea, she would have to save up $1,000 before we'd even consider her request for a used car, and surprisingly, she's halfway there. She's more responsible with money than I was when I was her age, though I was taking the bus after school back in 1975, working as a cashier to earn my spending money. I would never let her do that.

You can't put kids on the bus in Miami (way too dangerous), but maybe if she *does* get a car, she can work at the local ice cream parlor with all her friends. Once again, I am torn between my beliefs and reality.

I want so much not to spoil my kids, but sometimes, I just can't help myself. I continue to justify their sense of entitlement by comparing them to their friends, who are spoiled way beyond rotten, and that actually exonerates me. All the Bombshells agree that it's a vicious cycle every parent faces in that vain attempt to keep their kids grounded. It's all about picking your poison. When Chelsea wanted to go to camp for eight weeks, I refused to let her, because it was just too expensive. I lost lots of sleep over that decision, but I never gave in. You can't always get what you want. At least that's what my parents told me and I think I'm a better adult because I didn't.

So when Courtney started dropping hints about those hot new $100 Puma sneakers everyone in fifth grade was wearing (Samantha has them in three colors!), it wasn't even up for discussion. We bought the cheap copies at Payless for $14 and even bought a second pair because it was half off.

But then those business trips hit back-to-back, right about the time a nasty cold came bearing down on my little one, the same week she had to take those nerve-wracking school standardized tests. Leaving town was tougher than usual, but I didn't have much choice. Emilio was in grad school and I was bringing home the bacon; when it's sizzling, I have to bite, or we starve. So once again, guilt kicked in while I was working in New York, and the first break I had, I raced through three stores until I found those Pumas in pink, the one color I knew no one else in fifth grade would have. Plus, I bought both girls expensive Puma overnight bags, breaking my antidesigner rule just this once, trying to convince myself that Puma was not nearly as snobby as Louis Vuitton.

I'm not exactly sure who I thought I was kidding, but I'd spent years trashing those ugly, brown, plastic-looking purses all the girls in high school were somehow sporting for $500. As a testament to the strength of my brainwashing, my girls seemed to agree with my logic. The girls *did* go bananas for the Puma stuff, scratching their heads at my designer amnesia, not wanting to question why I broke down. I think they were afraid that if they asked, I'd take it all back.

Lydia laughed at my justification, but as we talked about how much is too much when it comes to our kids, we both admitted (shamefully) that guilt was the common denominator fueling our desire to please our children by showering them with material things. We've been trying to make up for not being there, but it's not working. When we both hit financial rough spots this year, forcing us to cut back on our spending, empathy never even entered our kids' minds. They had become accustomed to the good life, and it's been tough getting them to understand that the well sometimes runs dry. While each of us has chosen to spoil our kids in different ways, Lydia and I both learned the hard way that undoing our indulgence is going to be harder than we ever could have imagined. We just hope it's not too late.

So when I went shopping with my fellow Bombshells on New York's Canal Street, I was surprised to see Lydia and Annie get goose bumps as the sidewalk vendors whipped out the cheap Louis Vuitton knockoffs. And while Lydia really knows her daughter doesn't need any more designer purses, the $25 price helped her to justify her purchase, just this once. "They're really great copies," she mumbled sheepishly as she stuffed them under her arm. I just laughed in her face.

I had judged my Bombshell girlfriends pretty strongly that day and was emphatic as I stood on the street and preached against passing their designer idol worship to their kids. But on the day I sat in that airport in Jamaica, I was just grateful they couldn't be there to see all the junk stuffed into my carry-on bag. I'm not sure I could have proven my case.

Cuando Salí de Cuba

MERCEDES

Cuando salí de Cuba,
Dejé mi vida, dejé mi amor.
Cuando salí de Cuba,
Dejé enterrado mi corazón.

When I left Cuba,
I left my life, I left my love.
When I left Cuba,
I left my heart buried there.

These are not the words to the Cuban national anthem. But the song has become an almost sacred ballad of the Cuban exile community. That's how most Cubans, forced to flee their homeland for political reasons, feel about their mother country almost half a century after Communism ripped it from its foundation. But when my family left Cuba, I was only nine years old, and it all seemed so confusing. *"Mira ese cielo,"* my mami cried to me. "Look up at that sky, Mercy; you'll never see a bright sunshine like that for the rest of your life!" she implored, using my nickname.

Sure it sounds dramatic. But we are Latin. And, in our world, most good-byes are a little over the top. So as we stood at the front steps of the building where I had been born in the Vedado District of Havana, in what felt like the eye of the storm surrounded by neighbors and dozens of family members, my mother was begging me to look skyward and try to anticipate a life without the literal and metaphorical warmth of the Caribbean. And I did as I was told, mentally etching that image into my memory.

The day was overpowered by the bright sun as it shone through the trees that lined our street, the sidewalks I had played hopscotch on with my neighborhood friends, and the colonial convent of the barefoot Carmelite nuns across the way. Thirty years later I can still recall the long and teary good-byes of the adults, and the exciting trip to the airport in a convoy of beat-up jalopies.

The reason Mami wanted me to take a mental snapshot of the people and place I had known all my life was because it was all about to come to a sudden end, though I had no idea why.

The whole family had come to say good-bye, including every second and third cousin of a cousin. There must've been about thirty people in our entourage. My sisters and I were feeling disoriented, and, for the grown-ups, anxiety was building into the tension and fear that comes naturally when living in a totalitarian state. While I was ecstatic to be going on my first plane ride I was petrified at the same time. After all, the whole family was crying, and I had been told that we would never be coming back. Saying *adios* to *Abuela* (my grandma) was the toughest part.

She was already in her seventies, I knew she had a terrible disease called cancer and this would be the last time I'd ever see her. I loved *Abuela* above the four aunts, three uncles, and dozens of cousins. My other grandparents had already passed away and she was my sweetest delight. She was Mami's mother.

Abuela had always babied me. I was the sick grandchild, the skinny little girl who the doctors thought would die unless I was taken out of Cuba, moved to a different climate, given a better chance at life. I was the girl who suffered from chronic asthma and had been living in a hospital on and off for most of my childhood, the one *Abuela* made homemade taffy for, the one who got to sleep in her antique bed whenever I visited. I was Grandma's little girl.

I remember clutching a doll in my hands as I walked up the steps to the Cubana de Aviación Airlines flight. It wasn't even my doll. It belonged to my older sister. I had never had a doll of my own. The Cuban regime of 1972 had rationed toys, and my parents, opponents of the revolution, didn't qualify to buy their children toys or even milk. We had been kicked out of school as soon as it was publicly known that a maternal uncle who lived in the United States had obtained visas for us to leave the country after years of legal paperwork. Our parents lost their jobs, and the extended family had to share their small rations to keep us fed, malnourished as we were.

Our neighbors, many of them envious not to be sharing in our luck, looked at us as pariahs and didn't hesitate to inform on my parents to the Communist central committee because Mami and Papi tried to give away our meager possessions to family and friends before being forced to hand them over to the "revolution." In fact, those neighbors' snitching managed to delay our visas for several months. That's why the day of departure was also a big relief.

The flight was terrifying. We were aboard a twin-engine plane headed for Europe, and it shook like a frail paper plane in the turbulent currents for almost ten hours. My father kept assuring us that all was fine as we continuously lost and gained altitude, and my blind childhood trust somewhat eased my fears. Not so for my two older half sisters, each of whom was leaving one parent behind. Both cried and vomited for hours during the bumpy ride, as did my parents. The whole plane full of Cuban refugees seemed to be partaking in one last act of Communism: a collective wail.

At some point the plane landed for refueling on the Azores Islands. We were allowed to deplane and walk into the small airport. In a store window, in the middle of the night I spotted two anatomically correct dolls. I had never seen anything like it. I was mesmerized. I asked for them because they looked like real babies!

Of course my parents couldn't buy me the dolls even if they wanted to. We had been forced out of Cuba with one suitcase for a family of six; no money, no jewelry, no valuables. When we arrived in Madrid in the middle of December, we had only our Caribbean summer clothes. It was freezing. But we couldn't have cared less. It all seemed so beautiful!

The Spaniards were getting ready for Christmas, a holiday totally foreign to me, coming from a place that had banned all institutionalized religions outright. Of course, that didn't stop us from embracing the festivities immediately. Only weeks after arriving in Spain we found ourselves caroling with our hosts. We spent one evening happily crisscrossing our new neighborhood, arm in arm with new friends, our homesickness lost in laughter and song. They were a happy, helpful, hopeful lot: members of a Catholic charity organization that had received us at the airport with bags of groceries full of incredibly delicious food that we gluttonously devoured in those first days.

They introduced us to outdoor markets that boasted a wondrous new world of cold cuts and cheeses and baguettes and all kinds of delicacies I had never, ever seen in my life.

I remember smells and tastes above all else. The *dulcerías* or pastry shops with the smell of fresh bread and the old-time candy stores were my favorites. There were unimaginable sweets, gum, and hard candy.

Since we couldn't hope that our parents would spend money on such frivolous things as gum, my twin sister and I would treasure the small sweet pieces generously given to us by a girl in the neighborhood. After chewing on it all day long, we would carefully stick it to the wall overnight, only to pull it back off in the morning and continue sucking on it for days on end. And then, there was the chocolate . . . that sweet, dark, exquisite delicacy that had such a satisfying effect on my hungry spirit.

I was hooked. To this day chocolate and I have a very close relationship. I am a certified chocoholic. Nothing is more comforting to my body or my soul than a mouthful of chocolate. I always have a full supply. At home, in the office, in my purse, before an interview, after dinner, I've found nothing else that can psychologically take me home quicker than chocolate. And every morsel still brings back the taste of those early days of freedom, a reminder of the sweetness of life itself.

Madrid gave way to Las Palmas, a paradise island off the northern shores of Africa. I spent the happiest years of my childhood in the Spanish Canary Islands. While we missed our families and our native land, the memories of life in Cuba disintegrated in our minds. I went to school again, learned to ride a bicycle, read comic books, and eventually was able to afford to eat tin cans upon tin cans of a British chocolate that still makes me giddy when I occasionally find it at a local Miami store.

Spain was nurturing, welcoming, and generous. In due time, we were able to leave behind the Communist conditioning that had controlled our minds and ingrained itself in our way of life. We started to trust and laugh again. We began to be happy.

Three years later the visas were granted to come to the United States. It was hard to leave my equivalent of Eden, the only place where I'd ever felt truly carefree. Spain had given me a taste of a free childhood with television, travel, clothes, and all the food my heart desired. Though I never put on much weight, I never again felt deprived. Cuba had been full of hardship, a repulsed feeling of eating repeated leftovers: bug-infested rice and fried eggs, never enough to eat, limited water, occasional electricity, and impossible-to-find medicine to control my asthma.

Living there had been just as suffocating as my own disease. But my parents had a dream, to make it to El Norte, as we'd always called North America. So with no choice in the matter, we picked up again and left.

Our arrival in Chicago was even colder than our first winter in Madrid. It was the first time we had actually seen snow on the ground and we had a ball rolling around in it. Again, we felt a sense of freedom and reveled in our arrival at our final destination. Within two or three days my parents had registered me in school and I was attending the fourth grade. But there were no open arms waiting to feed my soul here. The language was completely alien, the other children utterly hostile, the weather so bitter that on my first walk home I thought my ears were going to crack open and fall off. We had no boots, scarf, gloves, or hats. We were still in a tropical state of mind.

Sadly, the first English word I ever learned was *spic*. It was a scary word and though I had no idea what it meant, I knew it was offensive. The other kids in my class kept chanting it as if it was some sort of death sentence. Just the idea of hearing it made me look the other way, cross the street, or linger out of earshot.

One day, that first winter, my sister and I were walking home from school when four or five sixth graders taunted us with that dirty word. They chased us across streets and through traffic. When they finally caught up to us, they began to beat us. We fought with the determination that comes from self-preservation, but with no clue as to why we were being punished in the first place.

Someone finally broke up the fight. The other girls left spewing hatred. My sister and I walked home dumbfounded, unable to understand why we had been so brutally abused. Although my head was bleeding and would ultimately require stitches, the open wound is not what horrified me. It was my ripped coat. I knew my parents had no money to buy me another one and the family had already made plenty of sacrifices just to acquire the one I was wearing. How would I explain "spic" to them?

I arrived home and apologized to my parents, explaining through sobs what had happened. They were livid. And although my mother had a Ph.D. in pedagogy herself, she didn't speak enough English to voice her disgust to my school principal and turn in the torturers. So we licked our wounds, consoled each other, and learned our first of many lessons in prejudice.

In the mid-1970s, America was a much more racially and socially divided place, even in a progressive city like Chicago. There we belonged to a new class of migrants. We were the unwanted, the aliens. It took time to adjust to a world that saw us as the underclass when our family and our culture had always placed us on the top tier.

So the word *spic* subconsciously followed me into adulthood, making me forever watchful in the back of my mind. For the fifteen years that I lived in the Midwest, as I went through school and daily living, I usually felt unwelcome, like an outsider or an outcast. It's a feeling that never went away until I moved to Miami.

I usually offer a welcoming joke to outside visitors when they first come to the magic city. "Welcome to the Republic of Miami. We're the closest Latin American country to the United States," I tell them. And I mean it in the best of ways. My friends who have grown up here don't understand the resentment most Hispanics have had to endure in other parts of the country, simply for looking and speaking differently.

When I told the story about my ripped-up coat in one of our Miami Bombshell meetings, Annie, more than Tammi or Sara, was the most amazed. "What?" she asked. "Don't we all speak Spanglish? Half of my sentences are in English, the other half in Spanish. *Pero, es natural.* I think that way.

"Being blond with blue eyes, I don't look Cuban. So I haven't felt the discrimination," she announced. And I guess she said a mouthful: to be different you have to look and sound different, as do most Hispanic immigrants like me.

However, this city is an experiment in belonging without full assimilation. And, unlike other cities, the so-called natives have mostly embraced the immigrant diversity. This has made Miami, in spite of all its poverty and crime, one of the most Latinized cities in the country. So, my "spic" Spanish is openly and freely spoken here by over two million Hispanics with experiences just like mine. Even Anglos, as American as apple pie, speak it with gusto. As a result, I feel a greater sense of belonging in this city than I have ever felt since leaving "my heart buried" so many decades ago. I'm finally home, and in the micro-Cuba that is Little Havana, the sun shines even brighter on me now.

Daddy's Little Girl

ANNIE

We all have pivotal times that make us revisit our lives. For me it was the new millennium. It started on Mother's Day, when my dad handed me a beautiful card that included an invitation for what was sure to be the trip of a lifetime. He wanted me to accompany him on a special trip that he had planned for just the two of us. He wanted to take me to cities he knew I would love: Prague, Budapest, and Vienna. Just the two of us. I cannot explain how completely off guard his invitation caught me. In my adult life, I had never traveled without my kids or husband, but I knew instinctively that I could not pass up the incredible opportunity. My father is my favorite person on earth, and the thought of having Daddy all to myself (sans husband and children) made me almost giddy.

Papi and I have a remarkable relationship that is difficult to put into words. I'm an only child and very close to both my parents, but I'm clearly Daddy's little girl. I feel very fortunate to be his daughter. He has never failed to be an incredibly loving, generous man who has always been there for me, no matter what my requests, needs, or desires might be. His unconditional love and support over the years has nourished an intense bond that knows no bounds. Saying no to Papi was never an option. I just had to go on this trip, but I had no idea how I was going to arrange it all.

I'm an extremely compulsive person so I had to make sure every possible scenario was completely covered. You would have thought I was preparing for a world summit. It started with a color-coded calendar for each of my kids. I included instructions on school uniforms, pickup and drop-off schedules, and extracurricular activities. I attached my detailed documents to the refrigerator door, which became the command center for my trip's operation. I was sure my husband and kids would welcome a break from the control freak. I myself could not wait to get on that flight.

I had no idea when the plane took off what a life-altering experience this trip would become. For the first time in twenty years, I had no one to focus on but myself. While the trip opened my eyes to some beautiful sights, most important, it reintroduced me to my inner soul. I had forgotten all about the woman I was before I had become a wife and a mother, and being with my dad, free of familial obligations, allowed me to reconect with the real me.

In the day-to-day "business," I had lost sight of myself. Dad just wanted me to disconnect from the harried world I inhabited, so he took care of every last detail of the trip. All I had to do was lock my arm in his and enjoy the ride; and enjoy it, I did.

We chuckled upon hearing that the others on the tour thought I was the young mistress of this presumably rich, older man. They could not believe that I was his forty-something-year-old baby, the parent of two kids, one a teenager. Strangers bathed me with compliments, and their praise began to breathe new life into me. Since becoming a mom I had been so wrapped up in the daily grind of parenting, working, and running a household that I had truly forgotten all about me.

The trip was monumental for both of us. We had plenty of time for ourselves, connecting with each other in a way I had never even imagined. I began to relax and live in the moment, as we enjoyed sightseeing and spending time alone over coffee, hot chocolate, or beer. I felt so very blessed to be sharing this time with him. How many daughters have the chance as adults to revel in their father's love and affection and feel like a child again? I was astute enough to know that this trip was an enormous gift that very few women in my world would ever have. My cup of gratitude was filled to overflowing.

My dad was still taking care of me, but this time, we were both grown-ups, discussing real topics and comparing notes on life. I was shocked that he could still read my thoughts and feelings, even though we hadn't lived together for more than twenty years. Even today, as I close my eyes, I can still see the sparkle in his eyes as I remember bits and pieces of the time we spent together.

He shared his joy over seeing me let loose, laughing and shining like I did as a kid. He said he couldn't remember the last time he had seen me smile so much . . . and until then, neither could I. Somehow Daddy woke me up, and I was never more alive than on the last night of our trip.

Every vacation must eventually come to an end and soon we had to bid farewell to Prague, my favorite of the three cities we had visited. We had spent all day sightseeing and despite his desire to keep going into the night, Dad's age and physical limitations caught up with him. He gracefully bowed out of the evening plans and encouraged me to join the rest of the younger crowd. Still being my overprotective papi, he reminded me to be careful and kissed me good-bye, as I assured him I would be fine.

My new friends and I packed into taxis and headed out for one last glimpse of this magical city, despite the inclement weather. The rain only made the city shine more intensely, and we all became so wrapped up in walking and spending time on the St. Charles Bridge that we completely lost track of time. When we arrived back at the hotel we were still not ready to call it a night, so we headed up to the lounge on the twenty-sixth floor to enjoy the view and have a few more drinks. The party continued.

Finally, we all reluctantly agreed it was time for sleep, because in just a few hours we had long flights to catch. I chuckled when I realized I was going to have to sneak into the room on tiptoe as I had done so many times when my partying had kept me out beyond teenage curfew.

But as the elevator doors opened onto the hotel lobby, there stood my tired old papi. His face was filled with despair and anguish. As I looked at him, I noticed that as I had grown up, he too had aged.

Once we made eye contact, Dad's expression quickly changed from fear to relief, and as he rushed to greet me, he checked his watch. It was his way of letting me know how worried he had been, and that he's still always going to be my daddy. I felt guilty that I had totally forgotten about the tender feelings within the heart of my dad. I had assumed that he would be sleeping. I guess no matter how old we get, to our parents we will always be children they love dearly, and for whom they will always feel responsible.

Once we got back to the room, Dad confessed that he truly believed I might have been kidnapped, and he had convinced himself he would never see me again. For hours my poor papi was preoccupied worrying about my safety and was unable to sleep. He felt paralyzed because there was no one he could call and no cell phone to connect us.

The tables had turned; Daddy had become the helpless child, and though I tried to comfort and reassure him that I was no longer that irresponsible teenager running out to the discos, he was not convinced. His response was as sweet as it was sad. "Yes," he told me, "but you are still my little girl, no matter how old you are."

At a Bombshell meeting, as I talked of my love for my father, I glanced over to see Lydia, with tears streaming down her face. My voice began to tremble as I tried to continue. Lydia had recently lost her dad and this one really struck a chord. Finally she composed herself, held onto Pat's hand, and told me how fortunate I was to have spent that quality time with my dad. She reminded us all to make each day matter, to continuously count our blessings, and to make sure that when the final day comes for each of our loved ones, we'll be comfortable (or as comfortable as we can be) in knowing that we had thoroughly enjoyed our relationships and had no regrets. Pat agreed, "Since my mom died I've gotten so much closer with my dad," she said. "He's always there for me, no matter what. I know I can count on him for anything I need. I know that his love is unconditional. Next month, for his birthday, I'm going to surprise him with a trip to Sedona. You see, Annie, I'm Daddy's little girl, too."

I will always cherish this trip with my dad for so many reasons. The photos captured the sights, but my memory holds the most precious pictures of all: time we spent together. My dad had once again breathed life into my soul, reminding me I was first a woman, before anything else, and a very special one, at that. And though his arms were one of the first to hold me when I came into this world, I know they won't always be here, but the gifts he has given me throughout my lifetime will forever remain in my heart.

Childless, by Design

PATRICIA

People sometimes look at me strangely when I say I've never wanted children. Does that make me a criminal? Heartless? Does every woman have to be a mother to be a complete woman? Forty-four percent of women in the United States aged fifteen to forty-four are childless. I'm not alone.

I love children and they love me. So do animals. I'm a magnet for both. But I've never wanted kids of my own. Why? Pain for one. Childbirth. Do I really want to gain fifty pounds and have my stomach stretch out so far I can't see my shoes? Do I want to be sliced up down there or have my stomach ripped open by a C-section? Do I want to risk hemorrhoids, stretch marks, and sagging breasts?

I always thought that if one day I should miraculously wake up wanting kids of my own, I would adopt. Lord knows there are plenty of kids who need good homes, and I know mine would be a loving one.

So why have kids? I love my life. I love my freedom. I can come and go as I please, most of the time. My cats and dog give me unconditional love. They don't talk back. They don't spend hours on the phone with boyfriends or girlfriends I think are trouble. They don't take drugs. They won't crash my car.

People sometimes make me wonder if this childless thing is normal. I'm constantly told it's not and that there must be something driving my feelings. We're taught by society that when you become an adult you marry and have kids. But that was never my dream. As a little girl, when I played "pretend," I was never a mommy. I wanted to be a movie star, a singer, or a dancer.

The closest I came to playing domestic was when I pretended to be Mrs. Paul McCartney touring the world with him. Sometimes I even pretended to be a soldier so I could play with GI Joes. But that was just an excuse to play with Manolito, the cute son of the family doctor who lived nearby.

My Bombshell friends, all mothers, tell me to look deep inside to find the real reason I don't want kids. Lydia and Mercedes, especially, keep telling me to dig deeper. They insist there must be some underlying reason I don't want children.

Lydia thinks that it might have to do with my being an only child and having lost my mom at a relatively young age. Maybe I fear leaving a child behind if something were to happen to me. The only thing that really rings true to me is that maybe I fear giving birth to a sick child or even having a child die. I can't bear to think of what it would be like to lose a son or a daughter. I'm totally devastated for months when I lose one of my pets, so I can't even imagine what it would be like to lose a child.

As I told this story to the Bombshells at our one and only weekend retreat, Lydia chimed in with a smirk, "Or maybe you've just been spoiled rotten as an only child and don't want to lose your peace of mind." Could be!

I think you generally feel younger, look younger, and act younger sans children. Although the Bombshells adore their children, I know they envy me from time to time. At one of our wine and chocolate Bombshell sessions, emotions flew as I defended my childlessness. "She has no carpools, no soccer games, no PTA meetings, no babysitting headaches, no sleepless nights, no sick days spent on children's doctor visits, no nagging compromises at every turn," says exhausted Tammi. "What's wrong with that?"

"Oh, come on," says Mercedes. "Those things aren't a burden! I adore my children and I love everything I do for them." Tammi's response (as she's laughing in Mercedes' face): "Oh Mercedes, if it was that euphoric, you wouldn't have shingles, or be begging for sleep every time I see you. Kids are awesome, and I wouldn't trade mine for anything, but try to imagine a whole week where you, and only you, are the center of your universe. Pat may really be onto something."

"I don't have to imagine," Mercedes bounced back immediately as she edged forward on her chair. "I remember for years I slept late, traveled the world, partied till I dropped and indulged my every whim, only to turn around one day and find my life felt empty because I had decided to delay childbearing."

"Oh Mercedes, puh-leese!" laughed Tammi.

"It's true," said Mercedes. "My life, to borrow a word from my daughter, is a million 'google' times better just because I had them. But I respect Pat's decision. We all make our choices. She's entitled to control her body. What we can't do is control destiny. That's why I always tell her 'You didn't want kids, fine, but the universe gave you a 101-year-old demanding grandmother, living only two blocks away and with no other siblings!" At which point, everyone just cracked up!

I believe there are too many people out there who have kids but shouldn't. They have no idea how to parent, love, and nurture. Is that acceptable? It seems our culture considers that more acceptable than a woman who never had children. I'm smarter than that; I made my choice—I don't want kids. I won't fall for society's preconceived notion that you have to be a parent to be happy.

I guess some folks will always think I'm selfish. I know I'm not. I give lots of love to my godsons and my friend's children. I'm just honest. I've never had that burning desire to be a mom.

I realize that I may regret my decision one day when I'm old and gray. I do sometimes wonder what will become of me if I'm left all alone, sick, and frail. The other day I asked Christine, Bombshell Lydia's daughter, if she would take care of me when I'm senile and decrepit. She said, "Absolutely." So I have nothing to worry about.

Childless. That's me! Call me crazy. Call me weird. Call me whatever you want. But if you call me, you'll probably get my voice mail because I'll be traveling the globe or partying, while you're home doing science projects, making nutritious brown bag lunches, or attempting to talk on the phone while your kids are yelling and fighting in the background and tearing your house apart!

Make Yourself Uncomfortable

SARA

On the verge of turning forty, I looked in the mirror and realized I had never taken a risk. I have done things that might look like risks, so this would surprise some friends who think they know me. But in reality, I had never put myself on the line.

I went to the safe college, took the safe job, and married the safe man. Some safety nets are harder to get out of than others.

I changed jobs and I changed husbands. I thought I had learned from the experiences of life.

My family considers me a success. Every year, on my birthday, I evaluate the year that has passed and determine if I've made progress. Invariably, I end up in tears on the phone to one of my parents, who tells me I'm crazy, lists my accomplishments, and then wonders aloud if I'm due for my period.

When I get into this funk, which is more often than I'd like, the Bombshells tell me I've got the "goods": a good husband, great kids, good family, good job, good friends, good sense, and good health. They go on and on about what I've achieved and urge me to see it from their perspective. It's a familiar conversation; I have it frequently with my mother, except then it's me telling her to look at all she has.

And it's not that I'm not grateful. After nearly dying due to a ruptured tubal pregnancy in my late twenties, I consider myself fortunate to be here, and to have all of the blessings in my life. But there's just something missing: I don't have a feeling of accomplishment. In my own eyes, I've failed, because I don't have anything I've created for myself. I spent my whole career making my bosses look good, and everything I have, I accept gratefully from my employer, every other Friday, with a bonus in March if I'm lucky.

To me, this is not a matter of perspective. I'm really not being hard on myself, though people tell me that I am. I want to do something that is important to me, maybe even important to others.

All around me are reminders of what I *haven't* done. I come from a long list of entrepreneurs. My grandfather, grandmother, mother, uncle, and sister all started their own successful businesses, but I've never been off the drug that is payroll—one that someone else has to worry about making.

This feeling started when my thirty-four-year-old sister opened her own business. Ellen is a free spirit with no apparent ambition, but an unending positive attitude. She tried several different careers—interior design, teaching, and real estate—before she decided to open a belly-dancing studio in Buffalo, New York.

To say there was massive skepticism is an understatement the size of neighboring Niagara Falls. But Ellen was an overnight success! Her business has taken her around the country, expanding into the space next door, and onto the front page of the local newspaper. More important, she is doing what she loves and building something all her own. I, on the other hand, am twenty-five years beyond getting straight A's and am still asking permission for a day off.

In our Bombshell meetings, the two entrepreneurs have me yearning for the grass on the other side. Tammi talks of exciting projects she is working on, or the fact that she took off Monday to shop and go to yoga. Pat's always busy with clients, yet still seems to have the flexibility to produce events for the causes that are close to her heart.

I think about what I would do on my own, and sadly, I'm not even sure. I tell myself I can't really think about it; it's not a reality. I have obligations to my family that prevent me from taking risks. I have a mortgage and bills. But I know the truth, and it's eating away at me one day at a time. Some days it seems to come to a head, and I know I need to do something about it.

In the course of this angst, I decided to start making myself uncomfortable, to begin to crawl out of safe spaces.

My first experiment with discomfort was attempting to fly on a trapeze. It's a Club Med contraption and it looks just like something you'd find in the Ringling Brothers' center ring: narrow ladders on each end of a rectangle leading to a platform, where a bar swings loosely through the air, and a giant net underneath spans the entire area.

After signing my life away, I carefully don a harness and start my climb up the ladder, barely the width of my hand. Halfway up, I'm told to turn myself around in order to climb over the net. This requires me to wedge as much of my foot as possible on the rung of the ladder, then pivot on that foot while swinging my other foot to the opposite side. Lots to remember while trying not to look down. Once up the ladder, I am forced to step onto the platform, which is maybe only a foot away but feels like a mile.

That's when they hook my harness to the ropes. Until then, the harness is nothing more than extra weight to hurl me to the ground if I should happen to fall. The Friendly Club Med Trapeze Man on the platform whispers soothing words. He tells me emphatically that he's got me, and that I must trust him. And I must. Because if I don't I can't fly.

If only he could understand I don't trust anyone. He sees me hesitate, grabs the trapeze bar, and signals for me to snatch it with my right hand. The trapeze is not long enough to be able to grab with both hands. In fact, I have to strain my whole body forward to reach for it, with Friendly Club Med Trapeze Man holding me by the back of my harness. The pressure mounts against my genitals and he holds onto me as I bend away from him.

So I do as he says and grab the bar, leaning forward as he instructs me. He tells me he's got me and his mellow directions take on a commanding tone as he explains that when he says, "Hep," I should fall off the platform, grab the bar with my left hand, and go flying through the air.

I consider going back down the ladder but am too embarrassed. If I can just get myself to fall off the platform, it's out of my hands, and I'll be flying.

It all seems so simple.

He yells "Hep" and I hesitate. I'm not ready, decide I'll make him say it again, and then I think "What am I waiting for? I just have to fall"—and so I do.

And I don't die. I even manage to enjoy the ride.

Every once in a while, life makes decisions easy for me: the store has run out of my size, or the dress that I fell in love with on the hanger looks awful on my body. But more often than not, I am forced to take control and make choices and trade-offs, especially about issues far more important than my wardrobe.

And sometimes, it's a matter of not thinking about it too long or too much, and just falling off the platform. When I grabbed that bar with my left hand and hooked my legs on, I realized I had underestimated myself. And it wasn't until I let go, hanging on the bar upside down by my legs, reaching out for Mr. Club Med Trapeze Man to catch me, that I really understood I won't know what I can do until I try.

So when I finally disconnected myself from the guaranteed paycheck and went off on my own, I figured I'd find out soon enough what I can do. I thought each experiment in making myself uncomfortable would get easier. But it doesn't; the fear never goes away, you just get more comfortable with the discomfort.

This time, there's no safety net. And even that can only protect so much. The rest, I guess, is gonna have to be up to me.

Yin and Yang

LYDIA

She's liberal and I'm conservative. She's pro-choice and I'm pro-life. She loves vegetables and I prefer doughnuts. She saves ducks and I eat them. We are very best friends, diametrically opposed in everything we do, but true soul mates to the core.

Pat and I have been sharing ups and downs since the seventh grade. Three decades of friendship seems inconceivable to my friend, who still deludes herself into believing she's not a day over thirty.

My, how the tables have turned through the years. I was always the popular one in school; Pat was shy and much more subdued. While I was a cheerleader, she was in the Spanish club. A fabulously slim size 4, I never had to worry about my weight, while Pat always carried a big Cuban *culo* (tush). Now she's the one sporting the trendy size 6 skintight pants (with her flat belly showing) and I just keep buying more stock in Weight Watchers. Life is so unfair.

These days, Pat's idea of fun is a late dinner (maybe three asparagus spears) followed by drinking and dancing the night away. I'd much rather go out to eat at seven, finish it off with a dessert tray sampler, maybe see a good play, and be home by ten, just about the time Pat's getting in the shower, getting ready for her night on the town.

But no matter our differences, Pat and I are bonded for life. Through marriages and pregnancies, divorces, children, dying parents, and all the joys and heartaches of life, our friendship just keeps getting better with time.

It's truly an unusual relationship. While we started out with the same beliefs in Catholic school, over the years Pat could no longer handle the guilt and completely transformed her ideas. She is now completely convinced she was an American Indian in her previous life and is very much in touch with all the energies known (and unknown) to humankind, while I remain a devout Catholic and practice religiously with only slight modifications.

I love to go to church, and I pray to Jesus, the Virgin Mary, and all the saints who I believe can keep me safe. Pat prefers to go to sweat lodges where she perspires until she almost passes out, and then believes the spirits have blessed her, while she visualizes eagles flying above her head. I too am a very spiritual person; I just don't don feather earrings and obsess about bonding with dead friends while swimming with dolphins. OK, so I'm exaggerating a little.

One night, many years ago, Pat and I went out for a quiet dinner, then took a walk through the buzzing streets of Miami. The outdoor cafés were packed with people eating and drinking and the night was crisp and delicious. At this point in our lives, we had both been married and divorced and were suddenly without any big responsibilities or Cuban curfews, happy to just be out and about enjoying each other. When we heard music blaring from a club, Pat insisted we march right in to join the fun. Pat has always been a great dancer, and I'm not, but I tried to let my hair down and fit in, as my friend did.

Within a few minutes, a very tall, good-looking gentleman asked me to dance, but I couldn't bring myself to say yes. I was happy people-watching from the corner of the room. But the man wouldn't take no for an answer and finally wore down my resistance. I felt like an alien dancing with the Jolly Green Giant, and although he was very suave on the dance floor, I couldn't wait until the song was over so that I could return to my self-imposed dungeon in the far corner. I told Pat, who hadn't stopped dancing since we arrived, that I needed to leave immediately; this was the last place I wanted to be. She tried to convince me to stay, but finally she acquiesced and we left the club.

We continued our walk down the busy sidewalks and it was on the corner that we made a sudden promise to each other. In full agreement that our friendship was as unique as our personalities were diverse, we made a pledge to make sure it always stayed that way. Like young children, we hugged each other, forming an unbreakable pact that would, in essence, commit us to each other for life. We agreed that, regardless of the place and time, whenever one of us needed the other, all it would take was a phone call and the other half would suddenly appear to assist in the crisis of the moment. That pact would put Pat to the test the very next night.

Shortly after midnight, less than twenty-four hours after we had sealed our friendship fate, I had a car accident. I was driving home from a school reunion and was rear-ended by a speeding car. My rear tire blew out, my trunk was smashed beyond recognition, and my car needed to be towed. I wasn't hurt too badly, but I couldn't call my parents, who were home with my son, so I called Pat. I was already exercising my rights under our newly formed agreement, and without hesitation, she was on her way. In less than thirty minutes, she arrived and took charge of the entire situation. I always knew my friend would keep her end of the bargain and I was just waiting for my turn to reciprocate. My part of the pact went untested for a lot of years, but we both knew it was rock solid. And then real life stepped in.

Years had passed; I was remarried and preparing a dinner party for fifteen friends when the phone rang. I had so much to do to get ready for this party and almost didn't answer the phone, but something told me it was Pat and I just had this feeling she needed me. She did. She was in severe abdominal pain and heading to the hospital. I remembered the pact and really wanted to help my friend, but didn't know what to do with my half-cooked dinner and the guests who would soon be appearing. I started to feel a major migraine setting in, but I called upon a good friend and left my husband to pitch in and have the party without me. I knew that Pat really needed me to be with her and sped off to meet her.

When I got to the emergency room, it looked like a scene from the Thursday night hit television show. Pat was in excruciating pain and after several hours of examinations, X-rays, and a myriad of tests, she was diagnosed with a severe kidney infection that required four days of hospitalization. I stood vigil for nearly ninety-six hours until the raging infection could be silenced and my poor friend's kidneys could begin functioning properly again. Pat has no siblings; her mother had passed away nearly fourteen years earlier, and other than her father, who was also there, I was truly her "next of kin."

Though Pat and I are the same age, sometimes I feel like I've become Pat's second mom. My life is so much more subdued than my friend's, and sometimes I can even feel and hear the voice of Daisy, Pat's devoted mother, who I think is reaching out to help guide me on how to continue raising her forty-eight-year-old wild and crazy daughter. My friend hates when I impose my own judgments on the way she lives her life, but I just blame it on Daisy.

Since Pat decided not to have children, she's counting on my daughter to care for her when she gets old and gray. Christine is fifteen and loves to be around her *tia* Pat, completely aware that she's so much cooler than I am, and a whole lot more fun.

Last year, Christine had to dress up as the Virgin Mary, and asked Tia Pat for some advice on what to wear. Pat tried to convince my daughter to go as a modern-day version of "Proud Mary" and dress hip with white jeans, a white blouse, and a psychedelic flower in her hair. Pat is anything but traditional, and even Christine drew the line that day, but it's the unique way Pat is teaching my conservative family to think out of the box that makes her so much fun to be around.

While I have three children, and now a beautiful granddaughter, Pat has a dog and three cats. It can really get annoying when she doesn't understand my responsibilities and assumes that we all want to live the carefree, responsibility-free life she has made her own for the past thirty years. She travels and makes impulsive decisions while I agonize over every one.

For some reason, Pat lives in a neighborhood that resembles Mr. Rogers's. Good karma, she calls it. Her neighbors, Bombshell Annie and Kathy across the street, happily take over Pat's animal and garden duties on a moment's notice when she travels. I live on the other side of the tracks. Mr. Rogers never stepped foot in my neighborhood, but if you look closely, you might see the Road Runner traipsing through my garden.

I schedule my trips around school calendars and live with the constant guilt that I can't make it to my son's baseball games or my daughter's basketball tournament, and as much as I love to cook, I just don't have the time. Pat thinks cooking is a complete waste of time and lives on ready-made foods prepared by the local gourmet markets at exorbitant prices.

She's always the first to tell me to take care of myself and to remind me that when I am not around, my family should be able to fetch their own meals. Pat thinks I should quit work and do something less demanding and often tries to impose her "single-person behaviors" on me, but I know that she is truly concerned about me and I love her for it.

Though our relationship sometimes has its ups and downs, it has lasted longer than any of our marriages, and ultimately, all of our disagreements work themselves out. We share our inner thoughts, dreams, and hopes for ourselves with each other, and we know that our deepest darkest secrets are sacred.

When my father was dying, I spent endless hours in the hospital to be by his side. Pat visited frequently, lifting my spirits in the midst of the sadness. Even my dad, in his final days, joked about Pat's native energy healings, after she performed one in his room, and he questioned if it was *Santeria* . . . Cuban black magic. Those were the days I truly understood the meaning of friendship, as she brought my Bombshell buddies in, laden with gifts designed to make me laugh.

Sara showed up with a talking teddy bear that spoke only dirty words, Annie brought a hand-beaded wineglass that she promised to fill when we were out of the hospital, Tammi brought rugula (those wonderful Jewish pastries filled with nuts and cinnamon), and Mercedes, who had to stay home with her kids, sent magazines to distract my mind.

I didn't have time for new friends when Pat brought these Bombshell women into my life, but on this day, I understood why my friend brought us all together. The compassion and love I devoured from these women that day is a feeling I will cherish for the rest of my life.

Dad died later that same night, and Pat stood with my entire family at his bedside as he took his last breath. As my family embraced in an emotional farewell, I was thankful to God for bringing Pat into my life and for keeping her there. And so was my family, who adopted her thirty-five years ago and will never let her go.

She is the yin to my yang, the Oscar to my Felix, the Laverne to my Shirley, and the love of my life. Old friends truly are the best friends.

The Worm

BOMBSHELL

I was raped. Not once, but twice. Once at gunpoint. I left him and it broke his heart. He went berserk and took revenge. He didn't shoot, but the wounds remain. He claimed he did it because he loved me and could not bear to be without me. So he forced himself into my body to be with me just one more time.

We dated seriously for several years. In hindsight, I always knew he had a violent streak. I had caught glimpses. There were signs of illogical jealousy, flashes of violent outbursts toward men he thought looked at me in a sexual way. I mistook his behavior for gallantry. So I ignored all the signs. I was in love, and in denial.

He was so handsome, strong, virile, and bright. We used to stay up till the wee hours of the morning talking, playing games, or watching movies. He was a bit bohemian, not caring about anything except the moment. And yeah, the sex was great. Problem was, he believed women belonged in the proverbial kitchen, pregnant and barefoot. I convinced myself that he would change and eventually accept me as a professional with hopes and dreams that did not, at the moment, include raising a family. It never happened.

We looked like an ideal couple. Two young people in love. And for a while, we were truly blissful. But as the hours and minutes of each day passed, I realized I was in a living hell. This man whom I loved turned out to be filled with insecurities and anger.

I did everything possible to reassure him of my devotion and love in order to keep the peace. I would make a conscious effort every time we went out to keep my eyes from wandering so he wouldn't jump to the conclusion that I was looking at another man.

On those rare occasions when I went to a girlfriend's house, I would call him continuously to reassure him that I missed and loved him. He would keep close track of my every movement to satisfy himself that I was not seeing anyone on the side.

I was just embarking on a career and trying desperately to make a name for myself. It was a constant struggle to decide whether to work late, as was sometimes needed, and then deal with my lunatic boyfriend or to leave early just to avoid a blowup. On those few occasions when I opted to work late, my heart palpitated when I saw him next—the all-too-familiar monster who was waiting for me in the shadows.

Being young and naive, I tried to play the role of dutiful girlfriend, sometimes even ironing his shirts, a real stretch for me. But I loved him and thought he would appreciate the effort. It was never enough. This man I loved actually became angry because I had not properly ironed his shirts. If I had the brains and balls that I do today, I would have shoved the scalding iron, the board, and the shirt up his ass. But I didn't.

After several years of living in a self-made cell, I found an escape. I did what he had unjustly accused me of doing for years. I met a charming man on one of my business trips; he was caring, sensitive, and sexy as hell. So . . . I cheated. *Why not?* I thought. *He assumes I'm doing it anyway.* He didn't deserve my loyalty, not after the emotional abuse he continued to heap on me. It was a one-night stand and I never saw the man again, but I received the momentary emotional gratification I wasn't getting from my boyfriend.

Somehow he learned the truth. Maybe I let him find out. I thought this was my ticket out. I told him it was over. At first, he didn't believe me and refused to accept it. After months and months of confrontations, he finally gave up and left my life.

I was able to breathe again. No more avoiding friendly hellos from men I didn't know. No more explanations! I was free. The cage door had been unlocked and I was liberated. I was able to do simple things like have dinner with my friends again, go for a walk on the beach after work, stay in the office and talk to coworkers at night. Simple things we all take for granted. I eventually began dating again. I had regained my life. Or so I thought.

I had just returned from a magical date with a kind and loving man I had known for years. We were just friends at first, until that night. We had made love for the first time and it was beautiful. It was a glorious Miami night, warm and sensuous and full of promise, and I allowed myself to believe that I could find love again.

I turned the key to my front door and headed straight for the couch. I sat there daydreaming, as I hadn't allowed myself to do in years. I was happy. That's when I heard the sound. Footsteps coming down the stairs. Who was it? I was terrified. I thought I was alone.

And then I saw him. I had forgotten to set the alarm and he had apparently climbed in through the upstairs window. He was crying, sobbing uncontrollably. And then I noticed the gun in his hand. My heart picked up that old familiar beat. My head swirled. I didn't know if I was going to pass out or throw up.

I'd never seen such anguish. I never heard a grown man moan with such agony. The gun in his hand terrified me, but the pain I felt in his heart drew me to him. I couldn't swallow. I tried to ask what he was doing and then I begged him to leave.

He didn't listen. He just mumbled that he couldn't live without me and couldn't bear for us to be apart. I thought he was going to kill himself.

This man I loved for years was now a stranger in front of my eyes. He was suffering immensely because of me. I had cheated on him, I left him, and now it was destroying him. It devastated me as much as it seemed to destroy him.

Slowly, I headed toward him, and gently wrapped my arms around him as tears overcame us both. We cried for a love that was lost, for a life we had planned together that would never be. We wept because we knew that from that moment on, it could never be the same.

I told him that I still loved him but that we just weren't meant to be. I embraced him with all of my being. And then he ordered me to undress. I thought I was hearing things.

"Take your clothes off," he said through his sobs. I didn't understand. He grabbed me by my arm and pulled me over to the dining room table as he climbed on top and kneeled. As he pointed the gun at my head, he repeated his command. The cold metal of the barrel shook me to my core. I trembled uncontrollably.

I still had not obeyed him. Somehow I had managed to keep my clothes on. I couldn't scream. I couldn't find the strength, and if I did, what would he do? Would he shoot me? And if the neighbors rushed in, would he shoot them? I couldn't risk it. Would he go to jail? How could I let him go to jail? He was a broken man because of me. It was my fault, or so I thought.

I begged him to leave and promised to keep this between us. He then released my arm, giving me a flicker of hope. But he kept the gun at my head. He grabbed a duffel bag that I hadn't noticed resting on the table and pulled out an Instamatic Polaroid camera. I was thoroughly confused. Then he opened his zipper and pulled out his penis.

"Suck it," he said through his tears. "Suck on it." *I have done this before,* I thought. He continued to sob uncontrollably. I convinced myself that if I followed his instructions he wouldn't hurt me. Maybe I can bite him. What then? Can I bite him hard enough to disarm him? Oh my God, but then I'll hurt him for life. I can't do that. I'm to blame for his pain. Oh God, the guilt.

As he grabbed my head and pulled me toward him, he put his penis in my mouth and started to take pictures. Close-up shots. His penis in my mouth. My face—his penis. This must be some strange nightmare that I will hardly remember in the morning. Sadness, anger, fear, and humiliation were fighting for control inside my body.

I didn't recognize his taste anymore. How strange and distant we'd become.

I was wearing a black miniskirt. As he forced me to lean over the table, the edge cut deep into my thighs. His hold on my head was sending a horrible ache down my back. We had eaten so many romantic meals together at this table. Candlelight dinners, soft music, and then love.

"I'm going to send these pictures to your office," he said. "I want everyone to see what kind of a whore you are."

Bite, I kept thinking. But I couldn't bring myself to hurt him. And then he stopped. He pushed away from me. After a moment he put the camera down, climbed down from the table, and dragged me to the bedroom.

I begged him to stop. But there was no stopping him.

I decided to close my eyes and fly away. Somehow between each horrible moment I remembered my soul. I focused on my Higher Being and the fact that I am more than my body. *He might hurt the shell of who I am,* I thought, *but he can't hurt the essence of me.* I don't know where this clarity came from. I have no idea how I was able to call upon such strength in the midst of such terror.

He threw me on the bed. And I took it. Over and over and over again, painfully hard, in my vagina and then up my ass. He then lifted me off the bed onto the floor and made me dance for him, a mock striptease, all the while with a gun to my head. He dishonored and abused my body and our past, but in that moment I decided he would not destroy my future.

As he finished, hours later, I remained motionless in bed. The physical pain and enormity of what had just happened began to pour down over me as something caught my eye on the wall. It was a five-foot-tall word, *WHORE,* spray-painted in black on my satin white bedroom walls. All I could think was, how come I hadn't noticed it before? And then he walked out the door.

I was ashamed of what had happened. I didn't want the outside world to know. I told my parents and a few close friends. It remained a hidden secret to everyone else.

I went to my girlfriend's house that evening. I was petrified to be alone. I didn't dare call my new boyfriend for fear that my ex would harm him. I must have dozed off early in the morning just in time to have my friend wake me; he was on the phone. She didn't know what to do.

He was calling to threaten me again with the exposure of the photos. He said that he would give them back to me, but only in person. When I refused to meet him, he swore that he would mail them to my office the next day. I panicked.

A delusional logic took over, and that afternoon, unbeknownst to anyone, I went to his apartment. As he greeted me at the door with photos in hand, he grabbed me, pulled me inside the apartment, and dragged me to his bedroom.

I was so exhausted emotionally and physically that I just didn't fight him. I didn't care anymore. *He can use my body,* I thought, *but at least I'll leave with the photos in hand.* I had to put all of this behind me, which I couldn't do with those photos floating around Miami.

So he raped me again until he had his fill. It was quick and to the point this time. No gun. No dancing. Just a very strong madman with a need to hurt me once again. And then he handed me the envelope and let me walk out the door, as any invited guest would do. I heard he moved out of town shortly after that. Thankfully, I haven't heard from him since.

I don't know what kind of lasting effects this has had on my life. Sometimes I think it didn't affect me. Other times I'm not so sure. I never really talk about it. I can't relate to it anymore. It seems like it happened to someone else.

I'm sure somewhere inside of me there's shame. For a long time, I was convinced I got what I deserved. Some part of me still believes that. I cheated on him, left him, and tore his life apart. I know that makes absolutely no sense. I know rape is wrong and there is no justification. Rape is not a crime of passion, it's a violent way to control and abuse another person. There is no excuse for rape. My mind understands that, but my heart still hasn't caught on.

I've never spoken to other rape victims about this. I'm not ready to go public, yet. I'm sure there are lots of women out there like me. You never hear about them though. You only read about the ones who are devastated, whose lives are ruined and scarred forever.

I am such a different person today. I have a tremendous sense of self-worth and would never allow myself to be violated like that again. I don't think. Who can ever really tell? I look back on my years with him and I don't understand who I was back then.

I remember once, when our love affair was just beginning, leaving a beautiful restaurant in Miami after a romantic dinner. We were walking hand in hand, looking out over Biscayne Bay with the Miami skyline twinkling in the background, when he turned to me and starting talking about his ex-girlfriend. The lights of the city seemed to dim.

He described her as a slim, long-legged, beautiful blond. He said, "It's a good thing you never met her, or you would have felt like a worm." A worm? What the hell does that mean? Is a worm ugly? Maybe he meant I didn't compare. I didn't ask him to explain; my love for him always found excuses for his hurtful behavior.

The pain stabbed so deeply I kept it crushed inside for years. If only I had understood these early warning signs, I could have spared myself so much unnecessary suffering.

A worm . . . my ass! What he didn't know is that this worm was actually a caterpillar that sprouted wings and learned how to fly, higher than ever thought possible.

four | Love, Lust, and Secrets

What is it about love, lust, and sex that makes us say and do such crazy things? When we started our Bombshell meetings, we stayed clear of these topics (for about two minutes), but it seemed that all roads led us right back to the issues that used to be inappropriate for women to discuss publicly. And there was no turning back.

Most of the "bombshells" we dropped had us confessing sexual secrets and desires to one another, as we tried to figure out why it's still so culturally unacceptable for women to talk openly about this kind of stuff. We giggled a lot, and some of us turned beet red, throwing our heads into our hands with embarrassment, because back then, we were still virtually strangers.

As our meetings progressed, it was clear that some Miami Bombshells had no problem admitting past affairs and sexual escapades, while others were shocked by some of the stories. But one meeting in particular revealed more than most of us could have imagined.

The six Miami Bombshells are sitting in Pat's living room, as our true confession sessions are starting to take on a whole new dimension. We've just started thinking that our stories might one day make for a great book. This meeting today, for the first time, has an agenda. As Lydia is stuffing her face with pastries and Annie is adding colored beads to her latest leopard-print cigar box creation, others are trying to pay attention.

We have trouble with that sometimes, as our get-togethers have become *way* too much fun. Pat, who was running this meeting, "asked" us (wink, wink) to be considerate and listen.

Lydia and Annie laugh at her, while Tammi and Sara roll their eyes and try to get focused. The first Bombshell clears her throat and begins to tell her story about a bizarre experience she had when a boyfriend went beyond acceptable sexual boundaries. "If I'm going to write about this, it has to remain anonymous!" declares this Bombshell emphatically, as she starts to describe her experience out loud.

Some of us don't take the story seriously and heckle the author relentlessly. Most of us don't realize that, to her, this incident was horrifying and traumatic and, certainly, no laughing matter. But it is no use.

One Bombshell, laughing so hard that tears roll down her cheeks, asks in amazement, "He put cocaine where?" Another Bombshell is now roaring . . . *"What?* You think twenty years later you're still feeling the affects of drugs? You have *got* to be kidding!" By now, the others can no longer contain their amusement. "It's *not* funny!" she cries. "It was horrible. . . ." But the laughter is out of control. Several Bombshells actually peed in their pants, including the author, who couldn't help but laugh through her tears.

Eventually, another Bombshell begins to read a story she's just now put on paper . . . a little ditty about a weenie that performed under the most unusual of circumstances. "Why do you feel the need to keep this story anonymous?" asks one curious Bombshell.

"Because, if I don't, the reader will think I'm a pervert."

"Well, you are!" scream two Bombshells from across the room, almost at the same time. By now, everyone is cracking up as the author flings a pillow in the direction of no one in particular. "But we love you anyway!" laughs another, who shakes her head and tries not to pass judgment on her friend.

Sharing our darkest secrets, deepest desires, and sexual truths with one another really *has* brought us closer. Through these confessions, we have learned that no matter our differences, as women, we all experience the same emotions when it comes to sex and relationships. And although some of us don't agree with each other's lifestyles, we try to respect one another and agree to disagree. Sometimes, however, that only comes after a heated debate or a reluctant acceptance.

Coming out of the sexual closet has helped all of us shed our inhibitions. We don't hear anyone complaining.

The Fight

LYDIA

It may happen in a dream, but how in the world does it happen in real life? Surely, it couldn't be happening to me. I was seated at a sporting event with my husband of more than six years when a woman approached me and said, "I've been having an affair with your husband."

Let's kick this story into rewind. Three couples, including my best friend, Pat; my husband; and me, had just finished a delicious dinner at Hollywood's fancy Diplomat Hotel that was demolished several years ago, along with the illusion of my perfect marriage.

After dinner, we all moved into the grand ballroom where a very special boxing match was about to be televised. It was being billed as the fight of the century, Frasier versus Tyson. By the end of the evening, I was convinced I was the one who had received the knockout punch.

As we entered the viewing area, our group had to separate because we couldn't find seats together. I was momentarily annoyed at this inconvenience, but in the end it proved to be a godsend.

We were waiting for the fight to begin when a tall blond woman came over and stood right next to me. "Hi, remember me?" she asked with a sweet smile. I could not immediately place her and while searching my memory bank, she identified herself as one of my husband's coworkers. Instinctively, I felt something was terribly wrong. I was having a difficult time focusing on what this woman was trying to say.

For some strange reason, my heart started to pound, and I was very confused, but I could never have imagined what would happen next. Without waiting for me to say a word, she proceeded to tell me that she had been sleeping with my husband for the past year, then whipped out a large stack of photos, giving me a narrated short story on each one. There they were in Cancún (where I thought he was on business). She even had a picture of him that I had taken on our most recent trip to Paris. (No wonder he made such frequent trips to the telephone during our strolls down the Champs-Elysée.)

Once she had finished her lengthy dissertation, she dropped the pictures on my lap and walked away. Very calmly, I turned to my husband (who had been sitting quietly observing the entire scene) and told him I wanted to leave. As I walked down the corridor three steps ahead of my adulterous mate, I tore the pictures into tiny pieces and left a trail behind me.

As we approached the valet to get our car, there she was again. Standing her sorry ass in the middle of the ramp, she created quite a scene as she began shouting details of her illicit affair with my husband. She was blaming me for being so stupid, and for failing to notice his infidelity for so long. After she had completed her barrage, she turned and angrily stomped off.

When we got in the car and drove away, I didn't know if I wanted to cry or die. As I looked back, I was horrified to see a multitude of strangers who had just witnessed a real live version of a soap opera in which I played the starring role. It was at that moment that I realized I was actually grateful . . . that none of my friends had witnessed what had turned out to be the most humiliating night of my life. What could I say? My husband too was speechless as he drove to the location where we had first kissed ten years earlier. He cried and cried and then begged me for forgiveness. But nothing he could possibly say could ease the pain I was feeling. In one night, I had forever lost my high school sweetheart, my husband, my partner, my lover, and my friend.

The following day was a total blur. I was completely numb and couldn't find a place for myself. And then the phone rang. It was Pat, who was calling to see why we had disappeared so early the previous night. She never knew that the fight of the century took place right at my seat. She ran right over, but nothing she said could ease the agony I felt.

Although I was emotionally drained, exhausted, and confused, after taking a week off to recover, I went back to work. It was there I learned that my charming husband's little mistress had decided to bombard me with the letters of their infidelity. I was baffled. Had she planned all of this or was this mean streak just a part of her personality?

As I opened the manila envelopes, I found very long love letters written by my husband to this demon. Pages and pages of sweet words, lustful words, and sexual innuendos. That's how the daily delivery of torture began; day by day, new letters, each more explicit than the last. Betrayal delivered first class, courtesy of the U.S. Postal Service. No extra charge. It killed me, but the curiosity didn't allow me to throw them away.

But still, I forged onward and I hired one of the best divorce attorneys in town. He was also very handsome, charming, and totally disarming. I used to look forward to our appointments at his office. Flattery was part of his style, and the attention he gave me was exactly what I needed. My self-esteem was shot, and he made me feel like a woman again. My very tight budget was not an obstacle to splurging on a new outfit just to impress him every time I had to see him. He pumped my ego and made me feel confident, which helped me face the divorce process with determination.

Finally, my day in court arrived and I came face-to-face with the "ditz" my husband was sleeping with, as she was called to testify. The attorneys asked her if she knew the definition of adultery. With a sly smile, she replied, "I'm sorry, how do you spell that?" The trial proceeded but their hot and passionate relationship did not. It fizzled and died. What a shame . . .

Ultimately, the money I was awarded was barely enough to cover my monthly electric bills. But finally, I was divorced, and free of the man who had stolen so much from me. And I was determined, with a new sense of self-esteem, to show the world and myself that I do not need a man to survive.

Round 2. Bring it on!

E-mail Hell

BOMBSHELL

We had been friends for years. And for as many years, I often wondered about the special connection that we shared. There was always this electricity between us, but we were friends, so we never crossed that line, especially since he was engaged. Neither of us thought very highly of cheating.

But one sweltering evening in Miami, that all changed. He came in for business, but it turned out to be all pleasure. On his last night in town, I joined him and his relatives for drinks. Half an hour or so into the evening, he shot me a "let's get out of here" glance, so we said our quick good-byes and slipped away and walked over to a quaint little restaurant in Coconut Grove. As we sipped on wine, we talked about our hopes, our desires, and our love lives. That's when he admitted that he wasn't really sure he wanted to get married. "What?" I asked him. "You just got engaged, what are you talking about?" He leaned in closer and touched my arm as I felt my skin tingle. "She's not the one I want to spend the rest of my life with," he declared. I was getting nervous. He stroked my hand and smiled. I looked into his eyes, and then he kissed me. Unexpectedly. Passionately. It took me by total surprise. My brain was not computing. But my heart was enjoying. What the heck was he doing? We sat there, speechless, as the waiter brought our food. We laughed nervously, both unsure of what was happening.

We didn't talk much as we nibbled on our dinner, neither one of us knowing quite what to say. As we left the restaurant, we walked hand in hand to my car. He kissed me again and said that he finally felt at home and that it had always been me. I was in a daze. I had no clue what he meant or what I was feeling. This was my friend, whom I cared for deeply, whom I always knew I was attracted to, but this had turned way too fast . . . and he had a fiancée. I drove home, alone, in a daze.

The next day, he left town and completely dropped off my radar screen. I thought the entire episode had been some sort of strange dream. A few weeks later, he finally called. He said he felt guilty about what happened, especially at a time he was supposed to be planning his wedding. "No kidding?" I said, but only to myself.

It was clear to me that although we never pushed past the boundaries of that kiss, we both knew there were feelings there we needed to address, but we just didn't know how. So we made small talk, and then hung up.

Weeks later, he reconnected, safely, through e-mail. For months, we wrote back and forth trying to figure out what "we" were and what had really transpired that hot Miami night. Was it love or just plain lust between friends? Our e-mails got intense. The writing got more and more tantalizing as we kept pushing beyond each other's limits. Our benign words were loaded with innuendo.

Months later, when we finally saw each other again, it was as if nothing had ever happened. He wouldn't even acknowledge the words he had spoken. I was eager to discuss our friendship and tell him how I didn't want a kiss to ruin it, but he didn't even want to talk about it, almost pretending we had never crossed the line. He played it cool and distant.

After that visit, he disappeared again for weeks. Not a word or call. And just when I was beginning to think he was nothing but an idiot who throws away his friends as easily as he discards old socks, I received an e-mail. I was thrilled. His note was innocent enough, but it was the reconnection I was longing for. I had not lost my friend after all.

And in that moment of euphoria, I forwarded his e-mail to one of our mutual friends, one of the other Bombshells. I knew she would be happy that he had reappeared in my life and I also wanted her to read between the lines and tell me if she thought there were any hidden emotions within his words. It was a very "girlie" thing to do. It was also very stupid and something I had never done before.

She read his e-mail, scrutinized it, and commented, writing down her psychological analysis of the hidden meaning she found in his words. She postulated on how she thought this man was obviously not ready to get married and was, in fact, calling out for help. "Change," she said, "is not something this man relishes." And then—she accidentally hit Reply All!

At the time, this Bombshell never realized what she did. So we went on with our normal lives for about two days. And then she, not I, got an e-mail, from clear across the world, from my guy asking her what she was doing reading the e-mail he had written to me and asking her why she thought I had sent it straight to her.

That's when she placed her frantic call to me. "Listen," she screamed. "Major @#*$! He sent me an e-mail asking me what I was doing reading his e-mail to you."

"WHAT?!" I hollered. My heart was about to implode. "What? How did he get our e-mails?!" I asked my friend accusingly.

"I don't know, but if you thought things weren't going well between the two of you before," she said, "they sure as hell are about to get a whole lot worse."

I about pooped in my pants. How could this happen? How did she forward her reply to me, to him? She had no idea.

She was hysterical. She told me she didn't respond to him, not wanting to stick her foot further down her own throat. So she resisted the temptation to reply yet again.

That's when I asked the earth to *please* just eat me up and swallow me whole! Now what? Should I kill my friend? Yes, but that would have to come later. My would-be lover now knew I had forwarded his private e-mail. How humiliating. How $%# $% embarrassing! Now it was up to me to figure out how to deactivate this time bomb. Days and days went by because neither one of us knew what to do, so we did nothing.

His friendship meant more to me than anything else, so I bit the bullet and called. He wasn't there, so I left a voice mail, "Hi, it's me, we need to talk. Please call me." And he did, almost immediately. I thought my heart would burst out of my chest when he told me he was livid and hurt by my breach of trust. All I could do was to tell him the truth.

I explained that it was a simple e-mail that I had forwarded to my girlfriend and that I didn't mean to betray him. I confessed that I wanted to share my excitement over receiving his e-mail after so many weeks of no communication. I was just happy that our friendship was not damaged and I had to share it with my friend.

Long story short, he married his fiancée. Eventually, after he tortured me with his contempt, he forgave me and our friendship blossomed.

My Bombshell friend insists she didn't send him the e-mail. She says that I'm the one who hit Reply All when I sent it to her. "I swear to you," she still insists, "I didn't send him that e-mail. You're both my friends for God's sake. I wouldn't want anything more than to see you two hitched. Why would I put that on the line? If I did it, I did it by accident, but I'm so sure I didn't do it."

I guess we'll never really know the truth. At this point, it doesn't really matter anyway. We're all still friends. We've shared each other's holiday celebrations since then and have moved beyond our childish indiscretions. As for me, I've gone back to writing letters the old-fashioned way, by long hand.

Maybe I should drop him a line . . .

Time of My Life

BOMBSHELL

It was my first day at work in corporate America. I had no idea what I was getting into. Literally. While this was the beginning of a very successful career, it was also the start of a personal adventure that changed my life.

The journey started in a country-and-western bar. The band was playing a tune I didn't recognize. Some of my coworkers were making fools of themselves trying to line dance, and even though I love to dance, I decided to sit out the song. And then the music changed. The pace slowed down and they started to play "Time of My Life" from the movie *Dirty Dancing*. It was one of my favorite songs and I was hoping that my new, very handsome boss would ask me to dance. As I glanced his way he was already walking toward me. I felt a tinge of excitement cross my heart.

As two strangers who had never danced before, we kept our distance and made it a point to discuss only work. But as the rhythms swayed us and the romantic lyrics penetrated our souls, it was clear that things were quickly changing . . . which took me by surprise.

When the music stopped, my heart continued dancing. We stood there motionless, looking into each other's eyes, but within seconds, we were interrupted by a coworker who asked my partner to dance. I walked away a little disappointed.

Several weeks passed with business as usual. I didn't see much of my new boss since he lived in another city. When we did see each other, there was never a mention of that night at the bar. From a professional standpoint, things were progressing and I was growing, learning, and loving my new job.

One afternoon, my boss called to discuss several pending issues, and we agreed to meet the next day at the office. He flew in the following morning and we spent the day going from one meeting to the next. By the time we were done, our stomachs were empty and our minds were fried, so we agreed to grab a bite and take care of additional business over dinner.

"Table for two," he said confidently to the maître d' as we arrived at a quaint restaurant in Coral Gables. We managed to talk about work for a few minutes, but there was definitely some flirting floating in the air. Halfway through dinner, he reached over and held my hand. I stared into his eyes and smiled. I wasn't going to play games, as we knew what we both wanted.

We left the restaurant before they even brought out the dessert tray. What we were both in the mood for was not on the menu. As we drove back to his hotel, we broke the awkward silence with small talk.

When we arrived, he invited me to his room for a nightcap. I felt embarrassed following this man I barely knew. To make matters worse, he was my boss. I resisted a sudden urge to leave, but changed my mind when he moved closer and kissed me provocatively, leaving me wanting a lot more. That's when he dropped the bomb and told me he was married. I felt disappointed and totally misled.

Although I told him emphatically that I didn't date married men, my words had no meaning once he pulled me toward him again. Our mutual desire for each other was overwhelming. It was irresistible.

I gave in. We made love over and over again. And so began the most passionate, yet painful episode of my life. I had never been the other woman, but it was a role that I fell into, head over heels.

We fell deeply in love and thrived in each other's company. We kept our affair a secret, and no one suspected a thing. The first year was magical. Though he lived more than four hundred miles away, we saw each other at least once a week and our love just kept getting stronger. We traveled together often, escaping reality, spending days holed up in hotel rooms, coming up for air only when room service knocked on our door.

As we approached the second year of our affair, our escapades became more frequent. We took greater risks, not caring about consequences. All that mattered was being together. But there was no escaping the truth . . . at the end of the day he had a family to go home to. As much as I loved him and wanted to be with him, I was tired of having to hide. I grew weary at the number of times he asked me for privacy so he could call his wife. After two years, I was still alone.

Eventually, I felt so dirty and cheap for being the other woman for so long. While I could not bear the thought of being without him, I knew it was time to let go. I was confused, but I knew exactly what I had to do.

I ended the affair over the phone. I couldn't bring myself to tell him in person. He did not make it easy for me and refused to accept my decision. He jumped into his car and made it to my house in record time. He was devastated when he showed up at my door, begging me to reconsider.

I'm not sure where I found the strength that day, but I was bound and determined to stick with my decision. The pain was excruciating for me, but paled in comparison to the guilt I had been feeling.

Fortunately for me, he left the company. However, his attempts at getting me back continued for months. He paid me other surprise visits and called me incessantly until I changed my telephone number. As much as it killed me, I knew I was doing the right thing. So why did it feel so wrong?

A Kiss Between Friends

BOMBSHELL

There is more to love than just love. There is acceptance, comfort, and familiarity.

Women love other women; they understand each other. This is not to say we don't like men, but that's not what this story is about.

My relationships with women have always been intense. I was the kind of teenager who had one or a few very close friends, rather than a mass of acquaintances. We would stay up late and talk on the phone until our eyes closed down the conversation, then put the phone by our pillows—keeping the line connected—until we woke up, picked up the receiver, and started the chat up again.

Years later, a close girlfriend surprised me one night as we were hanging out in my room. She leaned in and kissed me on the lips, then sat back, waiting to see my reaction. The kiss was shocking, startling, but not altogether unpleasant. I started talking quickly, about anything I could think of, while the butterflies in my stomach threatened to break free. We never discussed the kiss, and it never happened again.

That was the first time, but not the last, that I pondered how easy it would be to love a woman.

She came into my life at a time when I wasn't sure of who I was. She wanted to get to know me despite the fact I didn't know myself. We met through mutual friends and the connection was instantaneous.

Being with her was easy and difficult at the same time. My genuine self came out to greet her, to speak to this stranger who I intuitively knew would like me regardless of my idiosyncrasies, my sarcasm, or my moods. I knew this, I think, because I saw myself in her.

But she was also a bit like a crossword puzzle: challenging and frustrating. Exhilarating and fun. My brain always had to be "on," I always had to be thinking, and she let me get away with nothing.

We became close immediately and spent all of our spare time together. And when there wasn't any spare time, we created it, carving it off from other things we probably should have been doing instead. We dated other people and compared notes. But nobody we met was as interesting to be with as we found each other.

When an offer came my way to travel to Europe with a man I was seeing, I accepted. The first several days were a blur of planes, trains, and taxis, and by the time we arrived in Paris, he had determined he needed to go off and travel on his own. Staring at the depressing walls of the hotel room we had booked, I considered returning home, then decided to stay and see Europe alone. I figured I'd meet plenty of people like myself.

But that didn't happen. I met people—women and men from all over the world—but none seemed to be like me, to share my values or my sense of humor. I couldn't make a connection with any of them. My thoughts would always wander to my friend at home. I longed to be with her. I imagined that the two of us together would be all that we needed. And each day that passed in France, Italy, or Spain seemed to cement that feeling. By the time I was on a plane headed back to the States, I was convinced I was in love with her.

But if absence makes the heart grow fonder, then distance and being dumped make the heart exaggerate. Returning home to my best friend after that disastrous European trip, I realized that the relationship I had imagined with her didn't really exist, except in my mind. I believe the connection that women have with each other is sometimes so powerful that at times it can threaten to cross a romantic line. The common language, the shared experiences, roll up to an unspoken communication with which no man can compete.

This is where I lose most people. While all of the Bombshells can relate to the power of female friendship, the story, at this point, goes a bit off course for them. But one pipes in. "I sometimes feel like it would be easier to love a woman," she declares, emphatically. "If it wasn't for the sex part, I could completely imagine being a lesbian."

But it wasn't the sex that I was thinking about. In fact, I was trying not to think about it; it interfered with my perfect fantasy because it made me uneasy. What I couldn't stop thinking about was kissing her. The thought I was captivated with was the idea of folding her into my arms and feeling her softness. Of holding curves instead of angles. Of touching skin that is soft and sweet, rather than rough. Feeling the warm air on my cheek as she exhaled. Taking her face in my hands and softly kissing her lips, while thoughts that cannot be voiced passed from me to her.

The power of a kiss, to me, is breathtaking—literally. A good one can make me swoon. And the intimacy of that seemingly small act—that seemingly innocent act—can be so much more powerful than sex. I would rather my lover sleep with someone else based purely on a physical attraction than kiss them passionately; the latter would be a much greater infidelity.

We never did share the kiss. The romanticized notion of our friendship evaporated when I saw her and realized I had only the desire to hold her to feel the relief of being with someone who wanted nothing more from me than my presence. My friend and I stayed close, even to this day. Since then, though, I've found male partners who are very much in touch with their feminine side, and that makes me happy. But when I want to connect, to reach out for unconditional comfort, I always call a girlfriend first.

It's an Epidemic!

PATRICIA

Last week, a friend ran into my office, closed the door, and started sobbing uncontrollably. I thought her new boss had fired her, but actually, she's leaving her husband. After thirteen years of marriage, she's stepping out of the closet of denial. She can't live like this any longer, she cried to me. He's a great man but they're very different. She's alive and he's deader than a doornail.

The following week, my Bombshell friend Tammi called me wanting to cry on my shoulder. She too is a mess. She adores her live-in Cuban boyfriend, but they're just *so* different. She says she's overwhelmed with life and work and needs a time-out. Although she swears to me that he's the man for her, for now she needs to be on her own.

Two days later, I had lunch with another friend who was visiting from Seattle. She told me she had just asked her husband to leave, after only one year of marriage. She can't take it anymore. He's a great man but they're very different. She's alive and passionate, and he's as cold as Frosty the Snowman.

The next afternoon, I got a call from Annie, another distraught Bombshell. She's living in hell. Her husband, whom she still loves very much, isn't willing to let her step out of the comfort zone of being just mom and wife. She wants a little time for herself and for her girlfriends. She's sadly realizing that won't ever happen unless she leaves him. She can't take it anymore.

Damn, it's an epidemic!

Has anyone seen a living man around these parts? Breathing, with a pulsing heart will do. Give me a man who is *alive,* who enjoys life and wants to relish every moment of it. Not that we ladies are perfect, by any stretch of the imagination. We have lots to learn, and I know that we're not blameless when things go wrong. But damn, at least we're alive.

Give me a man who gets a hard-on from kissing his woman, as opposed to when gripping the steering wheel to his new car or thirty-four-foot cruiser. Give me a man who takes control, and I'm not referring to the remote. Find me a man who wants to suck the juice out of life instead of the beer can every Saturday night. Please send me that man who would rather spend quiet moments on the living room sofa with his beloved, instead of working and obsessing about it 24/7.

I want a man who can make me crazy with his hungry kisses and passionate desires by night, and still want my attention and caresses in the morning, as he brings me breakfast in bed. I need a man who cares about my dreams and aspirations as much as he does about his. I long for a man who'll say to me, "We'll do anything you want this weekend, sweetie," and mean it.

Men, listen up! Women in their twenties and thirties want to be wooed, wined, dined, and then gently loved. They want roses and love letters. They want fairy-tale romances with Prince Charming.

Women in their forties know there's no such thing. We just want to be kissed, a lot, and it doesn't have to lead to sex (or it could). We want to be loved by a real man of strength, both inner and outer. He doesn't have to be perfect, but he must be able to discuss world issues, spirituality, and inner emotions. We want a man to whom we can freely open up and reveal our true selves. We're famished for a man who won't judge us, try to change us, or guilt us into compromises.

As grown-up women, we need a man to see us as individuals rather than just as a wife or mom, and actually rejoice in that experience and celebrate it. We want men who will support us in our professional aspirations, no matter what's required of us. We crave a man who will make us a priority in his life, take us dancing and not complain about it. We want hot, unadulterated, intelligent, pulsating, hair-raising, first-date passion from the man we love.

Some of my friends still think the grass is greener on the other side. For their sake, I hope it is. I do suggest they first try fertilizing the lawn at home. Then, if that doesn't blossom into a beautiful yard, go for it. Just don't forget to take your weed whacker. Even the best-kept lawns have some weeds. As for me, the search goes on.

Limp

BOMBSHELL

How can you turn a light on without electricity? How can a pen write without any ink? How can he come if he's not hard? You can, if you're French! You can do anything sexually, if you're French!

I met a man. A French man. Sexy, debonair, with that, how do you say, joie de vivre? We craved each other. We wanted to be naughty. Far from home, single and free. On a Caribbean island, surrounded by trees. Give in. Why not? He's single. Me, too. What's his name? Who cares?

Hot, passionate, and disarming. French kisses. Sand in my shoes. French kisses. Unhook my bra. French kisses. Hand down my skirt. Sand in my panties. Oooh-la-la. But wait, what happened? Hot, still passionate, but drank too much wine. Oh no, can't get it up! What? He's French. They always get it up. Don't they?

French: Eiffel tower—long...hard...and erect. French: baguettes—long...hard...and erect. Isn't everything French... long, hard, and erect?

But not this Frenchman, he was tired. Too much alcohol turned his French baguette into a little croissant. But never fear, for the French man is here. He still had ways to make me hot, passionate, and wet with desire. Naughty. Dirty. Fun. Explosion...fireworks! *Vive la France!!!*

But what about him? This little croissant needs to be toasted, has to be kneaded into a French baguette. So I turn up the heat with no real hope of success, when to my surprise, the little croissant bursts with emotion. Overflows with joy. How is that possible???

Leave it to the French. How can you come if you're not hard? Leave it to the French. Soft and limp, yet present and performing. I'm in shock, in awe, and overcome with amazement.

And so, I propose a French toast to this man, his croissant and his café au lait.

Illegal Entry

BOMBSHELL

It was just sex. Lust. No more, no less.

We were in his office. He dragged out a large leather mat for us to lie on, as always, and threw it on the floor. The stereo was blaring a tango and the glow from the candles bounced off the dark walls. The mood was just right as we started to relax, making small talk and sipping red wine with our shoes kicked off right in the middle of his big, garish office. He reached over and kissed me hard, and between the wine and the warmth of his mouth on mine, everything got very hot, very quickly. This was how it went down every single time we met for four years.

Sometimes, the sex went on for hours. There were times when I actually fell asleep while he was inside me. He loved to make me moan with pleasure and reveled in the idea that I enjoyed every minute of it. There was no love anywhere to be found in our relationship, but I couldn't bring myself to break it off. It was way too much fun.

This night was supposed to be just like all the others. We took our clothes off, methodically, and began having sex in the same way we had done so many times before. I was on my knees and he was about to enter me from behind. But this time, he had a secret plan to come in through the back door . . . the forbidden alley, even though he didn't have a key. He knew anal sex was not my thing, and once I made it clear there was to be no unauthorized entry, we continued as usual, or so I thought.

But, somehow, some way, he got past security without my even knowing it. It's hard to believe, but I had no clue that he'd come in the wrong door, or that he was even inside of me. I couldn't feel a thing.

"I'm numb . . . my tongue is numb," I told him, completely confused and feeling very weird. My tongue seemed too big for my mouth. "Something's happening to me," I complained. That's when he stopped moving and calmly reassured me there was nothing to worry about . . . that he had simply put coke up my ass.

WHAT?

"Coke up my ass?" I asked quietly, not quite sure exactly what that meant.

Extremely confused, I craned my neck back toward him and asked, "What the hell does my ass have to do with my tongue?" He calmly explained how he put cocaine into his mouth, kissed me, and then applied it up my crack to numb me so I wouldn't feel him ram me from behind. Was he kidding?

"I'm still there," he said, very matter-of-factly. "Isn't it great?" he asked, so proud of himself. "And you don't even feel a thing?" He was right. I couldn't feel him. I was furious. As I shifted quickly, I left him no choice but to pull out.

How dare he? I felt utterly and completely violated. I'd never touched a single drug in my whole life—never even put a cigarette to my lips—and this guy put cocaine inside my body, up my rectum, without even asking? I was out of my mind with rage. I wanted to kill the son of a bitch.

I wanted to tell him how his actions had completely destroyed any sense of intimacy or trust I could possibly feel for him. But instead, I kept quiet, as the rage started to build inside my body, then calmly asked him to take me home. Immediately.

I was in a state of shock. It was one of the most horrific things that ever happened to me. Yet every time I think of it, I question how I could have ever even been with this man. What an *asshole*.

This whole incident made me really take a good, hard look at some of the decisions I have made for myself over the years. Sometimes, we trust people who just don't deserve it. We take for granted that most people we come in contact with are normal, and so many of them are not. Looking back, I cannot imagine what possessed me to think this guy was even close to being worthy. I spent four years

. . . more than two hundred weeks, screwing around with this psycho. Who knows what else he could have done to me when I wasn't paying attention. What was I thinking?

For the next several weeks, he continued to call. I could not imagine ever talking to him again and left all of his calls unanswered. As time passed, so did his attempts to reach me.

The deception was beyond belief. I can't explain the anger and humiliation I felt. And it hasn't gone away. The damage is irreversible, and for years I've worried about the long-lasting effects of having cocaine inside my body.

When I told this story to my fellow Miami Bombshells, one was appalled at how someone I trusted could violate me like that by acting out a perverted sex fantasy without my even noticing. A few of them roared with laughter, not just at how I could have allowed this to happen, but how I could think the drugs would still be affecting me. I was sickened to hear that to some of them, it was nothing but a big joke. But the joke's not on me anymore. Just telling this story was enough to empower me to put this whole episode *behind* me.

five | Going to Health in a Handbasket

Women are a special breed. We all know it. The female gender might as well be an entirely separate species. And when it comes to physical maladies, there are not enough words to explain to men what we experience. From hormones to pregnancy to a higher threshold for pain, women just *feel* differently.

As far as health issues go, there is always a minor affliction affecting one Bombshell or another. But, on occasion, we've had our serious scares. There was the time Tammi came to one of our meetings and announced she had skin cancer and was having surgery the following day. We all swallowed hard because, as Miamians, we know all too well the consequences of too much fun in the sun. Fear of cancer, or the onset of any other catastrophic disease for that matter, is just one more ingrained trait we Miami Bombshells have in common.

As we've approached those middle years, we've seen our bodies change and react to time in ways we could not have imagined. Body parts are steadily wearing down. Half of us are now dependent on reading glasses. Pat, Mercedes, and Sara still brag about their perfect vision. But Sara's came from Lasik surgery, so hers doesn't count.

Initially, it was our pregnancies that transformed most of us. We got stuck with alien bodies that gained an extra fifty pounds and left nasty marks after being stretched beyond the bounds of Lycra. And nobody warned us that if we pushed too hard in delivery, we could also end up serving our bladder on a silver surgical platter. That's what Tammi did. And she's still wiping up the spills.

The moment we became mommies, all of us Bombshell moms, except Mercedes, lost the bodies we had worked so hard to maintain. But, though our diva broadcast journalist may still be able to model down a runway, there was a time she couldn't hear her television cues because her pregnancies almost made her go deaf.

Annie spent a lifetime worrying about how her daughter's obesity would affect her health. She tried to protect her baby from the pain she herself had endured when she was young and chubby. That's probably why she agreed to let her desperate teenager go through gastric bypass surgery. And, although she may not be a mother herself, Pat's maternal instincts kicked in during day and night visits to the hospital to hold the hand of her Bombshell neighbor who, rightfully so, was a wreck.

Since we embarked on this project a serious case of the blues has hit each one of us. Most have been on antidepressants at one point or another to help us level emotions that, at times, threatened to suffocate us. But sometimes, despite the medicine, the anxiety turns into panic attacks. That's what happened to Lydia. This high-level executive can manage to profitably lead a department of forty-five people in an extremely competitive field. But, occasionally, she has had such dark feelings of desperation just running simple errands like food shopping, that she has been compelled to leave her cart full of groceries stranded in an aisle when she felt the walls of the building caving in on her. These episodes have led us to ask ourselves: Are we nuts? Did our mothers and grandmothers go through these cycles? Or is this the new normal for high-achieving, professional women?

One of our Miami Bombshell meetings brought these questions into the open. It began on a beautiful spring day with a backyard brunch. The rustic picnic table was set with antique porcelain inherited from Pat's great aunt in Hong Kong, and the champagne flutes overflowed with mimosas.

But the picture-perfect afternoon quickly turned into a collective crying fest. It was one of our earlier meetings, when we began sharing our life stories. Back then, much of our time was spent venting about excessive workloads and the huge pressure our great jobs impose on our lives.

Sara started it, detailing the loss of a painful ectopic pregnancy she had still not been able to come to terms with. We reached out to her, one by one, and the tears fell. Pat, who was usually the life of the party, had been hit by a double whammy. Her relationship with her partner was on the rocks and at the same time, this corporate VP Bombshell confessed, as she wept, "I'm devastated . . . my life is in shambles. My relationship is going down the toilet and at work they want me to fire almost my entire department. All they care about is the bottom line. I can't do it. I'm taking the buyout. I'm firing myself. I need to start fresh, on all levels." Maybe our hormones were in (or out of) sync that afternoon, as we all proceeded to come apart at the seams for different reasons.

And, as we all melted down, we found that our honesty begat unconditional group support. If there is strength in numbers, that afternoon we realized that sometimes, even though our mental and physical health is not perfect, it's nothing to be ashamed of.

The good news is that we're all still young at heart . . . which is why we all still party together every chance we get. Last year, Mercedes and her twin sister turned forty. For their birthday celebration, Mercedes' husband removed all the furniture from their living room and turned it into a disco, complete with glass ball and laser lights. A hot new musical artist, just arrived from Cuba, came to serenade the birthday girls, as did a full mariachi band. Then to top off the evening, a fabulous transvestite impersonating Donna Summer made a grand entrance (in full South Beach style), as all the Bombshells danced until 4:00 A.M. We're hoping it won't be our "Last Dance." But the acute pain we felt after boogying on four-inch platform shoes reminded us of how quickly we've gone from spring chickens to wise old hens.

I Gave Birth to My Bladder

TAMMI

It was a totally painless labor because I bribed the anesthesiologist.

I took the advice of a colleague who instructed me to call the maternity ward the night before labor was to be induced and ask which anesthesiologist was on duty the next day. Then I sent that doctor a huge basket of chocolate.

By the time I arrived the next morning, she was waiting for me. Usually, they start bringing on labor with an IV drip of Pitocin. But I got the epidural first. Unheard of.

I laughed my way through the entire five-hour labor. When Courtney was ready to make her debut, I couldn't feel a thing. It's not easy to push out an eight-pound baby when the lower half of your body is completely numb. So I did what I was told, put all my 180 pounds of pregnancy weight into it and delivered that beautiful child right out into the doctor's hands. The placenta was right behind her. And who knew one of my vital organs would follow? The doctor was just getting up to wash off, when I gave birth to my bladder.

The whole medical team was apparently in shock. The bladder is supposed to be pulled and stretched during childbirth but it's not supposed to exit the body. My husband and I were so busy counting Courtney's fingers and toes, examining every cheesy little fold on our delicious little newborn that we didn't even notice that I'd birthed the organ I needed in order to pee.

The doctor assured me it was no big deal and proceeded to shove my bladder back up where it belonged. As I cuddled my brand-new baby in my arms, I tried to picture my bladder suspended somewhere inside the cavernous hole that had been carrying a child for nine long months. How was it supposed to stay there? I wondered out loud. The nurses assured me it would be fine and told me that after my body had completely healed from childbirth, I'd have to come back so a urologist could "sew my bladder permanently back in." Huh?

Three months later, I was back in the operating room having my bladder stitched to my uterus with fishing wire. They told me it would hold for about ten years. What about after that? I didn't dare ask. They didn't tell me that over time, excessive laughing, coughing, or sneezing would make me pee in my pants, or that aerobic exercise was out, for the rest of my life.

I know plenty of perimenopausal women with bladder control problems. But I never thought I'd be depending on Depends while my kids were still in grade school.

Actually, I'm not quite there yet. So far, minipads suffice. But every time I feel that little gush, at least twice a day, it reminds me that I could be in diapers before I'm fifty.

My fellow Bombshells know that, and cut me no slack, especially during our meetings, when laughter often envelops the room. Once, as one of the girls shared yet another riveting tale of a certain sexual escapade, the mood went from serious to hysterical in an instant, and without any warning, I not only drenched my pants, I also stained Pat's new sofa. Lydia, who also leaks, helped me clean it up in a show of solidarity for what we call the "urinarily challenged." Lydia's problem isn't as bad as mine, though I am living proof that the bladder is no different from the wrinkles that mysteriously appear on our faces: it feels gravity's pull and eventually needs to be lifted. I hope Lydia defies the odds better than I have.

I never pass a restroom without stopping. But the trickles never stop, even when I think my bladder is empty. Carrying in the groceries has become a problem. My kids think it's funny their mom isn't potty trained.

I've stopped begging friends and family not to make me laugh, and I don't even pretend to do my Kegel exercises during sneezes. And jogging isn't even in my vocabulary anymore. Like the mother of a toddler who's prepared with a Pull-Up in case of emergency, I keep panties hidden in a Ziploc in my glove compartment.

I'll probably need a tune-up sooner rather than later. I've considered more surgery and even made that 800 phone call, inquiring about a new drug study designed to tighten my leaky valve. But until the urologist delivers the dreaded words, *urine trouble,* I think I'll live with the drips that come with the sagging breasts and varicose veins that come with the virtues of ripe old age.

Panic Attacks

LYDIA

Until you've experienced one, you cannot imagine how panic attacks can change your life. Though they strike thousands of people every minute of the day, when this monster descended on my life, I felt completely alone. From one second to the next, for no apparent reason, my close to perfect world came crashing in, and I lost complete control of everything around me.

I was thirty-one years old and had never looked or felt better. I was a bundle of energy, a fitness freak, constantly on the go. My career was just starting to take off and I was enjoying life as the single parent of a fabulous fourteen-year-old son. My love life was the only part that was a little unsettled. I felt trapped in a painful relationship with a man I knew, deep down, was not right for me, but the passion blinded me. The anticipation of the inevitable breakup affected every aspect of my life.

It was a gorgeous spring afternoon, and I was interviewing two women I had been recruiting for some time. I met them at a restaurant, which was busy with the sounds of waiters, dishes, and people engaged in lunchtime conversation. I can remember feeling on top of the world, ready to make these women an offer, when all of a sudden my chest tightened up. I hunched my shoulders involuntarily and felt as if everything around me was being sucked into a big, black tunnel. My vision became blurry. Then everything went dark. In a matter of seconds, my legs and arms got numb, and my heart began racing wildly. I was trying to gasp for air, but it was getting thinner with each breath. I really thought I was dying, drifting further and further away from the table. The women became alarmed and called for the maître d' when they saw my head drop to the table. I tried to talk, but the words just wouldn't come.

Somehow, I managed to mutter my doctor's telephone number, as I fell into a state of desperation. What was happening to me? I wanted my mother; I didn't want to be alone. My entire body was numb as I gasped for each breath. Someone managed to get my doctor on the phone and his voice was comforting as I tried, through labored breathing, to explain what I was feeling.

He told me to go directly to the emergency room, but for some stupid reason, I refused an ambulance. One of the women at the table offered to drive me to the hospital; it wasn't until I got into the car that I thought my life would end with a stranger driving me to the emergency room. I was petrified.

When we got there, the emergency room staff was already waiting for me. There were questions, tests, questions, and more tests. As they rolled me down the hallway I started to shiver, and my lungs just couldn't capture the air I was desperately trying to breathe. The nurse eventually covered me with warm sheets, and though I wasn't feeling much better, I didn't seem to be getting any worse.

After several hours and a battery of tests, my body stopped shaking, and I finally started to feel my arms and legs again. My heart began to slow down. Finally, the ER doctor came and calmly proclaimed that all the tests had come back negative. Every last one of them. I thought he was kidding. How was that possible? I felt like I was dying and there was nothing wrong with me?

When my own doctor called, I was hoping to hear some type of diagnosis identifying my condition, but his words shocked me. "You appear to have had an anxiety attack," he said, matter-of-factly. "Come see me tomorrow and I will give you some medication." I thought he was the one who needed drugs.

The following day, as I sat in his office, he prescribed drugs to calm me down. But they didn't work. The attacks continued, and I had to be taken to the emergency room again, twice within the next two weeks. I thought I was losing my mind and felt completely out of control. I lived with a paper bag in my purse in case I started to hyperventilate in public. I was ready to be committed.

The attacks were becoming more frequent, and the fear of getting them became even worse. I was afraid to leave the house, dreading a new attack. My doctor, a cardiologist and general practitioner, eventually referred me to a psychiatrist. A shrink. I couldn't believe it.

I swallowed my pride and made the call, but by the time I got an appointment, I had become agoraphobic: scared to death of public or open spaces. Being in a grocery store, a mall, or any enclosed public area would bring on another panic attack, so I just stayed home where I felt safe.

Driving was out of the question after I took my son to a drive-thru. Before I even received my food, I felt the need to hit the accelerator and drive away. My son started to believe what I feared most, that his once competent, confident mother was crazy. The attacks took over my life, and going to work became impossible. Just getting out of bed became a challenge.

I forced myself to go to the shrink, who also told me calmly that I was suffering from panic attacks, a very common condition. He too told me the fear of getting them again is ultimately the biggest problem.

A panic attack, he explained with much compassion, is a sudden surge of overwhelming fear that comes without warning or for any obvious reason. It is far more intense than the feeling of being "stressed out" that most people experience. One out of every seventy-five people will suffer from a panic attack at one point or another during their lifetime. I felt relieved to learn that I wasn't the only one whose life came crashing in three times a week.

An hour and a box of tissues later, the doctor prescribed medication that I would have to take in incremental doses over the course of one year. I left his office feeling relieved, confused, and frustrated, all at the same time. How could something like this happen to me? I had been invincible and full of confidence. And now I had to think twice before leaving the house? I told myself I could beat this thing with strength and with faith, but I'm not really sure I believed it.

The medication knocked me out. I slept on and off for two weeks. But once I came out of my stupor, I had an unwavering resolve to get back to normal as quickly as possible. My dad brought me every book he could find relating to panic attacks, and I quickly learned that once a patient can learn to overcome these situations, the attacks can disappear. The experts suggest taking control proactively, when you feel an attack coming on.

It was time to face this evil head-on, instead of trying to run away from it. I adopted breathing techniques and other measures to help me get through the rough times when I felt my chest tighten. I practiced them all and found that they made a big difference.

I did not recover overnight, but as time went on, I regained control of my life and things started to shape up slowly. My psychiatrist became a big part of my life, providing great support, giving me the extra push I needed when I felt like the rug was coming out from under me. One day at a time, I started returning to malls and restaurants and slowly resumed driving with my family and friends. Being with them made me feel secure and helped me take the necessary steps to return to wellness.

Eventually, I taught myself how to stop, look, and sail through an oncoming attack rather than trying to do battle with it. Step-by-step I was able to wean myself away from those horrific attacks and start to resume a normal life.

It had been fifteen years since I had my last panic attack. And then, a few weeks ago, out of the blue, I felt as if another one was coming on. I ran straight to my cardiologist, since I wasn't sure if, in fact, it was heart or nerve related. Sometimes the symptoms for both can be confused. After a battery of tests, he told me bluntly that it was probably the onset of a panic attack since any emotional change could trigger another episode. He was right; I had just lost an old friend who had died suddenly.

Then one day last week after my husband had left to take our children to school, I was all alone. I took a shower and dressed, and it started . . . suddenly a sense of panic started taking over my body. My heart was racing, I felt weak and restless, and I felt an internal heat rising up in my body. I was petrified of passing out. But somehow, through my hysteria, I knew that I was the only one who could stop this.

I took some deep breaths, walked around my bedroom for a while and started to pray. I began to exhale slowly, and little by little, I began to feel better. As soon as I knew I was somewhat in control I hurried myself up, got dressed, and got the hell out of the house. I didn't want to be alone.

I called Pat and before I could even explain what happened, she implored me to come right over. My lifelong friend, she remembered how debilitating the panic attacks had been fifteen years earlier and was waiting for me with a huge dose of love and a cup of hot tea in hand. We hugged and I cried out of desperation, unsure of what was happening to me; and then Pat gave me the name of a psychologist she thought could help.

Each day, I'm feeling a little better. This time the psychologist didn't think I needed therapy. She reassured me that I've learned to control these episodes. Nonetheless, I am always vigilant not to let my emotions get the best of me, and for now the monster is safely back in its cage.

Say What?

MERCEDES

By the time General Manuel Noriega's trial in the stately federal courthouse in Miami came around, I realized I had almost lost it. In the domed chamber, surrounded by the laws of man, I could no longer deny the laws of nature. I found myself unable to pick up the subtleties recited by the prosecution facing away from me. I couldn't hear the judge's muffled rulings. I was going deaf!

My first instinct, of course, was to deny it, then to hide it. I taught myself to read lips, as I felt more and more isolated in groups and conversations. My television work didn't suffer much, though; I could always do interviews and go back and log tapes with my earphones on at full blast. That was the same way I wore my I.F.B., the thingee we put in our ears to do a live show and hear the producer, director, and each other. As long as there was technology to aid me I was going to go it alone. But life has a way of presenting new challenges just when you think you've adapted to the old ones.

After ten years of traveling the world and establishing a firm career in Spanish broadcast news, I became pregnant. I felt totally fulfilled when I gave birth to the little girl I had always yearned for. My perfect life became even more perfect, or so it seemed. In reality, my world was crashing in around me. I couldn't hear my baby cry. The pregnancy had exacerbated my condition and left one ear worse than the other.

I tried to train myself to sleep on my bad ear so I could at least attempt to hear my baby with the better one. It didn't work. My husband, aware of my handicap, would inevitably end up tapping me softly in the middle of the night to wake me, so I could nurse our child. My despair grew deeper.

I knew I desperately needed help, if not for myself, for my little newborn, who needed her mother. I remembered a story I had once produced on cochlear implants and found the University of Miami physician I had featured, Dr. Thomas Balkany. After an evaluation, he told me what I already knew.

At age thirty-three, I needed hearing aids. I asked for alternatives, refusing to put those taboo little amplifiers in my ears for all to see under my chic and short hairstyle. There was only one other option, a risky operation to replace a bone gone mushy inside my ear with a tiny titanium rod; in other words, an implant.

I threw myself at the mercy of Dr. Balkany and begged for the procedure. But there was a catch: if it didn't work I would lose what little hearing I had left that could at least be amplified by a hearing aid. The operation also needed to be conducted half a millimeter away from the nerve that controls facial expressions to half my face. If that went wrong I would end up with facial paralysis, not to mention the end of my career. It was certain I would have to endure a metallic taste on my tongue for months or even years. And, at the very least, it could cause severe vertigo and send my head spinning for several weeks.

With the extreme fear that makes you reek due to nervous sweating, I tried to reason with myself. I had but a few moments before the wheelchair rolling me down the hospital hallway made its way to the operating room. I could still say no. I could still walk away, deaf but not deformed. But I didn't. In the numbness of an anesthetic drip that kept me semiconscious so the implant could be tested, I remember answering the doctor's questions. Repeat after me, *dogg, dog; bassseballllll, baseball; founnntainnn, fountain; ssssshoeee, shoe.* With that awareness also came the throbbing sting of a stretched eardrum. Fade to black.

When I opened my eyes, my husband shoved a picture of me holding my baby in my face. He was following my instructions. I needed to remember there was a deeper meaning for the risk I had just taken. Then I threw up. And I vomited for three straight weeks after that, going back to 110 pounds only three months after having a child. I couldn't hold food in my stomach; my mouth tasted as if I'd been chewing on aluminum foil; I couldn't open my eyes; I couldn't stand. It was as if someone had thrown me in a centrifuge and forgotten to turn off the switch. I just kept spinning. Even a gentle turn of my head would send me into a dive straight for the floor. But I could *Hear!*

The first test came as I picked up the phone. I purposely put it to the deaf ear and prayed. Through the thick cotton plug in my swollen ear the voice on the other side just rang in my head. Clean, clear, no more distorted sounds, no more pressure cooker hiss reverberating in my ear and intruding on my hearing, just the beautiful sound of a melodious voice. To this day I still can't remember whose voice awakened my dormant hearing. But it doesn't really matter. The magic wasn't happening at the other end of the line but inside my own head.

A thunderstorm roused me from a nap a few days later. I couldn't remember the last time I had heard a pounding tropical downpour, or the sweet honey softness of a baby's sigh. I sobbed out of happiness.

Five years passed and I had another baby. As predicted, the hearing in my other ear dissipated with the second pregnancy, and I submitted myself to another implant operation. But so much had changed. This time I began talking to people about my deafness, accepting my condition, embracing my limitations.

The surgeries could not restore my hearing to 100 percent. In fact, the last I checked, I could hear at 80 percent in one ear and a little less in the other. The hissing sound associated with my condition has returned and I am fully aware that in time, the implants may not be enough. Some day I may just need to wear the hearing aids I so disdained. But I'm no longer in denial, in fear of being found out. In fact, I've already decided that short, short hair isn't even that chic anymore.

I feel lucky for any extra week, month, or year that I can partake in a regular conversation, watch a movie at a moderate volume, or hear the crashing of the surf at the beach. As long as the seagulls call and my eyes instinctively reach for the sky, any sound at all will be music to my ears.

That's Why They Call It the Blues

PATRICIA

There's no time to be depressed, especially if you're a woman. Everyone expects you to be happy all the time, and when you're not, they tell you to snap out of it. Which makes you even more depressed, because you can't give yourself permission to be depressed. This is so depressing.

I've always been the life of the party. Hell, I'm the one who throws the party. I'm the happy-go-lucky one that others come to when they want to be cheered up. Recently my Bombshell friend Annie told me she was distraught when I cried in front of her. Why? "Because you're my pillar," she said. "What will I do if *you* get depressed?"

Well, I am depressed. There, I said it. I'm not even sure why, not exactly anyway. I have a great life. I was just able to leave my job and start my own company. I'm even profitable! I've been waiting ten years to do this. And now it is reality. Clients are knocking on my door! I have family and friends who love me. And yet, I'm singing the blues.

I guess many women—men too—suffer from depression at some point in their lives. But not me, not this crazy upbeat person. I'm not clinically depressed, I don't think. That's an actual illness. Aren't you supposed to be depressed all the time for that to be the case? I'm all right when I'm really busy. I feel good when I'm with my Bombshell friends just having silly fun. I'm fine when I'm dancing. That's always good for my soul. I feel happy when I'm with my pets; they always cheer me up. I just seem to be depressed mostly when I'm alone.

OK, I admit it, I'm probably depressed because I feel myself growing old. I actually have arthritis in one finger. That scares the shit out of me. Old ladies get arthritis. Not me!

I'm depressed because I feel fat and out of shape. Others laugh because I weigh 125 pounds. But for me, that's fat. I'm not as firm and tight as I was before, although I'm working on it. I'm depressed because I have no time for myself.

Last week I admitted to Annie that, for the first time in my life, I was taking the over-the-counter antidepression pill Saint-John's-wort. She turned around and said she was too. I had no idea. We laughed like idiots. She shared that she was feeling lonely and at a crossroad in her life. "I know I need to make certain decisions," she said, "but I'm not ready to throw in the towel yet; I want my marriage to work out. So the little pill helps."

Maybe it's not clinical and it's just a middle-aged crisis. Oh my God, is that possible? At forty-six am I really middle-aged? It turns out that many of my Bombshell friends and most other women in their forties I know are going through the same thing. Maybe it's in the water.

"It must be this darn perimenopause. It's driving me nuts," complained Lydia. "In addition to my very volatile body temperature, my mood swings are just too hard to keep up with. It doesn't take more than a second for my personality to go from that of a sweet and loving mother and wife to a bitter demanding stranger."

Sara took antianxiety medications when she left her job, sold her house, and started her own business, all within a two-month time period. She couldn't sleep and was barking at everyone, including us Bombshells. We were all grateful for her meds.

"I've never taken anything," admitted Tammi. "Though I could probably use something now—if only I had the time to find a doctor to go get a prescription."

One of our most difficult Bombshell meetings was when I actually spoke the words out loud, for the first time, and admitted that I was depressed. It happened over brunch in my backyard. We gathered around my teak table, drank mimosas, and munched on quiche, croissants, and fruit that I had set on antique china I hadn't used in years. I knew it was going to be an emotionally draining meeting, so I created a nurturing and comforting setting. After downing a few mimosas, I built up the courage to talk about my battle with depression. The emotions swelled up in me. I couldn't breathe. The tears began to flow and I couldn't speak. I felt like I was drowning. I persisted . . . wanting to get it off my chest, but it was impossible. As tears streamed down her face, Sara jumped out of her chair and ran over to hug me as the others cried in silence.

"What? You're depressed?" she wailed. "How can you be depressed? I had no idea. You're always so happy." Sara, being my newest friend, was the only Bombshell who didn't know I had been depressed for months.

In an emotional phone conversation with Sara the following day, she told me, "You're a role model to other women, Pat. When we look at you we figure if you're OK, we can be OK, too. That's not the same feeling that if you're holding it together we should be able to also, which would just bring us pressure. Your apparent control and happiness was empowering. Finding out that you were depressed meant that it might happen to some of us, but that it would be OK in the end."

I suspect the bouts of depression we face are necessary: to appreciate the highs we need to experience the lows. As long as it's not clinical, long term, and debilitating, there can be some value in getting in touch with our dark side—as long as we learn to get out of the quicksand moments that seem to swallow us whole, before it is too late.

Santana

PATRICIA

Carlos Santana healed my heart.

Last night sitting a few feet away from the man whose music has carried me from puberty to adulthood, the strangest thing happened. Right there in the Amphitheatre in Palm Beach, Carlos Santana played for me. There were thousands of people there, and I'm not sure if anyone else knew it, but I was completely convinced that this legendary icon was performing only for me. And I felt every single note.

For months, I had been suffering from a depression that had apparently been building for quite some time. The minutiae of daily life, and events that I seemingly couldn't control, were overwhelming me. Shit will *always* happen, but the emotions we attach to events are of our own making. I knew that, on an intellectual level, but before I realized it, I ended up depressed. That is, until Santana showed up and played for me.

I met Santana two years before that life-altering concert in Palm Beach. It was the first Latin Grammy Awards in the year 2000. He was nominated in the same category as my "other half" at the time, Nestor Torres.

We received word of Nestor's nomination just as we got off a plane in Denver. We could hardly contain ourselves. Then we heard he was up against Santana.

Knowing of my admiration for Santana, Nestor turned to me and asked, "So, who you rooting for?" We laughed, but I knew deep down he was serious. I've been a huge Santana fan for more years than I care to remember. Of course I wanted Nestor to win; he is the man I love and I know how much a Grammy Award would mean to him and his career. So I told him how proud I was and then sheepishly asked, "So, do you think I'll get to meet Santana at the ceremony?"

Understand, I'm not a groupie. I've worked in the entertainment industry all my life and I know that famous people pass gas (which stinks) just like real folks, and that most of them are as insecure and screwed up as the rest of us. But Santana is in a league of his own. He has talent, heart, and a mission, and his music has rocked my world for more than thirty years.

When Latin Grammy night finally came, all decked out and be-jeweled, on the arm of my man, who was nominated for the biggest prize in the music industry, I got to meet "the man." I felt like a teenage girl meeting her idol and I was speechless. What was I supposed to say? "Oh, I'm such a fan." PLEASE, how trite. "I love your music"? PUHL-EESE.

Problem is, I hear fans tell that to Nestor all the time. And it's sweet, but I didn't want to be just another adoring fan. I wanted to be special. So what did I do? I said nothing. I just giggled. I'm sure that made a lasting impression. *(Ugh!)*

Fast-forward two years; I heard Santana was due to play in South Florida one week before my forty-sixth birthday. So I dropped Nestor hints, subtle ones, like women always do. I left Nestor voice-mail messages and sent him e-mails for three weeks. They went something like this: "So I hear Santana's playing at the Mars Amphitheatre on March 22 at 9 P.M. It's an easy drive up I-95 to Palm Beach, two hours from home. Sounds like a great birthday present to me! I'm sure your friends in the biz could pull a few strings for you."

Sometimes, you just can't leave things to chance.

Lo and behold, he got the hint. Even rented a limo for the evening. I thought that was the icing on the birthday cake. But the big surprise was still to come. When we arrived at the theater, we were given backstage passes. I was floored. Our seats were incredible, front and center. And then, it happened. Carlos Santana played for me and only me.

I sat there, transfixed by his music, and it blew me away. The videos, the incredible colors, the lights, and the energy emanating from the stage made me feel like a passenger in a time machine, first to college, then back even further, to high school. I was carried away by the wailing of his guitar and taken back to a time when life was so much simpler and I had no real worries. A lifetime ago, or so it seemed. I was back in school, in my old house, in my little bedroom covered with posters. I remember being truly happy back then. I spent hours and hours sitting in my bedroom by myself, lights off, my comet lamp's white noise buzzing under the tune of my favorite album, *Abraxas,* by Santana. It was heaven.

And there I was again, thirty years later, mesmerized, watching this middle-aged man who was still at the top of his game. And that's when it happened; I felt a tinge of the happiness I knew as a young woman listening to his music. I actually recalled the emotion of happiness that had eluded me for months and then—I felt it! In a matter of minutes, Carlos Santana took my depression and turned it into joy. It was almost religious.

When the concert was over, I focused my attention on the man himself. Would I really get to meet him again? We were escorted to a holding area on the side of the stage along with radio people, photographers, and other well-connected VIPs. And then they called us: "Just the folks from BMG, please," they said. We were with Nestor's friend from Santana's record label, BMG. That was us!

Santana looked relaxed . . . he was among friends as we met backstage by the dressing rooms. When I snuck a look at him through his open dressing room door, there was an aura of peace and tranquility enveloping him. We waited a few minutes, and then, as if he knew the effect his music had had on me just moments before, he walked out of his dressing room and headed directly to me, held out his hand, and said, "Thank you for coming. Sorry I made you wait." Imagine that. This man had just changed *my* life and *he* thanked *me.* My mind was whirling.

I wanted to tell him that as I watched him onstage, I realized that I was responsible for my own happiness and that his words of inspiration—of love, peace, and unity—had touched my soul. I wanted him to know that I do "embrace my absoluteness" (that's a Santana saying that means to really honor and embrace how wonderful, unique, and beautiful our souls are). I wanted him to know that his music mysteriously peeled away the veil of depression that had been smothering me. But as he shook my hand and agreed to have his picture taken with me, all I could muster was "thank you."

So much had changed in the two years since I'd first met Carlos Santana . . . it wasn't that starstruck-college-girl-meeting-her-musical-idol feeling anymore. This time, I was an adult who had been battling real-life depression, meeting the man whose music reignited the ecstasy in her heart. He had absolutely no idea of the effect he had on my life that night. How could he?

So, I stood there, again, almost speechless, and just said "thank you." I guess that's all I really needed to say.

This morning, with the briefest hint of a smile touching my lips, I promised myself I'd sit down and listen to music for a few hours. *Abraxas.* I still have the LP and would hook up my old turntable. And somewhere in my bedroom is that old comet lamp.

But then the phone rang, and I had work to do. Tonight, no matter what happens, Santana will play for me again. As long as life doesn't get in the way.

The Big C

TAMMI

We all know someone who's dying from it; our guts ache each time we hear another tragic story. At our age, every strange bump or pain sets the voice loose. "Get it checked now or risk not seeing your kids grow up," it whispers eerily, as if someone is listening. So when the haunting becomes overwhelming, we go to the doctor, who laughs while telling us we're just fine (again). My fellow Bombshells Mercedes and Pat have each lost a parent to cancer. Both have had serious breast cancer scares. And Lydia? She's always afraid she's dying.

So when a colleague of mine, visiting her dermatologist for a facial, was inadvertently diagnosed with malignant melanoma, I figured it was time to get this thing on my nose checked. It was just a peely critter that I kept picking at, but by Valentine's Day, I realized I'd had it since Thanksgiving, so I scheduled an appointment.

The doctor noticed that I hadn't been using the Retin-A she prescribed to remove the lines from my tired eyes. The wrinkles were what brought me to the dermatologist every six months or so, and usually, she would give me a deep peel and send me on my way. This visit, it took a while to get her to really look closely at my nose, and she kept insisting it was nothing. I almost had to beg her to take a biopsy because she was sure the procedure wouldn't be covered by insurance and would be too expensive. Finally, she cut a small chunk from the top of my nose and sent it to the lab. I left, convinced it was nothing (again).

Almost two months passed, and life was so hectic, I couldn't even remember if the dermatologist had ever called. But I reminded myself they only call when there's a problem, so I didn't give it a second thought. The peely thing was still there, but I had eventually stopped picking at it, and it didn't bother me much anymore. New, uninvited additions to my face were visiting more frequently . . . another age spot wasn't the end of the world. Then I got the call.

"Ms. Fuller, um, we, um, got your biopsy back and it's um, skin cancer." I froze. "Excuse me?" I asked sheepishly, my voice quivering. "Yes, it's on your nose and it's got to come off, right away. It's a squamous cell carcinoma, but we don't know how far it's spread," the nurse told me, matter-of-factly.

That's when I remembered the biopsy was taken on that February Leap Year day. They didn't call me until April 23. According to my calculations, fifty-four days had passed.

"Why did it take seven weeks to figure this out?" I barked furiously at the nurse. My blood was beginning to boil. "We just found the biopsy results. Apparently, they'd been on the doctor's desk for a while," she embarrassingly admitted. "Must've gotten stuck under a pile of papers, I guess." What a lame excuse. Those life-threatening, nasty carcinomas had seven additional weeks to poison me, because this doctor couldn't keep her desk clean. I asked to speak to the doctor but was informed she would be tied up all day, presumably doing back-to-back chemical peels on rich old people. The nurse promised she'd call when she finished. I was livid.

I thought I was going to vomit. I was in an all-day seminar and could do nothing but wait to hear from the doctor, so I put the phone on vibrate and went back into the workshop. I tried to focus on the speaker, but my mind was reeling with thoughts of my impending death.

Who is going to teach Courtney how to use a tampon when she gets her period and I'm long gone? Who will Chelsea come to when she needs birth control? Mine was going to be one of those pathetic stories we hear too often, where the community helps out in the beginning, but after some time passes, everyone goes back to their business. I was already worrying about my girls, who would be left all alone.

By the time the doctor called, I had already thought about who'd do the eulogy, and how I could prearrange it so my daughters could stay in the house (moving, I'm told, is the worst thing to do to a child who's lost a parent). As expected, the doctor was mortified as she tried to explain what happened. She knew her office had screwed up, and she didn't know how to apologize, so she chose to play down the cancer. "I'm sure it's nothing," she told me with what sounded like confidence. That's what she had said fifty-four days ago when she took the biopsy, against her better judgment. "Let me take it out in the office. I have an opening next week. Not to worry . . . I'm sure it's nothing," she said again. She was serious.

I insisted she fax me the results immediately and took them to two doctors that same afternoon. Both agreed I needed surgery, and each thought I might need a skin graft, after the hunk of cancer was extracted. "They take the skin and cartilage from your ear," one doctor explained, as if it was nothing. I'd been single for six months and now I was going to look like a Picasso picture. If I lived. Unbelievable.

It didn't take long to find a reconstructive facial surgeon who fixes children born with genetic defects. The best in Miami, I was told, which is probably why he wasn't on my insurance plan. I couldn't have cared less. If I was going to die of cancer, I didn't want to look deformed in my final days. I wanted my girls to remember me as I was, even if I had to spend their inheritance to keep my face intact. So I told the doctor that if it looked like I was going to live five more years, while I was under the knife, he should use his plastic surgery expertise to get rid of the wrinkles around my eyes. Why not do something for myself as my life neared the end, I rationalized . . . but if the cancer was really bad, I told him not to bother. I didn't need to nurse one more wound while my hair was falling out.

Three days later, I was in the operating room, fading in and out of consciousness, as they carried slices of my nose off to the lab to see if the borders were clear. Just a few more minutes, the doctor kept repeating in what sounded like a wind tunnel. He was carving off pieces of my face as if it were a turkey breast. Then I passed out.

When I awoke in the recovery room, my nose was heavily bandaged, but everything had gone black. And then I got it. My eyes were bandaged too, which meant I was going to make it, and the wrinkles around my eyes were going to be gone, too. Miraculously, the doctor didn't have to graft my ear to my nose . . . seventeen stitches would hold it together, he promised, as long as I was careful.

My daughters took such good care of me when I got home, it was as if they knew this was a close one. We learned our lesson, too, about the power of the sun. None of us even goes out to get the newspaper anymore without layering on the SPF 45 sunscreen.

Every six months now, I make the two-hour drive to see a dermatologist who specializes in skin cancer, a man his patients call a pit bull. In two years, Dr. Kaminester has removed five more cancers that might have been well on their way to becoming melanomas. This guy takes off freckles if he thinks they might one day become precancerous. He's saved my mom's life a few times, too, and we bake him cakes every time we make the trip, just to show our appreciation. Dr. K has promised us both that if we remain vigilant, we'll never die of skin cancer, no matter how many years we've fried ourselves in the Florida sun.

Because of my paranoia, my poor girls have had to go under this doctor's knife more than once. Anytime they get a bump now, it's off to Dr. K for some digging and scraping. But their whining stops when I remind them how lucky we got. I escaped the Big C. This time, anyway.

No Stone Unturned

ANNIE

I would gladly shout out my age to the world, but I would rather die than share my weight. I avoid the gynecologist, not because of the awkward position and cold instruments, but because of the scale. I don't consider myself a compulsive person, but keeping my pounds a secret is truly an obsession for me.

I'm one of those people who eat to celebrate and eat to recuperate. Some people find it difficult to eat when under pressure; not this person. Food is a companion that has always been there for me, so throughout the years I'm sure I've gained and lost enough weight to equal an average-sized person. It seems that my self-image is highly dependent on the numbers on the ever-present scale.

As I grew up and thought of becoming a parent, I harbored many worrisome thoughts that my children would inherit my "fat genes." I hoped that my future offspring would inherit my best traits, and my worst would evade them. I desperately prayed that if I ever had a girl she would never have to deal with the weight problems I had faced: having thunder thighs or being called "chubby." These memories of my childhood remain with me: I avoided sports because I was self-conscious about my size, and I never felt as if I was as cute as my size 6 girlfriends.

And then my daughter, Jackie, was born and I felt truly blessed.

In her first few years of life, her size was comparable to others her age, although she would never have been known as skinny. As she grew older, however, I began to see the signs of weight gain, and I must shamefully admit, I began to judge her, as if she and I were one person: me. It was then that I became determined to take control of her weight.

At age ten, Jackie enrolled in Weight Watchers for the first time. I worked with her and planned attractive, nutritionally balanced meals together. We counted points and I set up all kinds of positive reinforcement systems for pounds lost and goals accomplished. But the pounds lost were few, and they seemed to reappear much more quickly than they had been shed.

I often had the feeling that she was more interested in pleasing Mom than she was in finding clothes in the junior department that would fit well and look good on her. My husband, however, always looked upon her as his darling little girl and didn't think the weight issue should be an issue at all.

I became hopeful when she got her period at age twelve. I had read that this hormonal time often causes young girls to lose their body fat. But this was not true for Jackie. In fact, she added another fifteen pounds to her expanding girth. I was devastated, and she pretended it didn't matter. She had good friends and a busy social life and the weight didn't seem to be affecting either.

She had a positive outlook on life but that still didn't stop me from carting her to almost every doctor and clinic in Miami to help her trim down. I knew I was projecting my own weight issues onto my daughter but I so desperately wanted to spare her the pain that had been my life for so many years.

At the same time, I was terrified that something could be medically wrong. There is a history of obesity and heart disease in our family, and I certainly was going to do all I could to prevent my daughter from dealing with either of these ailments. Deep within my gut, my maternal instincts were telling me that my daughter's weight problems had nothing to do with food. By the time she reached thirteen, we made our first trip to the endocrinologist and I asked the learned doctor for medications to help my daughter lose the ungainly pounds. Fortunately for all of us, he declined to go down that path with Jackie.

The summer before she entered high school (she was just fourteen), she rejoined Weight Watchers and really tried to be successful. By the time Jackie became a freshman, I could see her self-image fading. She could no longer fit into clothes in the junior department. She had to wear high-waisted jeans while her friends fit into the trendy low-rise jeans. She deliberately cancelled an important celebration dinner because she couldn't find anything that fit. That night she retired to her room, where I heard her anguished crying, and there was nothing I could say or do to get her to open her door.

Her daddy was always very supportive of her and although he wasn't denying her growing size, he didn't make a big deal about it. But then our outgoing daughter slowly became withdrawn. She no longer wanted to go shopping with her girlfriends or hang out at the mall. Worse, she had reached the age where boys' comments cut to the quick. I could read her body language when she returned home from school each day and I knew the days that their demeaning comments had caused her more pain and torment.

She resigned herself to become one of the guys since being a girlfriend wasn't in the picture. The boys invited her to hang out with them, as she was a good sport and lots of fun, but Jackie's rotund appearance deterred them from dating her.

I also began to feel self-conscious. Friends and family asked me why I had let my daughter gain so much weight. They didn't know or understand the truth: we had both been trying very hard to control Jackie's weight. My greatest hang-up was rapidly becoming my daughter's biggest hang-up, too.

I wish the outside world could have seen the behavior of this well-intentioned, caring mother. First I hid the cookies and all the other fattening goodies so she would not be tempted. When that didn't work, I eliminated all the "bad" foods from the pantry. I constantly watched what she ate; it must have been hell for her to have the "food patrol" on duty 24/7. But despite my incessant watch, and her attempts to cooperate, the weight loss was minimal and temporary.

The rejection she felt in high school fueled her desire to find the reason for the inability to control her weight. She shared with me how hard it was to fit in the group when the other girls were virtually half her size. I could completely understand where she was coming from. I had been there. We talked at great length, and together we joined forces to find a solution. This time she claimed responsibility and accepted the challenge.

During her fifteenth and sixteenth years, after visiting her pediatrician, three nutritionists, two endocrinologists, and an acupuncturist, she was enrolled in the University of Miami weight loss program for obese adolescents. The program was truly comprehensive and included nutritional training, counseling, behavior modification, and medication. She met with some success but it certainly was not the panacea we were expecting. I wasn't really sure this was the right path, but we were willing to try almost anything, including the effects of a new weight loss medication for teens. I fought with myself, realizing that I was actually giving permission for my daughter to become an adolescent guinea pig. My rationale was that a respected medical school was sanctioning it.

It was difficult to sit in the waiting room and watch one obese adolescent after another walk in with their parents, but I was willing to do anything to help my child. A year later when the program ended, she had lost ten pounds, certainly not the goal we had been anticipating.

The failures in the weight loss program made my daughter feel that she was destined to be fat. She began to tell me that we were at the end of the road, and that I had to accept it as she had done. She professed that God had made her this way and wrote a beautiful poem about self-acceptance that she read at a retreat. I cried when she showed it to me, but I refused to accept her message and plunged into more referrals.

I made more appointments for her, and I begged the doctors to give her something. I wanted a magic pill to help her shed the weight, but in my heart I agonized over the long-term effects of all her prescriptions. I also read an article in a magazine that caught my attention, on polycystic ovarian syndrome (PCOS), a glandular disorder that is often associated with obesity. We made another trip to a different endocrinologist where I asked him to please research this possibility. After the results of an ultrasound, some of my worst nightmares were confirmed. Jackie was diagnosed with PCOS. No matter what she did or what pills she took, there was little success.

I'm sure at times she hated me for putting her through all these programs. And maybe she even thought I was withholding my love because she was fat. But in reality I was in constant pain for my child. I felt I was a failure because I hadn't succeeded at making her thin. I was searching for that one thing that would make Jackie's body shape comparable to all the other girls. Isn't that what every mom is supposed to do?

My little fighter never gave up. She took Glucophage, Xenical, Bontril, Meridia, and Synthroid. And those were just the prescription meds. She also took endless over-the-counter useless drugs that made her violently ill. She drank protein shakes and cut all carbohydrates from her diet. The result, unbelievably, was twenty additional pounds.

I continued to blame myself because I hadn't found the answer. A friend summed it all up for me when she said, "You've left no stone unturned," as I continued to research the possible causes of the new weight gain.

Jackie had just turned seventeen when I cornered her pediatrician at a social function. At the time I didn't care that he wasn't wearing his hospital coat; my mission was relentless. I begged him to give me the name of a doctor who could help my child. He referred us to yet another doctor, a reproductive endocrinologist, a specialty I didn't even know existed.

I made the appointment for the following week. I never gave up hope, but as I dragged my daughter to one more doctor I felt torn inside. I wondered if in my quest to help her, I was really suffocating her and keeping her weight an issue. I could see the look of disappointment in her expression as I rattled off her medical history to the new physician. I listed all the programs and medications, and he listened attentively as Jackie sat and waited for me to finish. I could sense her frustration and so could the doctor. He tried to make us both feel better when he said that the love of a mother is so intense she will do whatever it takes for her to help her child.

After the complete examination, the doctor made his diagnosis: my daughter's weight problem was not food-related but rather a health issue. He explained that her weight gain was somewhat out of her control and that the previous diagnosis of PCOS was unquestionably a contributing factor to her obesity. My inner voices had been right all along.

The endocrinologist asked us if we had ever considered gastric bypass surgery, an option that had never crossed my mind. I was terrified by the idea of major surgery on my baby. She was only seventeen and a half. But with that suggestion, Jackie began to see the possibility of a future for herself.

That evening my daughter shared some of her pain with me. "Mom, do you know how it feels to be one of the fattest girls in school? Have you any idea how that makes me feel? Do you know how hard it is to try to be like other teenagers and go shopping in the mall, when nothing that my friends wear can even fit on my body? Do you know that I think people are looking at me and making snide remarks about the amount of food I probably consume? And I'm certain that I eat half of what most of them eat all of the time."

As she spoke I could not hold back my tears. I cried for her pain and I cried for mine, too. I held her tightly and wished I could make it all go away with a simple hug or kiss. I had suspected she was struggling with these feelings but I had no conception of the depth of sadness she was feeling. I also felt guilty because I began to believe that my own obsession with weight was tearing at my young teenager.

We began to research gastric bypass surgery, making phone calls and surfing the Internet. We had no idea that the process was so complicated. We went all over town and asked questions. I wanted to speak with people who had actually had the surgery, especially those as young as Jackie. I wanted to know if the surgical procedure could impede her ability to bear children in the future. I needed to know the success rate, the mortality rate, the rate and seriousness of anticipated complications, and any and all other pertinent information I could gather.

While in the "read and research" mode, I fell apart in front of my special friends, the Bombshells. They, as always, were extremely supportive and reminded me that the challenges we were facing were not to be minimized. Tammi told of her fears when, at sixteen, she'd had a "nose job" and wound up with an allergic reaction to the tape they had used. She assured me that my fears were justified but reminded me that we would soon be on the road to a happier life for Jackie.

Lydia and Sara both said that if they weren't such chickens, they'd be out looking for a doctor to take a "little nip and tuck" here and there for each of them. "Everyone fears surgery and this is a *big* one," said Pat.

We attended three different presentations on the surgery. We listened intensely and I became more confused than ever. Were they telling the truth about the safety of the procedure? Weren't they really selling the fantasy of being thin? What overweight person wouldn't try anything in hopes of fitting into society's norms? I looked over at my daughter's beautiful face, and I recognized her intense desire to fit in. How sad that most people judge others from the outside without ever giving the inside a chance to shine. I wondered if perhaps I, too, had misjudged her. I'm sure I had probably placed additional pressures on my own little girl.

We were fortunate to find a group of doctors close to home and ultimately made the decision to move forward. She was evaluated and deemed a candidate for the surgery. A new series of doctor visits and lab work began, as did the endless paperwork for the insurance company. I had promised my daughter that if the insurance coverage was declined, we would take out a loan and follow through anyway. After several long weeks of waiting, the insurance company approved the surgery as a medical necessity, and then we waited some more. Jackie had just turned eighteen.

It seemed our lives were in a holding pattern waiting for liftoff. For Jackie, my husband, and myself, each day seemed endless. After four months Jackie was given a date and with that my anxiety level rose even higher. I could not sleep at night and I did not want her out of my sight. I was terrified something would go wrong and the surgery would have to be postponed. I knew that I could not handle any additional delays. In an effort to do something that might make me feel better, I decided to donate blood for her in case of an emergency. But in my heightened state of concern, I forgot to eat and passed out at the blood bank. I just wasn't thinking straight.

Three weeks before the scheduled surgery date, the doctor's office left a message on our answering machine. When I saw the number calling, I went into panic mode. I felt certain that a glitch had occurred and they were calling to delay the procedure. Instead, they offered to do the surgery a week early if Jackie agreed to be part of a documentary on gastric bypass. Desperate to get it over with, she agreed to the offer and participated in the final tests and preoperation appointments with a camera crew filming her every move.

They interviewed her as she openly shared her pain and the difficulties of being overweight. She acknowledged how much it hurt when she was out with friends and the guys would step up to talk to the other girls and ignore her. Again, I cried as she spoke.

Finally, the day of the surgery arrived. In my purse I had a small statue of my patron saint that I carry faithfully with me. I squeezed it tightly as Jackie—now eighteen years old and a legal adult— signed all the necessary forms. I prayed long and hard, with my patron saint clutched tightly in my hand, for all to go smoothly. The surgeon arrived and took her away.

Family, friends, and the camera crew surrounded my husband and me as the surgery began. I wore a courageous smile, but on the inside I was tortured. I made hundreds of deals with God. I was willing to do anything to guarantee her safety. I sat in the waiting room flipping through magazines and newspapers but nothing seemed to be registering in my brain. Every time someone walked into the waiting area, my heart raced a little more quickly.

After what seemed an eternity, the doctor walked into the room and smiled as the TV cameras rolled. He announced that the surgery had gone well and Jackie was fine. As the doctor spoke I felt a huge pressure lifted from my chest.

As I walked down the cold hospital breezeway toward the postoperative center, I felt the tears roll down my cheeks. She was half asleep and had tubes in her nose. She looked tired and pale as I leaned over and kissed her gently. From somewhere far away, she murmured, "Please let me sleep." I smiled to myself thinking, *Jackie is just fine, she's already giving orders.*

I remained with her at the hospital as she was prodded and checked every hour on the hour. It was a long and tedious night with little sleep for either of us, as the hustle and bustle of the hospital continued around us. Her aftercare was carried out with kindness and compassion for the patient and the worried parents.

She was discharged after three days, and our journey continued at home. I was sent out to buy baby food for the patient and I smiled to myself remembering the last time I had "cruised" that aisle in the supermarket. It was interesting that my daughter now had brand preferences for her baby food.

A month after the surgery, Jackie told us her decision to have the surgery was now creating a bittersweet time in her life. She was delighted with her weight loss; thirteen pounds the first week and a continued loss of about two pounds each week after that. That was the good part. Postsurgical procedure limits the patient to soft foods and instructs her to begin her new lifestyle relating to food. The absence of solid foods for an extended period of time was the part that she didn't enjoy.

She had to learn so many things about her new body and about the foods it could process as she recuperated. She found that when she eats too quickly or the wrong foods, her body rejects what she has eaten and she throws up. This happens to most of the gastric bypass patients as they figure out what foods they can tolerate and which they are unable to process without negative results.

We had been warned that she might experience hair loss, one of the side effects of gastric bypass surgery, and this was an additional trauma for Jackie.

Fast-forward, three months. Jackie was back in school, and called home one afternoon. She sounded frantic, and I panicked, thinking something was wrong. With bated breath, I waited to hear about what new calamity we were suddenly facing. She started to giggle as she assured me that everything was truly fine. She was shopping with her friends at the Gap and was phoning to share the exciting news that she was able to fit into all the clothes she had taken into the dressing room.

Her only problem was that she could not afford to buy everything she wanted. It took all my inner strength at that moment not to say, "Buy it, buy it all." *I can easily handle this,* I thought to myself, as I smiled and hung up the phone.

I am watching my self-confident daughter returning to the

world each day. She was so brave throughout this long ordeal. Now she is learning to adjust and cope with her new way of living and eating. I am trying to step aside and offer my hand only when she asks, a whole new role for this mother. I thank my Higher Power and wish my daughter the best that life has to offer.

Mental Illness

BOMBSHELL

It's an affliction that paralyzes lives but is almost impossible to talk about. Cancer may be horrible, but sometimes it's easier to live with than mental illness. It's *certainly* more politically correct.

My husband spent years (and tens of thousands of dollars) chasing his tail, trying to figure out why he was fine one day and miserable enough to vomit up his frustrations the next. They told him he was a very sick man, but it was a diagnosis he chose to ignore. But the energy I spent covering it up for him was enough to make *me* crazy.

Mental illness has a lingo all its own: norepinephrine, seratonin, Serzone, Prozac, Paxil. The deeper you tread, the more frightening the maze of options becomes. The first time I walked through a metal detector to visit him in a psych hospital, I felt like I was entering Alcatraz. Though my husband wasn't "in" for committing a crime, the guards out front behaved as if they were doing me a favor by allowing me to visit. They even searched the cookies I had brought for him. "Oh, and one more thing, ma'am," the guard barked. "We'll have to check your purse . . . no razors allowed." As if.

There were thirteen different medications over the years with side effects worse than the symptoms; vomiting, heart palpitations, fits of rage, hallucinations, and rivers of tears. He couldn't keep track of what he was on, and I did my best to help, but short of forcing the pills down his throat, I was nothing more than a bystander. I kept at it, making appointments he failed to keep, researching new doctors and drugs he undoubtedly would dismiss. He didn't really believe he was sick, though he'd sweat profusely, refuse to eat (he lost thirty pounds in a month three different times), stand over me all night as I slept, and curl up in a fetal position, crying like an infant. He thought his dark moods and errant behaviors were driven by circumstance . . . work was crashing in on him and he'd lost money in the stock market. He wouldn't take his meds, but even when he did, they didn't help much. Treating mental illness is a crapshoot, but in order to win, you have to be a willing participant.

I tried to overcompensate, working longer and harder to give him a chance to relax, but that only made matters worse. His doctors called me an enabler, and my husband convinced me he'd be better off going to work, but in reality, he was completely unable to cope. His outbursts left the office receptionist in tears and sent potential clients elsewhere. His parents and younger sisters were very concerned about his health, and they worried about what people would think if they knew he was having a mental breakdown. They were convinced that if word ever got out, their brilliant, overachieving son and big brother would forever be stigmatized.

We had plenty of close calls, but eventually became pros at fabricating lies to make excuses for being late or not showing up at all: he's stressed out, not feeling well, stuck in traffic. Getting him out of the house was challenging enough; he'd rant and rave about business dealings that cost him his fortune (not true) and then would spend hours in the bathroom gagging on bile and eventually throwing up all his frustrations. The sounds that emerged from his withering body were horrifying.

We tried to live as normally as possible, but covering up his odd, spaced-out behavior was taking its toll on all of us. The kids started to withdraw, scared to death of what was happening to their daddy who didn't want to play with them anymore. Eventually, we shut ourselves in and kept to ourselves . . . trying to immerse ourselves in the rare moments we could share as a family. Ten months into breakdown number two, when I really felt his life was at risk, I was able to get a court order to get him committed, and after the mandatory seventy-two hour stay in the psych ward, he finally agreed to stay. But it didn't last, and he went off the meds as soon as he got home.

Mental illness doesn't go away by itself, and getting the patient to agree to stay in a hospital is never easy. Once, his sister and I took him to a facility clear across the country, against his will, physically dragging him through airports, begging and pleading with him not to run away. This last time, my guts had been through the wringer, but I'd never had more hope, and I really felt we were so close to getting him the significant help he needed. More than a dozen hours later, he agreed to stay, as long as I left him my credit card so he could call home. They take all your worldly possessions when they lock you in to one of those places, so the credit card offered some comfort. The phone bill was $300 the first week.

Ten days into this hospital stay, he called with what seemed like some encouraging news. I'll never forget the way my heart jumped when he told me he finally snapped enough to realize how much he was hurting the ones he loved most, and how much he had to live for. He admitted his life was crashing in on him and his career was shot, but he said he couldn't bear to lose me. He begged me to support him and to help him pick up the pieces of whatever he had left. Finally, some hope, I prayed, and promised him the universe. For years, he had been in denial, blaming his mental ups and downs on everything but the chemical imbalances in his brain. Now, he told me, he finally understood.

The doctors too gave me so much hope. They were optimistic, and so was I, until they finally allowed me to visit. When I walked into his room looking for my handsome husband, what I found was a very broken man, latching onto me, crying, begging me not to leave him there. I fell apart, and I loved him so much, but I just couldn't give in to him anymore. So I devised a plan to keep him going . . . something for him to daydream about when he was at his lowest moments. Sex! At least we still had that.

Psych hospitals are like prison wards. But there are no conjugal visits. Someone is always watching and listening, but that didn't stop me. I whispered some seductive words into his ear, convincing him to meet me in the bathroom, where I'd be waiting to make wild, passionate love to him. It was a pitiful experience, nothing like the lovemaking we'd shared together for so many years. And to complicate matters, I had my period, and the bloodstained towels could've cost him weeks of "incarceration" if discovered . . . they'd surely think he was trying to harm himself. So, after our tryst, I dutifully shoved the soiled towels down my pants, smuggling them to safety. We laughed and he agreed to stay, but he eventually checked himself out of there and there wasn't anything I could do about it.

Even during the most tumultuous years of life on this evil roller coaster, I never gave up hope of seeing my husband whole again, despite threats and desperate attempts at taking his own life. I really believed in my heart that one day our love and our family would be enough to will him well.

Of course, neither of us really understood that dealing with mental illness is an inexact science, and it takes more than just the desire to conquer it. You can never stop experimenting with the meds until you find the one that jump-starts the chemicals in your brain and lets you live again.

My husband was unlucky enough to be dealt a bad genetic card, predisposing him to mental illness, and it was hard to see that sanity was usually just right around the corner, through therapy and medication. But it was. It took a lot of years for me to realize that only *he* could take himself there. I continued to search for the right doctor, the one who would push the right buttons. There were dozens. Fighting with insurance companies, begging for appointments he didn't want to attend, and grilling doctors who thought I was too pushy (maybe I was the problem, one told me). It was the most frustrating, time-consuming job I had ever undertaken, and I was never ready to accept the idea that no one could help him.

Eventually, I found a doctor who experimented enough to find the right combination of medications that could stabilize my husband's brain. With psychotropic drugs, as they are called, it's all about the biochemical combinations and how the central nervous system responds to them. Getting him to buy into "just one more" try was anything but easy, because medicines only work if taken as prescribed. His record of compliance wasn't great, but through his tears, he finally gave in, only after I promised not to leave him.

It took nine years of experimentation before this one doctor finally got it right. He was diagnosed as bipolar, a real-life chemical imbalance. He would have to take medication for the rest of his life, just as a diabetic takes insulin. The only difference: the stigma. He still doesn't talk about his dependence on lithium. But he promises to take it religiously. Because now, my husband says, he finally *does* get it . . . and knows his whole life depends on it. I pray he does.

six

To Love, Honor, and Oy Vey

None of us entered adulthood expecting that men we loved so much could shatter our hearts into tiny pieces. As children, we had bought into the Walt Disney myth that Prince Charming would charge through the storm on his white horse and take us into the eternal bliss, with love conquering all. But life isn't that predictable.

Partnerships are never simple. Whether they are marriages, live-in lovers, or affairs, we've all learned lessons from them, often the hard way. Sometimes, becoming someone's other half can prevent us from being whole.

When we first came together in the spring of 2001, we were all firmly committed to loving partners who had brought joy to our worlds for quite some time. But now, four years later, three of us have asked those once wonderful husbands and boyfriends to move out. Tammi, Annie, and Pat have been to hell and back over the past year, but they might not have had the *cojones* to make such difficult choices without the unending support and love of their fellow Bombshells. Whenever there is a wayward Bombshell falling apart, there is always another one there on the phone or the computer, ready to throw in a life preserver.

In the summer of 2004, it seemed to all happen at once. Pat ended her relationship with her live-in boyfriend of twelve years in an amicable and even loving parting of ways after mutually deciding to transform their romance into a friendship. And though this was something they both wanted, the grief associated with the breakup was overwhelming for Pat.

Tammi's torrid romance with her live-in Latin lover hit some rough spots after three years and she decided to move into a new home without him, calling their breakup a "time-out." "Sometimes," she says, "you've just got to step back to see if the fog lifts, and whether or not love really does supersede all the daily power struggles." They're dating each other now, hoping that one day they'll meet their destiny together. But when they first separated, Tammi was devastated and inconsolable.

About the same time, after twenty-four years of marriage, Annie and her husband began divorce proceedings. Annie, who always believed in, and wanted, the proverbial white picket fence, finally admitted to herself, her friends, and especially her parents, that hers was not a picture-perfect life. "I guess I'm not June Cleaver anymore," Annie told us, with resolve in her voice. "The guilt sometimes still overpowers me . . . and I wonder what I did wrong. But in my heart I know that we just went our separate ways."

Ironically, on July 4, Independence Day, Pat was grieving over the loss of her relationship. Still in bed at 11 A.M., she just couldn't drag herself out to face the day. An exhausted Tammi, who had flown in from Colorado on a red-eye the night before, called to check in on her fellow Miami Bombshell. After hearing her friend's trembling voice, she jumped into her car, crossed county borders, and was at her door within forty-five minutes. A tearful Pat greeted her.

As they hugged, there were no words. Almost immediately, Tammi started to cry as well, as she too was grappling with some big decisions. They climbed the steps to the second floor and literally fell into Pat's bed. Half an hour later, after consuming almost an entire box of chocolate, Tammi answered the phone, only to hear fellow Miami Bombshell, next-door neighbor Annie . . . in tears. "I'm drained," Annie, whined. "I can't take it anymore." Pat grabbed the phone and ordered Annie to "get your butt over here right now!"

Two minutes later, Pat, Annie, and Tammi were lying on Pat's bed, consoling each other and laughing at their pathetic selves.

The following month as we're sitting at a Bombshell gathering, talking about love and love lost, Tammi says through teary eyes, "When it comes to friends, Pat, I don't know what I would do without you. When I'm down, no matter where you are or what you're doing, you check in, sometimes to the point of annoyance, even when I don't even think I want to talk. But somehow, you always show me the light ahead." At this point, Pat is crying herself, and she blows her nose as she declares, "No Tam, you're the one who's always there for me. Even if you're in the midst of madness, I can always count on you to come to my rescue and crack me up, my friend."

As Tammi and Pat hug each other, Annie, who has not yet decided if divorce is the answer, is in her own world today and, looking at no one in particular, announces, "There are positive things from my marriage, but sometimes I feel overwhelmed because I feel like the CEO of this relationship. My husband just sits back. I wish someone would take care of me for once. At some point over the past twenty years, I lost my identity."

She continues, as emotion rolls over her face. "I followed this cookie-cutter life. I was this perfect little person; straight A's, went to college, and then got married. My life was on preset and I followed the path. I don't know if along the way I really made any decisions. I just did what I was supposed to. Guys . . . I don't know what I would do without all of you," cries Annie.

At this point, Lydia stands up, intent on breaking up the wallowing session, and belts out a James Taylor song at the top of her lungs (in operatic style): "When you're down and troubled . . . and you need a helping hand . . . and nothing is going right . . . you've got a friend: . . . "Usually, when we least expect it, Lydia can always make us laugh at ourselves.

We have found that no amount of patience, compromise, or understanding is sufficient when love simply withers away in a tired relationship, or one day you wake up to discover you have a roommate, instead of a lover.

That's not to say that love can't endure. When a relationship is healthy and strong, it can survive life's unexpected ups and downs, even redefine the meaning of happiness. Mercedes' relationship with her husband fell into place in the early years of adolescence, and more than twenty years later, she still sings his praises, providing optimism to the rest of the group.

As Mercedes told the Bombshells about her devotion to her husband, Sara can't help but poke fun: "Come on, give me a break, you mean to tell me you've never ever wanted to have sex with another man?"

"I never said that, Sara," answered Mercedes. "I've had my fantasies; I've wanted to be with other men, and many men have wanted to be with me as well. But I take my marriage very seriously, and although I've been tempted, I can't imagine having sex just for the physical pleasure, if I can't bring the passionate love part into bed as well. That's what I already have with my husband."

Whether in transition or in it for the long haul, our relationships help define us and sustain us, and through them, we have learned the most significant lesson of all: that loving ourselves is just as important as, maybe even more so than, sharing our love with Mr. Right (or in some cases, Mr. Right Now).

Climb Every Mountain

TAMMI

Before I knew better, I flirted with danger every chance I could. On vacation, while the others would choose to float down a winding river's easy route, I would grab another thrill seeker and head right for the blazing rapids. I spent my South Florida childhood under the sea, with my spear gun, coming face-to-face with sharks and barracuda more times than I can remember. I wasn't having fun till my life flashed before me. And the rush got more intense with each escapade. Once, I even jumped out of an airplane at ten thousand feet and am still an active, card-carrying member of the Mile High Club. Adventure was my middle name.

Then I became a mom. And midlife set in.

Two delicious little girls brought a whole new dimension to my world, but parenthood came with a brand-new set of rules. My foundation was rocked when I landed smack-dab in the "responsibility" chapter of the book called my life. My mom chalked it up to growing up, because, for the first time in my life, fear reared its ugly head and I began to worry for my kids; it was up to me to keep them safe and healthy, and I had to do that for them. Without giving it much thought, risk taking just disappeared from my radar screen. Sacrifice was what motherhood is all about; at least that's what my mother kept telling me. And I believed her.

My new reality became filled with fifty-hour workweeks and nannies who would rather watch Spanish soap operas than my kids. Our family would consume more than the recommended daily allowance of Happy Meals, and homework always seemed to dictate our plans. Even if I wanted to, I couldn't find the time, or the energy, to pursue all the thrills I'd chased in my twenties and early thirties. Finding my car keys was enough of a challenge. I no longer had to comb the wilderness for adventure. It was waiting for me every night behind the front door.

I did get cranky the day I was resigned to trading in my luxurious car for a minivan, knowing the only free spirit left in me was my bra (and even that went from a 34C to a 38A after two kids!). I was hoping my lust for adventure would come back later in life, but growing up meant that eye contact with the sharks through the aquarium window would have to suffice. If my kids were happy, I too was going to be. And I thought I had myself convinced.

But as my girls grew and I told them stories of my glory days, they seemed so fascinated with the woman I used to be, so different from the mom they knew, and questioned why I had become so "boring." I tried to tell them that a good mother need not risk her life for a lousy thrill or two.

Then I went rock climbing.

Actually, it happened by accident. My husband and I were vacationing in Vail, hiking the mildest of trails with the kids on our backs. The scenery was breathtaking, but we weren't exactly battling the forces of nature with gourmet burger joints perched on the mountaintop. When we came down from our moderate hike, I felt cheated. The next day, I begged my husband to cancel his golf game, then left him with the kids and set out to find some true adventure in the Rocky Mountains.

It didn't take very long. I made a few phone calls and stumbled across a group of journalists searching for the secrets of the Vail Valley summer experience. I was invited to tag along the day they'd try climbing a seventy-foot wall of granite. Straight up. The idea intrigued me, but I didn't know if my mushy body would comply. I was in a little over my head, but reminded myself I *had* been an athlete once, even if it *was* when Jimmy Carter was president.

Rock climbing's premise is simple. We're all born with the urge to climb. We start with steps, then try to flee our cribs. We graduate to monkey bars and trees, fences, and eventually, our boyfriends' bedroom windows. But by the time we're teenagers, most of us give up climbing in favor of talking on the phone or hanging out at the mall. I never knew how much I'd been missing until I met that wall at Camp Hale, Colorado, one chilly July morning seven years ago.

Melanie was our guide. Her first job was to gain our trust, as she was the one who would hold all our lives in her hands when we ascended this huge rock, operating the fallback ropes. When we first arrived, Melanie ran up that wall like Spiderwoman (without ropes) to thread our lifelines through the large anchor already bolted into the rock. We were amazed at how easy she made it look. We listened to instructions, hooked into our ropes, and crossed our fingers.

Facing the rock was the scariest part. From where I stood on the ground, looking straight up, there didn't seem to be any ledges to hold onto. But Melanie was my belayer, the person who controlled the ropes, and she talked me through it. From the moment I hooked my rope into hers, there was an unwritten contract of connection between us. At least that's how Melanie explained it. The harder I tried to climb up this rock wall, the more encouragement she'd shout up to me. The higher I climbed, the tighter she'd pull my rope. This was supposed to make me feel secure enough to push myself to the limit. It didn't.

So I held my breath, triple-checked the ropes, and made myself a promise to never look back. And then, almost as if someone had put a torch under my tush, I began my ascent, moving up and across the rock as if I'd done it dozens of times before. Like a ballerina on pointe, I felt like I was dancing up this wall of granite, resting on edges no more than half an inch wide.

To move on rock, you must find those hidden hand- and footholds, then pray your body is gymnastic enough to reach them. Mine was now twisting and stretching in ways I didn't think were possible, but I was so pumped, and miraculously, my body was hanging right in there with me. I struggled, panting, with my legs quivering spastically, but eventually, I made it to the top. Everyone on the ground was applauding the old, fat lady, but for me, the thrill of victory was beyond intense, right up there with having a baby. Even more unbelievable: I realized that day I still had it in me.

As soon as I hit the ground, I begged to go up again, this time on a more challenging route. But the next climb was a completely different experience. From the very first foothold, it was clear my dance was over. I was so tired, and I just wanted to rappel myself down to the bottom, and take the safe, easy way. The same route I'd become so accustomed to following in so many aspects of my life lately, even in my marriage. Should I push it?

There was bound to be some strength left in some hidden crevice of my aching body, though I was still not sure it would be worth the effort. I'm a grown-up lady, a mommy and a wife, I rationalized to myself, and nobody really cares if I climb up a stupid mountain anyway. That's how I looked at everything back then. The status quo didn't really seem so bad . . . and I had gotten proficient at taking the path of least resistance, especially when it came to expectations about my marriage. It was what it was, I thought, and though I was still unfulfilled, I wasn't being abused and life wasn't so bad. Who was I to think it was supposed to be any better than this?

You know the ending. I made it to the top of that huge rock that day, and that climb ultimately changed the way I lived my life. I became a better mother, and a more tolerant wife (for a while), feeling those warm, fuzzy things that wash over you at the end of a good Disney movie, when the odds are overcome, and adversity makes for better people.

For whatever reason, tackling that mountain made me feel happier, for the time being, anyway. My attitude changed, and so did the way I looked at my life. My husband was a great guy, and I decided I wanted to grow old with him by my side, living happily ever after like my parents were.

The following summer, I was picnicking with the kids on Vail Mountain, and I ran into Melanie, the rock-climbing instructor. She invited me to climb with her again, reciting back the vivid details of the day I tasted victory on that huge, intimidating rock. My marriage had improved so much and I didn't think I needed it anymore, I told Melanie unconvincingly, but she told me she taking some athletes up a new rock, and my oldest daughter convinces me to join them. I barely sleep, thinking that now I'm a whole year older, seven pounds heavier than last year, and worried that I won't make it up again. I almost felt relieved when my three-year-old woke up with a miserable cold, but my husband convinced me to go, promising to hold down the fort. If only he knew the can of worms he was opening.

It may sound petty, shallow, and superficial, but that rock-climbing adventure made me see that I needed more out of my days on this planet. I wanted to live and taste every single morsel of life, and I begged my hubby to join me on this exciting journey.

I told him that when I turned forty, I was going to be happy, even if it killed us, though that wasn't really what I wanted. I just needed to play more, feel more, love more, and worry less about tomorrow. I wanted to move to the mountains and start a whole new life with him and the girls.

But my husband just didn't have it in him. He needed to secure our future, he told me, and took great pride in working hard to make it happen for us. Let's work now and play later, he'd plead with me. And for three long years, we really tried, therapy and all, but I became so depressed that life became unbearable for me.

It wasn't until I couldn't see any light left at the end of that long, long tunnel that I did something about it. The year I turned forty, my mom was diagnosed with a rare disease, and for a few days, until we got completely informed, we weren't sure if this was the beginning of the end for her. During this traumatic ordeal, when Mom should've been more focused on her own stuff, she took me aside and asked me to make her a promise. She cried at what she was afraid might be her final request. If anything happened to her, she told me, I had to promise to get divorced. Imagine that. Mom told me that I was too young to ignore the emptiness I felt inside and worried sick about the walls I was building around myself. She wept with sadness when telling me that my misery was taking a toll on my kids and that until I was happy, they would never be. She assured me I'd be fine once I got over the guilt of leaving my husband. I wasn't so sure, but my mom could see my grief and frustration and knew that I'd be OK even if I remained alone for the rest of my life.

As my fortieth birthday approached, my sisters and friends grappled to find an appropriate way to celebrate this rite of passage, knowing I was hardly in the mood to celebrate. Despite my tearful protests, they insisted on planning a girls' weekend at my cousin's sprawling ranch near Aspen. The fourteen people I loved most on the planet were schlepping in from all over the country to try and cheer me up. As the weekend approached, I tried desperately to pull myself out of the funk, and I vowed to show the people who loved me a great time. It was the least I could do.

The weekend was unbelievable. It was two years before the birth of the Miami Bombshells, so Pat was the only one I knew at the time, but she, along with my sisters and some lifelong friends, dropped what they were doing, flew to Aspen, and filled me with so much love over those few days, it made my head spin.

They roasted, toasted, inebriated, and resuscitated me until, astonishingly, I began to breathe again. I'm still not quite sure how they did it, but somehow, these women brought me back to life, giving me the courage to take that first step, to climb up the next huge rock, head-on.

I had no choice but to leave my marriage, and while my pals warned me that I was most certainly going to slip and fall along the treacherous path, and would probably get pretty banged up along the way, they practically promised there was no question I'd make it to the top of the next mountain, where a whole new life was waiting for me.

They could not have been more right.

I Married a Monster

SARA

Mine was a wedding you would never forget. If you were lucky enough to get inside through the velvet ropes at the front of the television studio, you would have a vivid memory of that night.

Both of us had been married before. Since we hadn't been so good at getting married—actually, staying married—the first time around, Bill and I wanted the second time to be different. We decided to plan an untraditional wedding. Not the untraditional "top of the mountain" wedding that has now become traditional for those who want to be untraditional. But *really* break the convention. We aimed to do the opposite of traditional, in everything about the ceremony and party, in the unspoken hope that the end result—the marriage—would be the opposite of what had come before.

First-time brides have so much hope, so many romanticized notions, and they all begin with the wedding. Small decisions like the color of napkins take on ridiculous import. Not unlike second- and third-time parents who no longer boil a pacifier when it falls on the floor, I knew the first time around was full of unnecessary precautions and ridiculous worry about insignificant details. We wanted this wedding to demonstrate what was really important to us: celebrating with friends and family and having a good time.

I had a vision: I wanted to give my friends a chance to wear their old bridesmaid and wedding dresses a second time. I imagined a giant party with a dozen brides and twice as many attendants. I didn't want to be the center of attention (been there, done that) and figured no one would be able to spot me in a sea of bridal wear.

Our friend Mara asked me about our plans one night, and I told her my idea. She said, "If everyone is going to come in costume, why don't you just get married on Halloween?"

Halloween was perfect. For years, Bill and I had dressed up on every Halloween, doing Gilligan's Island, the Spice Girls, or Sonny (me) and Cher (him—he's taller). We'd have a Halloween wedding and all of our guests could shed their life's masks and pretend to be someone else.

I was willing to trade the fairy-tale wedding for the fairy-tale ending, but that didn't stop me from imagining that Cinderella and Prince Charming would be the perfect costumes for the bride and groom. Bill's idea for a costume was to go as Frankenstein and the Bride of Frankenstein. On the positive side, I didn't have to worry about having a bad hair day; it was guaranteed. On the negative side, I wouldn't be a beautiful bride, though I might be a blushing one. And so, if only for the sheer drama, we planned a Frankenstein wedding.

We didn't allow it to be called a wedding. Instead, we decided it would be our first annual anniversary celebration, so we named it the Halloweenaversary. We eschewed all things expected: no flowers, no caterer (just pizza and sushi), no attendants, no registry, no wedding dress; even the invitations went out on e-mail. It was held at a local television studio on Lincoln Road (a pedestrian mall) on South Beach. Just inside the door, a television camera with a green screen projected our guests into the movie *Young Frankenstein* as they entered. We asked not for gifts, but for donations of toys that would be given to kids who needed them.

The guest list included Dr. Frankenstein, Igor, and Frau Blucher, for starters. We had a King, Queen, Prince, and Princess. Also, a Keystone Cop, three flappers, Dracula, Wonder Woman, Bat Girl, and an escaped prisoner. For every villain, we had several superheroes. The year was 2000, and our most creative guests came dressed in the perfect political costume: one with leaves all over her, and the other with one arm missing, a screw in his head, and blood dripping eerily from his wounds. They were Bush and Gore.

Igor walked me down the stairs (not aisle) while the crowd cheered and screamed. Bill and I took our places, but before the ceremony began, I unveiled my final surprise. The three flappers joined me and became my "Pips" as the song "Wedding Bell Blues" blared from the formidable sound system.

"Won't you marry me, Bill? I've got the wedding bell blu-u-ues."

The ceremony was short and sweet, performed by a make-believe king in nondenominational language. We had written our own vows so we'd be certain they didn't create expectations that were impossible to live up to. I promised to bitch and moan, overreact, and lose my temper. He promised to procrastinate, never ask for directions, and generally annoy me. And then love each other madly for the rest of our lives.

But even without the pressure of "love, honor, and cherish," the wedding day jitters got to both of us. The informality of the event and ceremony aside, we both knew the size of the commitment we were making to each other. The question hung in the air: having tried something already and failed at it, why would you do it again if you didn't have to? We didn't plan to have any more children, why were we making it legal? my mother had asked me, and I didn't have a good answer.

I wondered what I would do if Bill found out what a terrible person I could be and left me. I couldn't believe I was putting myself in a position of so much vulnerability.

I stood on the stage shaking, sweaty palms crushing the paper on which we had written our vows. I looked into the crowd of cheering friends, terrified, and wanted to turn and run.

But when the king asked me if I would take Bill to be my husband, I said, "Yes." When His Highness proclaimed us "Monster and Wife" we kissed, and hugged our kids. And then in a cracking voice that might have given away my anxiety, I grabbed the microphone and said, "Let's party."

It was indeed a memorable wedding, but I would never have chosen it had I not already had the "other" kind: the big kind with the big dress and the big hair, big flowers and big meal, along with the big bill. I know from having had it that it's not really about the wedding at all. A wedding is something that happens one day in your life. A marriage is what happens every day after that.

And so, the next day, as we held the signed marriage certificate and prepared to put it in an envelope, I voiced the fear I had been feeling.

"Let's not send in the marriage certificate," I suggested.

"But then we won't be married," replied Bill, smiling. He thought I was kidding.

"Everyone will think we're married, but it won't be legal, and then if something went wrong we wouldn't have to get divorced."

"You're serious," he said, tone changing from playfulness to concern.

"I am," I said, tone changing from tension to relief.

We held the certificate for a couple of days before we ultimately mailed it; we are truly and legally married. You can't run from marriage because you're afraid of divorce.

Bill and I have been able to stay true to our vows. He's been lazy and I've been awful and yet we can't wait to wake up together. We may not have looked like Cinderella and Prince Charming on our wedding day, but now the masks are off, and we are living—for the most part—happily ever after (though I haven't given up hope on the castle).

The One and Only

MERCEDES

There are very few people I would trust with my life. In fact, I can count them on one hand. They are the few who would come to my rescue in times of trouble and single-handedly fight an army to secure my happiness and well-being. They are the ones who actually expect an honest answer from me when they ask how I'm doing at the beginning of every morning. Those are the people most of us call family or best friend; in my case I call him my husband.

I met him in my junior year of high school and felt embarrassed to date him because he seemed like more of a grown-up instead of a kid like me. He was already in college and looked at least ten years older, though in reality there was only a four-year age difference. He had a mustache and beard, was already balding, and weighed at least a hundred pounds more than I did. He had the air of a confident man who knew who he was and what he wanted and wasn't afraid to ask for it.

Although it didn't take long for him to ask me out on a date, it took me a while to say yes. I just didn't think we looked right together. I was the beautiful swan (or so I thought in my self-absorbed teenage mind) and he . . . well, the duckling in polyester pants, mismatched sweaters, and galoshes who only listened to my parents' salsa music.

As fate would have it, it was that same music that brought us together. Tom was an industrial psychology major at Loyola University in Chicago. Yet, he somehow finagled the Communications Department to grant him control of six hours of airtime for its Sunday radio programming. In that time slot he launched an experimental radio show in Spanish he called *Dimension Latina* that is still on the air today! We didn't know it then but that little college radio show set the stage for a national radio revolution that in the last twenty years has swept the radio industry and turned Tom into one of the most sought-after Spanish radio executives in the nation.

But we knew nothing of destiny then. I showed up at WLUW 88.7 FM one Sunday afternoon to audition for the news job. I wanted to be the voice of the five-minute cut-ins at the top of every hour. I had no experience to speak of. To make matters worse my Spanish was *malisimo*. But I had passion and drive.

Though my parents only spoke to me in Spanish, my whole other world revolved around English, so my diction and vocabulary in my mother tongue were probably those of a twelve-year-old.

Somehow though, Tom saw the fire in my belly and gave me my first chance at broadcasting. Within a month of having met him, I was in awe of his brilliance and humor, his sweetness and charismatic ability to lead. It didn't take long for me to start seeing him with different, more loving eyes, until one day I just went home and nonchalantly announced to my mother, "I'm going to make that man love me." It wasn't hard. He was already there. Tom and I became inseparable. I applied to Loyola, scrapping applications to Columbia's and Northwestern's schools of journalism, just to be with him.

I adopted Tom's passions, his work ethic, his Latin-ness. He introduced me to an underground club-scene culture he frequented to promote his radio show and to interview ascending singers who eventually became salsa legends. I watched and learned. We went to beat-up dance halls in some of Chicago's most dangerous neighborhoods, where you ran as much a risk of being shot by dueling barrio gangs for wearing someone else's *color* as arrested for wrongful association. The air was usually so thick with pot smoke that it would often trigger my asthma attacks. I never smoked or took drugs, so these outings really shocked me at first. But Tom was with me so I felt protected.

Little by little those somewhat illicit escapades sparked my love for a culture that was much richer and more complex than those weekend gangsta facades. More than the rich pulsating music, I rediscovered a warm welcoming community and a glorious heritage that had been snatched from me in my childhood when we fled Cuba.

Together Tom and I witnessed salsa history in the making. I saw the great Hector Lavoe arrive at the Aragon ballroom at two in the morning drugged out of his mind and crooning like a songbird. I guess you could compare him to Jim Morrison of the Doors from a different genre. I got to attend concerts by Ismael Miranda, El Gran Combo, Johnny Pacheco, Tito Puente, Willy Colon, Rubén Blades, Eddy Palmieri, and many others. Salsa, Tom, and I were growing up together.

And then Tom invited me to a concert by the great Celia Cruz. I had never heard of the famous Cuban singer who, like us, had fled Communism, so I had no expectations. I spent most of the night dancing with friends as he interviewed the musicians backstage. When she finally came out and started singing, her melodies bewitched me as if she were a beautiful mermaid. I unknowingly gravitated toward the edge of the five-foot-high stage and found myself gazing up in adoration of this old black goddess. She was dressed in a long red lace gown, wearing impossible four-inch heels on too heavy a frame and belting out her famous hit "Bemba Colora," or "Red Lips."

In a moment of surrender my hips started to swing uncontrollably, my eyes closed, and I looked deeply inward to a place I had long forgotten. As the song rolled off Celia's lips like a powerful lullaby, it rocked my essence. In that instant I understood where I came from, why drums move me to where my roots were planted long, long ago.

The disco queen in the faded jeans and long hippy hair became Latina again, and Spanish became the language of my heart. Celia Cruz is possibly the best gift Tom ever gave me because through her, and the difficult life she had endured, a total understanding of myself followed.

This concert gave me the sense that Tom was not going to be a temporary infatuation. We had lived parallel lives. He too was part of the Cuban diaspora. We had both been whisked away to Spain to escape Communism and later resettled in Chicago. We shared the same values and now the same dreams.

I married Tom on a beautiful Sunday afternoon in June of 1986 right out of college. I cried all the way down the aisle. He was crying, too, as he held out his hand for me. I had not anticipated that we would be so emotional. But dozens of family and friends wept with us out of pure joy that day. Ours was a marriage of love, above everything else.

I was very young by today's standards, only twenty-two. And, even then, I knew Tom was all I would ever want or need in a man. More than twenty years later, Tom's the only man I've ever made love to, a rarity according to the rest of the Miami Bombshells and the most natural thing in the world to me.

That's not to say I haven't been tempted. The offers were fierce when I first made it onto the television scene. Men I met at many assignments wanted to date me. The fact that I was married only

made it more of a lure. There was the young and handsome judge
who sent me his home phone number with a bailiff from the bench
as I covered a trial. There were police officers, attorneys, coworkers,
and the occasional viewer who would send letters or flowers to the
TV station I worked for. Some of them actually found my home
phone number and left messages, one time even inquiring about
me to Tom.

But I was never interested, always strong in my commitment to
the man I loved—until I took a business trip to one of those exotic
faraway destinations I always visit with excitement and trepidation,
for love of its beauty and fear of its dangers.

He was a journalist like me, an American who spoke Spanish,
covering the same assignment in the magic of the Andes, appropri-
ately for us, a place of conquest and conquistadors. The sparks flew
immediately. I found him handsome, intelligent, eloquent, and fascinating. He shadowed my every move and hung on my every word.
I felt hopeless and afraid. For the first time in years I really felt vul-
nerable, and terrified that I could easily fall into the arms of an absolute stranger. I was flustered and overwhelmed.

One night after work we had dinner alone by a burning fire. We
spoke through the night until we couldn't fight off sleep any longer.
Our conversations were full of flirtatious innuendo in English,
Spanish, and that universal body language.

All I really wanted to do was give in to the emotions that were
enveloping me. But I refused his offer to spend the night together,
even to kiss me. I went to bed in a cold hotel room fantasizing about
what I did not dare act upon.

We flew home together on an interminable flight that only deep-
ened thoughts of intimacy. He spoke softly in my ear, inviting an affair that I secretly contemplated with every passing mile. His breath
lingered in my senses. His words burned into my mind. Yet in one of
the hardest acts of self-control I've ever had to endure, I refused to
touch him, to betray my values and my marriage.

For months we stayed in touch. We spoke breathlessly on the

phone often and I actually maneuvered to see him on another assignment in another city. We had dinner again, a long conversation, and another difficult good-bye. We wished each other a happy life, knowing there would really be no repeat rendezvous.

Again, he pleaded for at least a kiss. "What does it matter if I'm never going to see you again?" He asked defeated. "I can't cross that line," I answered looking into his deep blue eyes, as I allowed myself to caress his face just this once. And with that I quickly left him, not looking back, afraid to shatter the fortress I had built around me.

For months, the pragmatist in me wrestled the romantic and won. My phone affair had been a fun distraction that I hadn't played with in a long time but one that felt adolescent and immature. I refused to get sucked in any deeper, to compromise my commitment to my husband and my real happiness, and called it off.

It was devastating. I was heartbroken. And I struggled with the fact that though I craved this relationship I had to let it escape, never to know what could have been, how it would have felt, whether it may have even survived or made me happy. Though I had not even touched this other man in a sexual way I had engaged him. And the guilt consumed me.

I dug into my soul to figure out where my marriage stood and what it meant to me before I could decide what it should mean to my husband or this other person. I still didn't have children so they were not a factor in my decision.

When I figured things out, I took Tom to dinner and briefly told him what I had been going though. I didn't offer details. I only told him that I was again choosing him, not because I had to but because I loved him. I did not want to lie to Tom or to myself.

It took a lot of self-analysis to understand the rectitude that informs my character and the strict moral values by which I live my life. I don't come from a strict religious background. I don't go to church and am not fanatical about anything except maybe personal responsibility. I believe everything we do in life is a choice and our choices carve our destiny.

I try never to lie. In fact, the very nature of my work is transparency, honesty, and finding the truth in situations and others. I believe in purity of heart; I admire loyalty and could not tolerate betrayal in anyone important to me, let alone in myself.

Yet, ultimately, these were not the deciding factors underlying why I've been with the same man for about two decades, to the exclusion of anyone else. Tom has remained my one and only for the simplest of reasons. Because he has loved me the way I've always wanted to be loved, with attention and devotion and care and great tenderness; because he listens and actually hears, and understands and nurtures me. He has all the qualities that I cherish in a man and in a partner. And he's loyal too.

On the eve of our fifteenth wedding anniversary we flew to South America, where life always seems more intense for me, and booked a long weekend in an old Indian village away from our busy lives. I planned a secret renewal of our wedding vows and a simple ceremony in the colonial chapel in the local square.

But the night before the ceremony was supposed to take place I asked Tom, just in case, if he would marry me again, given the chance. My beautiful husband hugged me and softly kissed me over and over and assured me that he would marry me again a thousand times "for the chance to become an old tree with you."

The next evening he laid his head on my shoulder minutes after he realized the mass we were attending was intended for us, the "foreigners who have come this far to consecrate their love for each other." When the priest asked me to come up to the altar and read from the Bible to my beloved, I couldn't. The broadcasting expert was too choked up in happy tears to get a word out. My loving husband, on the other hand, stood proud. He read a beautiful love passage that in our hearts proclaimed the love that binds us.

That second wedding, by ourselves and in the company of only two good friends, felt as honest, wholesome, and profound as the first one. The town mayor, who helped coordinate the surprise, invited all the villagers to the ceremony. The whole town turned out to cheer us on and wish us a happy life together. The teenagers who were bused in for the choir serenaded us on the church steps. We went off singing and dancing on the dark cobblestone streets, celebrating our blessings once again.

Inside I confirmed that this one man, this one and only experience of love, was enough to fill my life forever. I knew I was one of the lucky ones, to have been able to stay happily married to the love of my life. It was a happiness I had learned to protect and defend and, therefore, had earned.

I Do

ANNIE

By the power vested in me by the State of Florida, I now pronounce you man and wife, and so the journey begins. The journey is a series of revelations that evolve as the years pass.

I met my husband when I was just nineteen and a naive college student. He was an older man, seven years my senior and already established in the real world of business. I saw him as a mature, wise man who would love me and take care of me forever and I thought that we would live in the storybook world of "happily ever after."

We dated for several years before we married. Believe it or not, when we married and moved in together, it was the first time I had ever been away from home. I fell more in love with him with each day that passed. Looking back on the day I said, "I do," I realize that I had no idea of the complexities of marriage that would confront us both. I was so excited about having my own home and eventually having kids that I never thought of the reality of it all. I was simply following the sequential plan I had imagined, which included high school, college, marriage, and finally motherhood.

It has been twenty-two years since we exchanged our vows and, boy, have I changed. I have matured and grown into an accomplished career woman with hopes and dreams. I no longer fear the big world out there; in fact, I love the challenges it presents. I like feeling independent and being able to care of myself.

And the marriage has also changed. It's very multifaceted, as is life, and presents many obstacles. It means learning to effectively manage a relationship, children, and a career and still find time for myself. Often I feel like a professional juggler, trying to keep "all the objects" in the air at once.

As a forty-four-year-old woman, I know that I want more, and I deserve it, too. This is the arena that presents the greatest dilemma for me. I know that I am the only one responsible for my personal happiness.

Still, I seem to be so intent on pleasing my husband, children, parents, bosses, and friends that I wind up with no time and less energy for myself. These feelings manifest themselves as stress, guilt, and periods of total anxiety.

When my husband and I were first married, our lives were simple. We had very few obligations and lots of time for each other. We took wonderful vacations and found time to nourish and fulfill each other's needs. He was the center of my universe and I was the center of his.

As our children arrived, they added a magnificent dimension to our lives, but they also added major responsibilities into the equation of love and marriage. When the children were small, there were so many demands that I'm not certain we made enough time for each other. I think this is where our marital journey began to hit some rocky roads as we began to travel in different directions. We became so absorbed in nourishing the kids that we unintentionally neglected our own needs as a couple and as individual people.

We never stopped loving each other but we also did not put enough focus on ourselves. I guess we became complacent as we settled into a routine. Looking back, I realized that not only was I neglecting our relationship, I was neglecting myself as well. My personal growth had been put on an extended hiatus.

The years have passed, the children have grown older, and we are now trying to reconnect to each other. We still share love, responsibility, and commitment but somewhere along the way we have each evolved as two entirely different people.

We are now consciously working to find time to be together and also individual time alone so that we can each continue on our personal journeys of self-fulfillment.

I think my husband feels that the distance or the differences between us mean I no longer love him, or that we have drifted too far from each other, but this is not true. We have both changed and matured, but we continue to be connected, on a slightly different level. I have talked to several friends and it seems that many of us are going through similar changes in our relationships. I seem to be fighting an inner tug-of-war all of the time.

Within our Bombshell world, only Mercedes and I are in our "original marriages." She has often reminded me that the job of keeping a marriage that was begun when we were blinded by unrealistic youthful expectations is not an easy job. What an understatement! Each of the other women is traveling on similar pathways to fulfilling their personal goals and identities and just talking to them always makes me feel more empowered with my life.

I have discovered a joy in writing and I truly enjoy spending time by myself. I still love my husband but I also need my own space. I often find myself hiding the new me from my partner and then I don't feel that I'm being honest to either one of us.

In my mother's world, the role of the woman was to stay home, take care of the children, dote on the Latin husband, and forget about personal needs, wants, and desires. Well, this is the twenty-first century and the world is very different. I'm concerned that he may think we no longer belong together. I know that my newly found self-confidence will make me a better person and I want my husband to understand that it is okay for me to have interests beyond our own little world.

Many husbands feel that if their wives step out of the traditional role within the home it will change the relationship in a negative way. It may change the relationship, but I feel that it will be a positive change and an enhancement of the marriage. I believe it's advantageous to continue to grow as individuals and then we can return home and share our growth with our partners.

I want my husband to realize that I just want to expand my horizons. I find comfort in knowing that he is there for me, just like I am there for him. I want to continue to grow beyond our cocoon and comfort zone so that when I return I can share my experiences with him. I want to feel like more than just a wife and a mother; I want to be me.

I don't want to feel guilty every time I choose to do something for myself as simple as having coffee with a girlfriend, walking the beach alone in the early morning hours, or curling up with a good book. I want him to understand that I am not excluding him from my life, I am just enjoying being me for the moment.

My marriage and family are very important to me. I find warmth and comfort in our lives together. But can he understand my need and desire for new growth and interests? Will he consider them a wall between us? I know that following my dreams and aspirations will enhance my life, and I hope I can lead him to search for his own personal goals, which I hope will ultimately enhance our lives together.

Postscript:

Two years have passed and as hard as I tried, we just couldn't make it as a couple anymore. "I Do" is now "I Don't, Anymore." And so it goes . . .

The Last Supper

ANNIE

I've always been a devout Catholic, but never in a million years did I ever think I would personally participate in the Last Supper.

A few weeks ago I grudgingly accepted my husband's invitation to dine at an upscale restaurant in Coral Gables. It was his attempt to celebrate the signing of my Miami Bombshells book deal and an effort to try to revive our failing marriage. But it did not feel genuine to me. I have become increasingly skeptical of his intentions over the past few years. In my heart I knew the evening would not accomplish what he wanted. He really would have liked a new beginning, a fresh start to our marriage. But I knew better; too many years of pain and anguish had written our history together. Still I was willing to give it a try. The pacifist acts again.

As I dressed, I tried to be open-minded and to defuse my negative thoughts. When we entered the restaurant, I was overwhelmed by the faux decor. The ostentatious wall treatments, maroon velvet pillars, and baroque gold candelabra were suffocating, as they seemed to parallel my faux relationship. All I saw were men who smelled of affairs, despite having their wives sitting next to them.

We sat at the bar while waiting for our table. I ordered a glass of merlot in an attempt to help me relax and enjoy the evening. Apparently my sense of discomfort and discontent was obvious, and he tried desperately to quiet my uneasiness. If only he had tried so hard years ago.

The conversation strolled into our past. Questions emerged that were difficult to answer. The man sitting across from me yearned to say something that would spur hope, but I felt that there was very little left for the two of us together. I shared my feelings of sadness and loneliness. I admitted that I had not been happy for years and that I could not go on for another two decades feeling like this. A rush of emotions swirled through my mind as tears began to flow. I felt like vomiting, figuratively and literally.

I wanted to purge all my years of pain and splatter them right in front of him on the table. But I could see the same pain in his eyes that I had kept locked inside me for so long so I kept the thoughts to myself. Our lack of ability to communicate suddenly became extremely obvious and I realized that this had been a major source of our problems.

He apologized for not knowing I had been in pain and admitted he never intended to hurt me. In his mind, he believed that he had always been there for me. My perceptions were very different. We both see the recollection of our years together from diametrically opposing points. I have all these pent-up feelings of having had to deal with so much by myself. I said that I felt as if I had been carrying this huge backpack of responsibility and that I could no longer deal with it. I needed to lighten the burden and regain my life.

The night ended with a stroll down Miracle Mile. I would have liked to stroll all night, anything to avoid going home together. Eventually exhausted, we drove home in silence and although we shared the same bed, we were truly strangers.

I cannot remember the last time I was able to let my guard down with my husband. Lately our relationship has become so stressful that I constantly find myself on the defensive; I never know what will happen next. To say that there were never any good times would be untruthful, but the heavy angst seems to surface over and over again. I also know I am tired of having to think before I speak to avoid a confrontation. This walking on tiptoes has to come to an end. The more honest I become with myself, the more I realize how intense the dishonesty is in our relationship.

The only thing I want is peace. I want to feel that I can make a decision without having to worry that I may upset my husband. He claims that I am overreacting; however, I feel that I am simply responding to the pattern that has been established. I find myself telling him half-truths to escape his anger. I'm tired of investing so much energy to engage in a simple activity. I find myself attempting to justify my every move. I think having an illicit affair would be easier than walking in my own shoes.

My husband keeps asking why I can't be happy going to work and coming home; why is it necessary for me to find a life beyond those parameters? He doesn't see that I'm also a person, not just a wife and mother. He is content to return home from work, eat dinner, and watch TV, preferably with me at his side. This is not enough for me.

I should not be made to feel guilty every time a simple activity takes me away from home. I would like to leave for a short time, have some fun, and return. His needs have already been met, now it's my turn to fulfill my own. I have never neglected anyone, except myself.

The morning after our dinner from hell, my husband broke down and cried, asking for forgiveness. I was numb, as I sensed his heartache, knowing the pain all too well. For years he had been oblivious to my pain and now as he suffered, I was the one unable to nurture. Perhaps we were both so wrapped up in our daily lives that we missed each other's cues. Right now I am overwhelmed with a flood of emotions. I am unhappy, I am afraid, I am angry, I am lonely, I am scared, I can't sleep, and I see myself at a huge crossroad. I need to make a decision, but I feel paralyzed.

Guilt creeps up on me as I toy with the idea of divorce. But it's not a new thought. I've been in denial for more years than I care to remember.

JOURNAL: FEBRUARY 11, 2000

How long has it been since I have been happy? I have a smile on my face but it doesn't feel genuine. My heart tells me that there is more to life than what I am experiencing. My relationship is deteriorating (or maybe I'm just beginning to notice it) and the depths of my sadness seem to predominate my life. As the old song asks, "Is That All There Is?"

I'm feeling scared, alone, depressed. My life is lacking in good quality. I need to find strength to focus on the positives but I'm not seeing much of them. I try not to dwell. . . . I want out. I don't think my mind and my soul can go through another episode. I feel like running away but I know that that's not the answer. Where would I go, anyway? I am really hurting . . . oh, God. . . .

Our relationship is not improving. In fact, it seems to be sliding downhill rapidly. After months of begging, we finally went to marriage therapy. I felt that that might be a positive sign, but after two sessions, he has decided to quit. He claims that nothing is wrong with him, the problems are mine.

I have just returned from a three-day writing retreat with the Bombshells and I could not believe that wonderful experience would actually lead my marriage to the brink. He asked me to choose between the book and my marriage. My answer may be a big surprise to him.

Under great duress, he returned to therapy with me last night. Ironically he now wants to attempt to fix something that is completely damaged, with no extended warranty. I gathered all my inner strength and told him that was no longer an option. I openly admitted that I want a divorce. I will see an attorney today and develop a game plan. I pray that I find the strength to fight this battle.

Valentine's Day

SARA

There are innumerable things I love about my husband: he is generous, attentive, affectionate, spontaneous, and fun, to name a few. In full disclosure as I take inventory, I am compelled to say that he makes sure I know he loves me every day, at some point in the day. But there are two things about my husband that threaten the equilibrium: he doesn't get things done, and he won't engage in a good fight.

This Valentine's Day, we had agreed not to buy each other presents. Instead, we went with friends to a couple's massage class. I, understanding the universal language of women, had known instantly that our agreement really meant we were to buy small, special gifts "just because." So I ignored what we decided and bought something small: pajama bottoms with hearts for him, and a very small sleeping outfit for me that pronounced my true love.

As I got into bed that night in my slinky teddy full of hearts, I realized I hadn't received anything from him. Nothing. By then I had figured out I wasn't getting a gift; but I expected a card—at the very least. I mean, nothing? On our second Valentine's Day? That was simply unacceptable.

"You're going to sleep?" I asked. This was not so much a question as a declaration of war.

"I was going to try. Why, do you want to talk?"

"Yes, I want to talk. I want to know why you didn't do anything for me for Valentine's Day."

No answer.

"I mean, you couldn't take five minutes and go to the drugstore to get a card?"

No reply.

"Aren't I a priority to you? I can understand why you haven't done the other three things you were supposed to do for the past month, but this is different. I'm your wife. You didn't even think about it?"

He was nonresponsive.

OK, so maybe I put a little too much emphasis on holidays. I figure, every other day of the year I do for everyone else. On my birthday or Valentine's Day or Mother's Day (or Flag Day? No, that doesn't fly), they can do for me.

And maybe I am a little high maintenance, but only because I provide a high level of maintenance to my family. This wasn't about a card, of course. It was about validation. And I needed mine tonight.

Fight, dammit. Fight with me. Come up with an excuse so I can tell you how ridiculous it is.

"Sara, don't you know how much I love you?"

"Yes, but it's *Valentine's Day.* I mean, it's the one day of the year when you're *supposed to do* something to show me how much."

Silence.

This fuels my engine, and I can't stop myself.

"OK. Then help me understand. I really want to understand. Did you not get me a card because you didn't think it was important?"

(What is that on my leg?)

"Did you intend to get me a card but didn't find the time?"

(Ouch, what is that sharp edge under the covers?)

"Or did you just forget altogether?"

(Goddammit, what the hell is scratching me?)

In a rage, I threw the covers off me and my eyes fell upon the object of my annoyance: a small, pink envelope. Inside, I felt awful, embarrassed, and ridiculous. But ego had the best of me, and I couldn't back down now.

"Why didn't you tell me there was a card?" I demanded. "You could have saved me a lot of screaming."

"Give it a rest, Sara."

Hallmark had written: "Sharing a life, sharing a love . . . it's wonderful with you!"

I couldn't leave it alone. I asked, but he wouldn't tell me why he just lay there suffering my verbal abuse while I ranted about the card. Perhaps his real Valentine's Day gift was watching me make a fool of myself.

In his own handwriting, it said:

"To my best friend, my lover, my wife . . . you make *every day* Valentine's Day."

A wonderful sentiment, to be sure. And it did make me cry. But I don't want every day to be Valentine's Day; I need some days to feel extra special.

But it was late, and the battle had taken a lot out of me, so I sighed, kissed him, and gave up.

Sometimes you have to live to fight another day.

Double Life

BOMBSHELL

I just got an unexpected holiday greeting from an ex-lover. He called to wish me a Merry Christmas. I recognized his voice immediately after several years of no contact. My heart stopped.

How can it be that after so many years I'm still paralyzed by his voice? This is the man I was in love with for most of my life. This is the man who I believed to be my soul mate, the same one who led me to a life of sin.

He was my high school sweetheart. The first man I ever loved emotionally and physically. We shared classes and those adolescent hormonal emotions that forever remain ingrained in your mind as the best and the worst of times. We dated throughout high school. But my college years away from each other separated us.

I was a young and restless college student. I dated; I partied and experimented. But somehow I just couldn't get him out of my heart.

I flew back home every chance I had. On one of those trips I decided that I wanted to see him and no one else. When I arrived at his house I was introduced to his new friend. At that moment I had wished the earth could swallow me. I could feel my heart pounding; I could only hope that they did not see how distraught I felt. I was in shock; I had always been so sure of him and his commitment to me. But my position had been filled.

Many years passed, and along the way I married. I did not see him again even though we lived in the same city. Every so often, I'd run into mutual friends. Though his name always came up in conversation, I hesitated before asking for the details I so desperately wanted to know.

After about ten years I took a risk. I wanted to see him again, so when I ran into a mutual friend, I offered my number and prayed it would reach him.

After a few weeks, he called me. At first I did not recognize his voice, but within seconds I knew my plan had worked. I immediately was transformed into a young giddy high school girl all over again. We both spoke as if the years had never passed. But it didn't take long for reality to sink into the conversation. We were both married. We said our good-byes, but clearly without closing the door behind us.

Little by little we began cracking it open. It started as friendly phone calls and an occasional lunch. That was safe enough, or so we tried to fool ourselves. But soon it was like being back in high school; I felt the same desperate need to see him, to hear him, and especially to touch him. I started to long for his phone calls. That's when I knew I was in trouble.

Our encounters became an escape and I was a fugitive from my own life. We made love every chance we could. The sex was amazing, but the intimate connection is what fulfilled my desires. Our affair allowed me to run away from my daily grind. We shared our frustrations and tried to figure out our spouses and our kids. I began to lead a double life. Initially it felt right. We were the only thing that mattered. There was us and only us. Sometimes planning the escape was part of the fun. We were consumed by years of repressed love. We became a part of each other's lives in as many stolen moments as possible. It lasted for years.

It wasn't easy covering my tracks. I took lots of showers in the middle of the day. I couldn't risk leaving traces. There were elaborate excuses, to my husband, my bosses, and myself. There were countless hotel rooms, motel rooms, and the back of the car. Our mission was to meet anywhere we could and whenever we could.

After a while, primal lust gave way to the real world. The guilt sank in. How could I have been unfaithful? How could I have lied to my child? How would my family feel if my secret got out? Would my husband understand I was seeking comfort and an escape from the daily routine? Would he understand that unfinished business needed closure?

I was trapped. I couldn't leave my husband, but I did not want to disrupt my pretend world either. My home life gave me the security I needed. Peace and comfort can become addictive. The weird part is that I still loved my husband and didn't want to leave him. I'm not sure how I was able to compartmentalize my life for so long. I had attempted to live a lie, a fairy tale, but as everybody knows, eventually make-believe stories come to an end.

My lover figured it out. He knew my heart was still at home and I was not going to leave my husband, so he ended it with me. Eventually, he summoned up the courage to leave his wife, although it had nothing to do with me.

Losing him for the second time was even more devastating. I ended up on antidepressants, lonely and despondent. I had lost my only true refuge. I found myself grieving in silence and secrecy. It almost killed me.

But eventually, the wound *did* heal. That's why that holiday surprise phone call knocked me for a loop. It seems he hasn't quite gotten over me he said. He still misses me and still holds a place for me in his heart. His voice no longer has the same disarming effect on my heart. It doesn't hurt anymore. Although I didn't know quite what to say, I invited him to a lunch that he politely declined.

Thank God! Some doors are better left shut. Lest our demons decide to barge in.

seven

Do You Believe?

All of us Miami Bombshells know that it's not necessarily important *what* you believe, but *that* you believe in something, and that those beliefs bring you comfort and peace when you need them. It's taken a while for that philosophy to form; some of us have searched more eagerly than others, a few going along for the ride.

The leaders in the pursuit for spirituality are Pat and Mercedes, who may very well be the *angeles guardianes* (guardian angels) in our group. Mercedes, though the rest of us usually don't know about it, will do special prayers for the group before or after our get-togethers, especially when things get tough for one of us. And she's not shy about handing out power objects to help the others deal with personal trauma.

At one point or another, Pat dragged Tammi and Annie to her sweat lodge with Raoul the Brazilian Indian. Pat has this thing about Indians, swears she was one in a previous life. Pat was wearing feathered jewelry trimmed in turquoise long before it hit the Limited or J.Crew. Although she does aerobics once in a while, it's the monthly Lakota Indian lodges where she sweats pounds off her J.Lo *pompis* in an attempt at cleansing her spirit.

For the most part, Lydia and Annie are still the quintessential

Cuban girls, consumed with Catholic guilt, whose spiritual paths consist of going to Spanish mass on Sundays to pray for the good, ward off the bad, and beg for the forgiveness of all their sins. At a recent Bombshell lunch gathering, Annie admitted, "Lydia and I may not believe in all the myths and superstitions of our Cuban Catholic culture, like putting our purses down on the floor will make us broke, or pinning an onyx stone to a baby's clothing will ward off the evil eye, but we still repeat them anyway, just in case. You have to respect that stuff."

"You guys are so guilt-ridden and programmed to believe what you were raised to believe," quips Pat.

"Maybe," replied Lydia, "but I did feel the Virgin Mary when I traveled to Conyers, and that's no more weird than what happened to you and Mercedes in Peru."

Tammi and Sara? They still roll their eyes when Mercedes and Pat start talking about their mystical experiences in the middle of the Peruvian Andes. They're those twice-a-year synagogue Jews who didn't believe in much of anything until they had children and found they had to pass on their values, even those they still hadn't settled on, to their rapidly forming offspring. Tammi's opened her mind a lot recently. At first we thought it was the yoga, but now we're convinced it's the lover and spiritual partner she had been living with who is lighting the way. She's even agreed to let Mercedes and Pat do a spiritual sage cleansing of her new home. "It can't hurt." If only she could find the time.

Sara's philosophy is rather simple: she believes in whatever makes her feel better. It gives her comfort to think that everything happens for a reason; otherwise, she'd obsess about the "whys" and "what ifs" (actually, she does that anyway, but she'd do it more). She's amazed at the complexity of the world and wouldn't be surprised if all of the things that Pat and Mercedes talk about are real; she just needs a little more proof. But, if you listen closely when Sara's around, you might hear her spirituality banging at the door.

Revelations from the Virgin

LYDIA

Planning our first trip away with our three-year-old daughter, I had no idea that the next few days were going to change my life forever. This was to be a spiritual journey to Conyers, Georgia, a small town where apparitions of the Virgin Mary were supposed to be taking place, and we wanted to see this miracle for ourselves.

We spent our first night in a delightful bed-and-breakfast and got up before dawn to try and beat the crowds, which were getting bigger each day as word of this spiritual vision began to spread.

The ride to Conyers took us off the freeway and down a country dirt road framed in beautiful, lush vegetation. The day was crisp and the cloudless blue sky added to a calmness that started to wrap itself around me. When we finally arrived at our destination, we parked inside a maze of cars and carried our cooler and sleeping bags through shaded pathways that took us to an open field. We had no idea what we were looking for, but the excitement began to build as we approached the cottage where the apparitions had been said to take place. We claimed our spot among the hundreds of people staking out their few feet of space. My husband was completely skeptical of the whole thing, but standing by me devotedly, as I waited for this epiphany that was sure to come.

Only those who were physically inside the cottage would experience the actual apparition. The anxiety began to build within me, and I began to sense the anticipation of the crowd as they waited patiently to see if a miracle was really going to occur.

And then, out of nowhere, it *happened*. Someone announced that we should look up at the sky, so we focused on the sun, astonished that we could actually stare at the blazing star with our naked eyes. A gray halo began developing around the sun, and, within a few seconds, it began to pulsate and spin wildly. We looked at each other in awe, as the people around us seemed to be enmeshed in their own sacred moments. Each person reacted differently and many fell to their knees crying at the sight of the unexplained halo in the sky. Surely this had to mean something, though we had no idea what. Minutes later, when I finally looked away, I noticed that everything appeared to be surrounded by a golden orb. It was as if I was looking at the world through fourteen-karat-gold-tinted glasses. My rosary, the trees, the leaves, even the people all looked as if they had been dipped in gold. A wonderful sense of peace took over my mind and body, but it scared me to death. I didn't need to go into the cottage to see the Virgin Mary. I was feeling her spirit right here in the middle of this field.

"You're so silly," my doubting spouse told me. "It is just the reflection of the sun." And just as he was finishing expressing his customary lack of faith, I heard a voice, which seemed to echo from inside my head. It told me, over and over again, "You are pregnant. You will experience difficulties and there will be some problems. But you will be fine." I didn't know if I was imagining things or if I had been overly inspired with the whole experience and was allowing myself to be carried away, but it scared me to death.

I was in total shock. To begin with, I don't normally hear voices in my head. More important, I had absolutely no plans of having another child. I was almost thirty-eight years old with two children, the eldest already in his twenties.

When I recovered from the incident, I told my husband what I had just heard. I knew he would think I was overreacting, and I was right. He didn't believe any of it and told me so.

It was hard to believe this strange phenomenon was just a hallucination; it just seemed too real. When we left the field, I insisted that we go to a drugstore to buy a pregnancy test. With grave doubts and some reluctance, my husband agreed.

When we returned to the hotel, much to our surprise, the EPT results were positive. They said that I was pregnant. But Mario wasn't convinced so he went back to the pharmacy and purchased a second kit, which confirmed the news again. We were both caught off guard.

During the next few days of our vacation, I started to feel ill. I was getting more and more debilitated as each hour passed. Morning sickness hit me 24/7 and the flight back home was a nightmare. I tried to think positively but it was hopeless. I was sicker than I had ever been in my life.

Once we reached home, I got worse and worse. My clothes were becoming looser each day, and the accelerating weight loss was becoming a concern to my husband and to all our family and friends. I visited a specialist who assured me it was just a bad case of morning sickness. All I craved were Popsicles and ice chips, which I lived on for weeks.

Sixteen weeks into the pregnancy, I finally began to feel like myself again. The constant nausea was fading, and for the first time, I could walk into a restaurant and not gag at the smell of garlic and onions.

When it was time to go for an amniocentesis, my husband and my niece (typical Cuban entourage) filed into the room. The discomfort was minimal but the feeling of the long needle penetrating my womb was chilling. The doctor was pleased with the simplicity of the process and proudly announced that the baby was a boy. My husband and I were thrilled.

I followed the doctor's orders and stayed home for the rest of the day, relaxing and watching TV. And then it happened. I started leaking. I was terrified. I immediately called the doctor, who sent me right to the hospital. My mind was fast-forwarding to all the worst-case scenarios.

By the time we arrived, the discharge was pouring down my legs. I was whisked away for a sonogram and I began to question the technician about his findings. He advised me that only my doctor could provide me with that information, which wasn't the consoling news I was hoping for. My worrying nature took over and my entire body started to shake.

When the doctor eventually came in to see me, she delivered the bad news. My baby's amniotic sac had ruptured and lost a large amount of fluid. She gave me two choices: to terminate the pregnancy immediately or risk having the sac seal itself back up. She warned that if I opted for the latter, I would risk the possibility of a dangerous infection, which could ultimately be fatal. Her recommendation? To end the pregnancy.

But that was not even an option. I believed in my heart that my unborn son deserved a chance to live. I wanted him to get to know the world I loved and to be a part of our tight-knit family. I wanted him to have the chance to be my son, and me, to be his mother.

I spent the next few weeks on total bed rest. I took my temperature every thirty minutes to make sure I wasn't getting an infection. That was the greatest risk; if an infection set in, the pregnancy would need to be terminated immediately.

I was now in the hands of a neonatal specialist, and every single week, sonogram after sonogram, the amniotic fluid was measured with positive results. Day by day, the tiny baby in my womb struggled to survive.

My husband and young daughter teamed up to keep me comfortable. They catered to my every whim and pampered me as only family can. My husband was concerned that he would hurt me in his sleep, so he moved to a sleeping bag on the floor of our room. My daughter joined him with her Minnie Mouse sleeping bag and they watched me sleep, my belly moving with each breath. Mario taught Christine to rejoice in each pound I gained, and we were all happy to see that I was making progress.

On July 19, 1994, my beautiful son, Andres, was born, weighing in at more than nine pounds, measuring twenty-one inches long. During that difficult pregnancy, it was my deep faith in God that gave me the strength to believe all would turn out OK. I truly believe it was He who blessed me with this gift of life. On that gorgeous day in Conyers, Georgia, when the Virgin Mary delivered the news that I was pregnant, I really wanted to believe, but wasn't really sure

I could. It was the last part of her direct message that gave me hope and helped me endure the darkest hours of that tough pregnancy. Eventually, the mother of Jesus promised, I would be fine. And thanks to her, Andres is.

Spirit

PATRICIA

I was raised Catholic even though my mom was Jewish. She was pretty much forced to convert to marry my dad, otherwise his mother threatened to boycott the wedding. How's that for tolerance?

When I was young, I was given the choice: be Catholic or Jewish, but not both. I chose Catholicism. I have no idea why. It's not as if they taught me about both religions, then let me make an educated decision. I think I picked it because most of my Catholic friends were having cool Communion parties.

We had little money when I was growing up, so I went to public school for most of my life. But for four years, I went to the very Catholic St. Patrick's on the very Jewish Miami Beach. The best thing that came from that? The sisters I met. Not the nuns, but the dear lifelong friends I made there.

I never really got into the whole religious thing. Mass was always a bore, but I made it through by playing the guitar in church, which made it bearable. I just never understood the "we're born as sinners" thing. You mean to tell me we're "bad" even before we're born? At least give me a chance to be wicked, let me have fun being bad, *and then* call me a sinner. I can deal with that. And let's not even get into who is doing the sinning at church these days. I wonder what God has to say about that.

They never really explained to me *why* women can't be priests. Or why we have to go through a priest to talk to God. Why can't priests get married? And why can't we get divorced? And why can't women living in poverty with five children use birth control? I don't get it.

I guess I'm culturally Catholic, but these days I call myself a Universalist. I believe in the underlying principles of most religions. Maybe if we gather the essential wisdoms from all faiths and meld them all together, then we'll get a little closer to the Real Truth.

I believe much more in spirituality than in religion. In my opinion, religious institutions have one major downside—humans lead them. Usually it's greedy humans with a thirst for power, money, and control.

And if you don't believe what others believe, or if you misinterpret their teachings, watch out. See how quickly turning the other cheek becomes slashing each other's throat, literally or figuratively. Talk about a dichotomy. That's why I've been pursuing my own path.

Since I was a child I've had this mysterious connection with the Indian tradition. I didn't exactly grow up socializing with them in Havana. In fact there are no Indians left in Cuba because the Spaniards killed them all. And we Americans didn't exactly break bread with the Miccosukee or Seminole tribes who we've practically pushed out of South Florida. The closest we've come to embracing them is going to their casinos to gamble, or on their airboat rides to peek at their world as if they were some sort of circus freaks.

But the connection was always there for me. When I was four, I collected pennies and gave them to my mom, asking her to send them to the poor Indian children. Today I understand where that came from.

Time and experience have led me to accept the idea that there's more to life than what meets the eye. I've also grown to believe that if reincarnation is a reality, then I'm sure I've been Indian at least once in my past lives.

A few years ago, my Bombshell friend Mercedes told me about a precious little New Age store called the Fairy's Ring in historic

Coral Gables where they offer weekly Reiki sessions. That's when skilled masters donate their time to perform energy healings on people who need them. I was curious.

I wasn't familiar with this form of healing, but since I'm always looking for alternative spiritual viewpoints, I gave it a chance. My mind was more open those days but I didn't want to be completely surprised or overwhelmed, so I did a bit of research and learned that Reiki is one of the most common and ancient forms of energy healings.

It involves direct application of chi for the purpose of strengthening one's energy system. Chi, according to my readings, is the underlying energy force of the universe.

All a Reiki master actually does is place his or her hands upon the person to be healed with the intent for healing to occur, and the energy is supposed to begin to flow. It sounds strange, but I've been told that "intent" is the most important part of the process.

I decided to give it a chance. I walked into the Fairy's Ring, a bit apprehensive, but trying to remain open to the new experience. I was greeted by an Indian man with the most intense and piercing eyes I had ever seen. He was short, about five foot six, with long, thick black hair slicked back into a ponytail. But what drew me in was his wide beautiful smile. His skin was the color of a strong cup of tea. He looked native, as in Native American, but had an accent that I could not place. His name was Raoul.

He was one of the Reiki masters I had come to see. He was born in the Brazilian Amazon but truly embedded, spiritually, in the North American Indian tradition. We immediately connected, and I was fascinated by that, as if I'd known him my entire life. My early childhood preoccupation with Indians was finally coming full circle, and I could actually sense that through him, I would be learning and experiencing more of the native traditions that captivated me.

The Reiki session with Raoul was wonderful. I joined a group of about ten people and we sat in a circle, closed our eyes, and meditated as the Reiki masters took their turn on each one of us. Raoul performed Reiki on me. The heat emanating from his hands was intense. When it was over, I felt wonderful. I had come into the session agitated by a workweek that was overwhelming. After the Reiki session, I felt much more at ease and completely relaxed.

Reiki became a weekly thing for me; and whether it was all in my head or it was real, I didn't care. I felt good after Reiki, and that's all that mattered. As Raoul and I got to know each other and he learned about my interest in the Indian ways he told me about his "other life" as a Fire Keeper in a Lakota sweat lodge and invited me to attend.

Eventually, I accepted his invitation. Dressed in shorts and a tank top, I arrived at my first lodge, a bit nervous, not knowing quite what to expect. As I walked up to the small crowd that was gathered, Raoul greeted me warmly and then introduced me to Grandmother Barrett Eaglebear, a striking, tall, and imposing Cherokee woman.

She is the holy one who "pours the water" at this traditional Indian sweat lodge (called an "Inipi" in their native Lakota language). She embraced me and immediately recognized my need to evolve spiritually. She comfortably welcomed me into the family.

As others came up to greet me, I noticed what looked like an igloo in the middle of a small open field. This igloo was made from willow branches and canvas. Raoul explained that the way the branches are set up invokes the four directions, representing the entire universe including all the living beings: the two-legged, the four-legged, the winged, and the finned; all the things of the world are contained within it to be purified before they can send a prayer to what he called the Wakan Tanka (Great Spirit/God). It's all part of the Indian rite that literally means "renew life." It's a very powerful way to pray and connect with God, All That Is, Spirit, or whatever you want to call It.

The Inipi calls on the power and spirits of the four elements—earth, fire, water, and air—and it honors the never-ending circle of life. The ceremony, full of Native American tradition, cleanses, purifies, and heals those who participate.

Raoul, the Fire Keeper of this lodge, is in charge of the fire and the heating of the stones that are to be used in the ceremony. It is a position of honor to be a Fire Keeper. The stones represent the great power of God, which gives life to all things. They are heated in a sacred fire outside the lodge until they turn molten red. I was getting a little worried as I noticed how hot the stones actually got, when Grandmother Eaglebear motioned that it was time to enter the lodge. She told me to follow her in. I took a deep breath to calm my nerves and followed her lead.

I got on my hands and knees and crawled in on all fours. The ceiling was so low there was no other way. Everyone else came in after us. Once inside, we sat around a pit in the center of the lodge, which was really a big, circular tent. Grandmother explained how the pit represents the center of the universe, and after everyone was squished together inside, Raoul carried the rocks into the lodge. One by one, the sacred stones were placed within the pit and it started to get hot.

The canvas flap to the lodge was then closed and we sat in total darkness and prayed to ourselves. The place was heating up fast and there were so many people in there, my heart started to beat faster and faster. I concentrated on breathing slowly and tried to concentrate on not passing out. That would be just too embarrassing.

When Grandmother began her beautiful prayers in Lakota, I began to calm down. It was too dark to see, but I heard her pour some water over the burning rocks and with that came the steam; scorching, intense, blistering steam. I felt like I was in an old Turkish bath, but this was so much hotter, and the feeling much more intense.

In the Inipi, the steam is so hot that you sweat from pores you don't even know you have. I wasn't sure how I was going to be able to breathe, until I realized that "sweating" is as much an act of spirituality as of self-control. I'd been told that if I panicked, I should bring my face to the dirt and breathe from down there. Since steam rises, the air near the ground is always cool. Somehow, I slowed down my breathing and was able to keep from passing out.

Throughout the lodge, we prayed openly and to ourselves. The others sang songs in Lakota and we all rejoiced in life. We cleansed our spirits as well as our bodies through the sweat and prayers. At the end of the ceremony, we smoked the sacred pipe as Grandmother explained to me, the only newcomer, that the smoke carries our prayers up to Great Spirit.

When it was over, after about thirty minutes, I crawled out, and felt as if I was leaving a womb, feeling alive, happy, and rejuvenated (and soaked down to my panties!). It was an exhilarating and spiritual experience that I knew I would soon make a regular part of my life. Entering that Indian temple was a life-altering experience. As they say at the lodge, "There's only one thing that will change after you sweat: everything."

This experience jump-started my connection to the Indian tradition. And through it, I felt like I had finally found my roots. Although it took forty plus years for me to find this path, I really felt at home.

I've even dragged a few of my Bombshell friends to the sweats at one time or another, figuring it would be a terrific experience to share. At one of our Bombshell meetings, Tammi confessed that she let me take her because she figured that at the very least, she might lose a few pounds. I rolled my eyes, ". . . but I never dreamed that I'd get anything spiritual out of it," admitted Tammi. "I didn't exactly buy into all the weird rituals but I tried to keep an open mind. When I crawled in, I just let go and I really felt like I was the only one in the tent. I could have stayed in there forever."

"Wow," laughed Sara, "she converted!!!"

"Very funny, Ms. I'll believe-in-whatever-works-for-me-today . . . it was actually a very powerful experience."

"She's right," agreed Annie, who went with Pat to another sweat. "Being a Catholic, I hoped that I would not be committing a sin, so I convinced myself it was just like a prayer group . . . in a very unusual setting."

Everyone cracked up. Tammi chuckled, "Oh Annie, you're so guilt-ridden."

Annie agreed. "Yeah . . . you're right, but it worked for me. Inside the sweat as they prayed and sang in Lakota, I prayed an 'Our Father.' The whole experience was actually very moving, and left me feeling physically and emotionally cleansed."

My Bombshell friends, for the most part, have come to accept this part of me, but my family, of course, thinks I'm nuts. They constantly remind me that they wish their White/Catholic/Jewish/Cuban daughter would find a different, more sterile spiritual journey, one that doesn't involve strange energy healings or releasing bodily fluids in a sweat lodge alongside "them strangers." Actually they should be happy I'm not on drugs to help me cope with life, and I only hope that one day they will come to respect my attempts at spiritual growth.

So, now . . . I sweat and I continue going to Reiki. One night, during a Reiki session, I had a vision. As I sat in meditation, I saw Raoul and myself, as Indians, smoking a pipe in a sacred ceremony in front of a tepee. We were not alone.

An eagle circled above us and a wolf stood watch. In my vision, Raoul was wearing an exquisite camel-colored Indian jacket, with unique colored beading and long fringes hanging from the sleeves.

When the session finished, noticing the blank look in my eyes, Raoul asked, "Where did you go?" I told him what I'd seen and described every item in detail. That's when he took me to his car to show me something he had brought from home, and planned to show me after the session, something he had made years before. It was *exactly* the same jacket I saw in my vision. I cried.

Last year, at one of the sweats, I was honored when Barrett Eaglebear presented me with my own prayer pipe. The beautiful red stone pipe had been made by hand with love for me, by none other than Raoul.

The circle closes.

All these "unusual" experiences are helping me to find my own way. I try to create value with my life and to be happy. I attempt to connect with Spirit, the earth, and all living creatures every day, somehow. Now, I have even learned to perform healings so I can help others. I urge my friends to sweat, chant, pray, meditate, read, or do whatever feels right to them. The important thing is to dedicate some time every day to whatever daily discipline can help feed their souls. Most important, I remind them to be open for whatever comes their way. Because it wasn't until I was able to open my mind that I shut out the doubt.

Epiphany

MERCEDES

I'm not some evangelical missionary out to convert the world. In fact, I don't purport to exact much change in others, other than in myself. I actually started off as your run-of-the-mill atheist. Black and white, yes and no, just the facts, ma'am. Not even a Jesuit College education could convince me of the preposterous idea of a Higher Being meddling in my affairs. That's probably one of the reasons I became a journalist, because I only cared for the facts.

But eventually I was humbled, brought right down to size. I inadvertently stumbled into an experience so wondrous that it brought my whole set of beliefs tumbling to a thunderous crash and turned my carefully constructed world upside down. It was April of 1994. I had been sent on a press junket to a place in South America that had always captivated me. What I didn't expect was that this time, it would beguile me.

I'm on the train again on my way to Machu Picchu. Funny, I've been dreaming of this place ever since I left in April and now, only a couple of hours away, the anxiety I felt leaving Miami somehow left me. I feel at peace, happy. That angst of the past few months has become an obsession. I am gripped with understanding just exactly what happened to me the last time I was here, what was it that was so intense, so real, so unbelievable in my capacity to comprehend as to make me think that I was going crazy, what, what, what? What the heck was that?

This begins the story of what brought me to come back to the land of the Incas. I got off the plane in Lima at five in the morning. It was the red-eye and I was exhausted. I met up with the group, half a dozen or so journalists from different parts of the United States and Latin America. American Airlines was sponsoring the trip to promote its South American routes.

The government of Peru had just captured the elusive Abimael Guzmán, a bloodthirsty leader of the Shining Path movement, and was trying to attract tourism after decades of corruption and domestic terrorism had eroded the economy. My network thought the time was ripe to revisit the country, from a foreign correspondent's point of view, even though we had a bureau in Lima. The reporter who was scheduled to take the trip couldn't make it, so I was asked to fill in at the last minute. It was a "see what you can bring back" kind of a deal, no built-in agenda or even set stories to investigate.

I met up with Pat San Pedro, the American Airlines liaison who had put the trip together. We introduced ourselves with half-hearted pleasantries and went over to the hotel to sleep for a couple of hours, shower, have breakfast, and start a tour. Everything seemed normal enough. We saw the great square in old downtown Lima surrounded by the Palace of Government, the cathedral with the famed conquistador Francisco Pizarro still entombed inside, and the beautifully wood-carved Spanish balconies that make this one of the most well-preserved colonial main squares in Latin America.

We visited the gory catacombs in the basement of another church, the gold museum full of Incan artifacts, and the trendy Miraflores and San Isidro Districts and ended the day at a cocktail party hobnobbing with presidential advisers. Naturally, I put in the most persuasive request I could to interview then-president Alberto Fujimori and went back to the hotel to finally get some sleep.

The next morning we arrived at the airport by 5:30 A.M. and were in Cuzco an hour and a half after that. The flight was breathtaking. Even though I'd been to the Swiss Alps, the French Pyrenees, and the Rockies in Colorado, no other mountain range had ever had the capacity to awe me as the Andes did. And Cuzco was at the center of it all, the belly button of the world according to the Incas. This was the city where one of the greatest Indian empires was built and lost, and where great spiritual traditions were not only born but also, unbeknownst to me, still practiced.

At the hotel we drank coca tea to ward off *soroche* or altitude sickness. We toured the colonial city, including the impressive Cathedral of Santo Domingo where the old Qorikancha Temple shook off its Spanish façade and revealed its Incan foundations during an earthquake a few decades back. According to legend, this was the beginning of the unraveling of an ancient prophecy that would one day be revealed in front of my rolling cameras. But I don't want to get ahead of myself.

That night, as we tried to get some sleep before the 4:00 A.M. wake-up call for the train to Machu Picchu, my life began to change. I couldn't sleep. A repetitive word kept hammering at my awareness without my even knowing its meaning. It was *oraculo,* the Spanish word for oracle. Because I hadn't yet studied much Greek mythology, I really didn't know what it meant, let alone its translation into Spanish. But it just didn't let up, strangely keeping me up all night. The following morning I was intrigued to learn that no one else from the group had slept either! We all just chalked it up to the altitude.

Before I left Miami, I had contacted Univision's Lima bureau for information on someone to interview at Macchu Picchu. I was planning to do a historical piece on the place. But the bureau didn't send me an anthropologist or archaeologist who specialized on the ruins. Noooo, they sent me a foul-smelling Qechua Indian named Q'enqo who spoke broken Spanish and whom I'd briefly met the previous day at a visit to Saqsayhuaman, another historical Incan ruin in Cuzco. I had thought him a little slow in the head after he told me to warm my hands by the huge boulders that make up the monolith. He claimed the rocks absorbed heat during the day and could warm me in the Andean evening, as the air grew colder. Duh!

He later told me that there were special priests who worked at these "holy sites" to tap their "magical" powers and could do incredible things like heal a person who was sick far away in another country. I dismissed him as a third world nitwit. He offered to introduce me to such a person and I said *muy bién* just to be polite, "tonight after dinner." But I quickly changed my mind, blowing off the appointment without as much as an afterthought. I lingered after dinner enjoying conversations with new acquaintances. I didn't think that in this place, Western punctuality or even courtesy calls were necessary. After all, this was the land of *mañana* and these were just Indians. Who would even care?

Sure enough, when I saw Q'enqo again the next morning he didn't even seem offended. He showed up at my hotel lobby and was happily waiting to accompany me to Machu Picchu, dressed in frayed rags that reeked of urine. Phew! The rest of the group looked at me in disbelief. Could I not come up with someone better, more dignified to put on TV? I was unapologetic, as is usually my nature. But I did catch myself becoming irate as the train conductor forbade my guest from riding with me in the first-class section of the cabin and instead herded him like a steer to the second-class compartment. There was a clear class chasm in Peru I had never experienced, though I knew it existed. Indians were considered second-class indigents even if they were clean, well dressed, and educated.

We finally made it to Machu Picchu. It had been a cloudy day that in no way detracted from the majestic beauty of the trip. The train meanders through the jungle as it winds its way around the Urubamba River, a tributary of the legendary Amazon. There are sections of the trip where you can actually see portions of the old Inca Trail, a precursor to our highways. The road was built throughout the Andes and was used by the Incas in sort of relay races to move goods and information across their vast kingdom throughout most of South America.

After zigzagging the mountains in the 1950s-era steam engine train for about three hours, we arrived at Aguas Calientes. There we took a bus ride to the top of the world.

We went into the ruins with a small group of tourists. It was late and we only had that afternoon to film since we'd be returning the following day. The cloudy skies didn't clear up and as soon as we set up the gear to start the shoot it started to rain. "Damn." I was tired, sleepy, hungry, and not so thrilled about this stinky Indian following my every move. We waited. The rain stopped. We set up again. It started to pour. We stopped again. Then, my cameraman had a novel idea. He cynically joked that the Indian ought to be able to do some kind of a rain dance to stop the downpour.

I, of course, concurred, and mockingly suggested this to Q'enqo. He agreed! "Sure, *mamita,* I can do that," he told me. Well, if I wasn't having a lousy day already the whole *mamita* thing almost took me over the edge. *Mamita* literally means little mom, but it also has sexual connotations meaning "babe" and let's just say where I come from I wouldn't let anyone call me *mamita.* But, I was very far from where I come from and from what I thought I knew, as I was about to find out.

Q'enqo opened the shoulder bag he had been carrying, took out a half conch, what I mistook to be dried herbs, and set them on fire inside the shell. He then took out a flute and started to play a five-to ten-note repetitive melody. It poured even harder. We took cover one more time and sheltered the equipment. He went inside a small hut and continued his ritual. After about a half hour, the rain stopped. And this time it stopped for good. We came out of hiding, set up the gear again, and got ready to interview him. I joked that whatever he did worked. "It would've worked a lot sooner, mamita, if you had only had faith." Me, faith? I rolled my eyes at the insult and started the interview.

"So, I hear Machu Picchu was the seat of Incan political power. What can you tell me about how this place was run?" I asked.

"No, mamita, this was the Temple of the Virgins of the Sun," he answered.

"The what?" I asked.

"Young girls were brought here to live and learn how to become priestesses. Then they were taken to the sundial, where they would look up to the sun and a golden ray would impregnate them. The one who gave birth to a boy with a third eye would later help that boy to rule the kingdom," he told me.

Sounded to me like a new twist on the Virgin Mary begetting Jesus through the Holy Spirit. "Well that's not the story I've heard. How do you know this, being that the Incas didn't even have a written language?" I inquired.

"Because I hear them talking" he said.

"Who do you hear?" I prompted him.

"The people who lived here," he answered.

"What do they say?" I asked, beginning to lose my patience.

"That we're in the first world and that in many, many years, when we enter the third world we will all have feathers."

What is he rambling about? was the thought swirling in my head. Did our bureau send me a nutcase on top of someone with an obvious lack of hygiene?

Just as Q'enqo said this, a small black bird came flying up from the ravine next to where we were sitting, circled behind his head and in front of my face. The camera, of course, was rolling. I have it all on tape. *What a weird coincidence,* I thought. But it piqued my curiosity. After we finished, when I asked to take generic video of him in the ruins for editing purposes, Q'enqo insisted on taking me to the sundial he had discussed earlier and then to another altar, one he thought I especially needed to see.

I came before the Pachamama stone late into the afternoon. Q'enqo told me that this was a very special altar because it was female. He then offered to do a coca reading for me in front of it. I acquiesced, to put it on tape, as I had already figured out that I was going to have to produce a much more folkloric type of report than I had anticipated. He pulled the coca leaves (the herbs I had seen earlier) from a small pouch and threw them onto a piece of woven cloth. "Two children," he said. "Your family is fine. You are going to be fine." *Yeah right,* I thought to myself, *my father has cancer, he's probably dying, and I neither have nor want any children.* Whatever!

"What else does the coca say?" I asked in jest.

"That you don't believe in anything, mamita, that you don't believe in anyone."

"Well, you finally got something right," I said without much care, in my best holier-than-thou attitude. "Thanks for everything, I'll see you at the train station tomorrow," I said waving him off.

"But I need some money, mamita," he protested.

"I'm sorry, I don't pay for interviews," I reprimanded him.

"It's just to stay at the *albergue* (mountain hut) and to buy bread and tea," he answered softly in a Spanish as tattered as his clothes.

"I can only give you ten dollars, and it'll be a present not payment," I said, becoming even more arrogant, if that was possible.

"That's enough, mamita," he smiled.

"And if I'm going to pay for your stay overnight, then I'll need you again here first thing in the morning to shoot more video."

"That's fine, mamita."

I was up again up at 4 A.M. We had decided to stay at the Pueblo Inn in Aguas Calientes instead of the hotel right outside the ruins. It was another half-hour bus ride to make it to the top before the sun came up, and two hours before the place opened up to tourists. We wanted to shoot the stillness of Machu Picchu in its solitude and its majesty.

Our hope was to recapture its serenity without the throngs of tourists, water bottles, and trash, knowing quite well that our report, beamed to about a hundred million viewers across the United States, Canada, Latin America, and parts of Europe, would only generate more visits and contribute to the eventual decimation of this ancient jewel.

And, for one small moment, we did capture the unspoiled essence of a time and a place before the white man "discovered" (to the indigenous people it had never been lost) one of South America's best-kept treasures.

We entered Machu Picchu as the first rays of daylight began to foretell the coming of a very bright and crisp winter morning. We were at a higher altitude than the clouds, and their mist shrouded us in the mystery of the mountain. Several lazy llamas were lying sleepily at the entrance to the ruins and they reminded me of sentinels guarding the passage to a forbidden secret. Q'enqo was the first one in. He stopped at the narrow stone passage that is the entrance, held out his arms, and touched both sides of the walls. He turned full circle and then entered. He warned us to do the same so as to "not bring anything into the ruins or take anything out."

"What could you possibly be talking about?" I asked.

"*Espíritus,* mamita," the Spirits, he said.

I had the cameraman follow him to shoot more video while I planned to relax in the ruins for the rest of the morning. But just then Parisina, one of the other journalists in the group, who had become fascinated by everything Q'enqo had said during my interview, asked me to join her at the Pachamama stone. She wanted to meditate at the altar but was afraid to go alone. So, I indulged her, just to spite the old Indian and prove to myself that there was nothing special about the place. I climbed up on top of the altar, deliberately profaning it, and just stood there. But, despite my best attempts at sneering at the alleged supernatural powers of Machu Picchu, I began to notice a strange attraction.

Before long, I started to feel the mammoth stone pulling me in, almost magnetically. It was a very strong, yet gentle draw. I put my arms on it, so as to resist, but the force of the pull continued. So began an invisible tug-of-war, a mano a mano with the Pachamama until I was face-to-face with her, my nose crunching under my breath. I was feeling light-headed.

A crazy notion came over me that at that moment I could either fly or get out of my body as I had heard some people claim they could do. But my mind kept saying, "No way is this really happening. Get a grip." Yet I couldn't or wouldn't escape the attraction. I stayed there until suddenly my head started pulling away from the wall, but my waist remained somehow attached to it. I started arching backward with my arms extended in an open and embracing pose. Farther back my body went, and I was convinced that I could just let myself go and levitate over the Andes.

The overarching caused my body to tremble and my throat to let out guttural and embarrassing sounds as a soft yellow orb swirled in my mind's eye. I don't remember how long I stood engulfed in that bizarre daze. But the feeling eventually diminished and brought me back to my senses.

I had no vision, except for the true conviction that I could have let go and flown. Of course, my reasoning, objective, journalistically trained mind tethered me down. It kept saying. "This isn't possible, this isn't happening, you're imagining or hallucinating and you're going to fall . . . Stop." And I did, out of fear of the unknown. But not without feeling that I had somehow connected to an energy, a power, a state of consciousness or reality I had neither expected nor ever believed actually existed. Until that moment.

The euphoria of the experience gave way to exhilaration, then to a realization that I had maybe stumbled into something strange and real and mind-boggling. Then it gave way again to fear and finally to denial. But that denial was hard to reason with after hearing stories from others in the group who experienced some pretty riveting experiences of their own. Pat had also witnessed some pretty unusual events, I came to learn.

Pat had left Machu Picchu late that morning with two rocks. Wandering through the ruins thinking of her mother, who had died of cancer, she felt compelled to pick up these stones that she claimed "called out to her." I didn't learn about this until I got to Cuzco, after I confided details of my extraordinary Pachamama experience to her. The rocks she took were both shaped in the form of triangles or had trapezoidal lines in them. "They look like small pyramids," I offered casually.

That night, our last one in Cuzco, we all met again in the hotel lobby to go out to dinner. Pat was anxiously awaiting my arrival to show me her forehead. "Oh, my God! You have a pyramid on your forehead," I screamed. Other members of the group had also seen it and were waiting for my reaction. I gasped, and couldn't believe my eyes. It looked as if someone had pressed a cookie cutter against her skin and made the deep indentations. "Yes," she said, "I noticed them as I came out of the shower."

"Well, don't worry about it too much. You probably just got too much sun," I added, trying to convince her and myself that it was nothing unusual.

We laughed off the pyramids at dinner. But the lines never waned. In fact, Pat seemed tired and weak until she excused herself to go to the bathroom. After about a half hour, when she didn't return, I went to look for her. I found her vomiting up her innards and looking like death had warmed her over. I helped clean her up, she excused herself, and we all went back to the hotel.

Throughout the night, Parisina and I stayed with Pat in her room and tried to nurse her back to health. I really felt the need to help this woman, though I barely knew her. I offered some of the medicine I had brought with me, but nothing worked. Pat continued to vomit for hours. She later confessed that she felt so horrible that night, she actually thought she was about to die and was embarrassed at the thought of how difficult it would be for the rest of us to transport her body from the Andes to Lima and back to Miami.

After a while, Parisina, who had also experienced a strange encounter with the Pachamama, and had talked about it on the train, asked about the stones. "You shouldn't have taken them out of Machu Picchu," she told Pat. "That is sacred ground. They need to go back." I jumped in to help this poor woman, who, at this point, was grayer than anyone I had ever seen. "Well, we can't very well go back to Machu Picchu; there has to be another way," I rebutted. By this time, a couple of hours had passed and Pat had stopped vomiting so violently. "Where are the stones?" I asked her. She pointed to a little pouch next to her nightstand and I handed it to her. As she opened the bag and let the stones fall into the palm of her hand, the vomiting resumed, almost immediately. I grabbed the stones with a cloth, not wanting them to touch my own skin, and gave them to Parisina to take outside.

While she was gone Pat's condition worsened. She kept checking her forehead with a small makeup mirror, and the lines were still there. You'd think that being professional, intelligent women with cameras at our disposal, we would've taken pictures of her forehead or even called for a doctor. But it didn't even cross our minds. Somehow the idea of dialing 911 for pyramids on the forehead was hard to explain, even to ourselves.

So, I took a leap of faith, my first one ever. I picked up the phone and called the man that Q'enqo had mentioned, the one he had offered to introduce me to, the one who could heal from a distance, the one I so callously stood up like the royal bitch I had been throughout this whole trip. Q'enqo had given me the man's phone number, and in that reporter instinct that never fails me, I had written it down. I dialed it. A woman answered. "No, Victor Estrada is not home. He is in Arequipa," she told me.

"Señora, I need his help, there's a very sick woman he needs to see. She has very unusual symptoms and they seem to be getting worse. We're from the States. We don't know who else to turn to. Can you please give me his phone number in Arequipa?" I begged.

The woman was very kind and she obliged. I called the man, and after a short while someone put him on the line. "Hello, you don't know me. Q'enqo told me about you and in fact I agreed to go see you with him the other night and then cancelled on him. I'm sorry I stood you up. But now I need your help. There's this woman . . ."

"What's her name?" he asked, interrupting my pathetic apology."

"Patricia San Pedro."

"Yes, I know. I was expecting your call, put her on," he ordered. It turns out that the San Pedro is a hallucinogenic Peruvian cactus that when specially brewed by a shaman is drunk for vision quests and divination. Victor Estrada was one of those shamans and during a later conversation admitted to having been taking the San Pedro brew that night at the time of my call. A coincidence?

Estrada told Pat that her reaction was a cleansing and that it was good. He told her it was a blessing and that she should pray. He would also keep her in his prayers and, since we were coincidentally taking a plane to Arequipa in four hours, he would come to see her in our hotel later that day. He assured her it would be fine to keep the stones because one day she would heal others with them.

We were so exhausted by then, that his words, strange as they sounded, eased our fears. We all hugged and I followed the others in a prayer that was strange to me. I then stayed with Pat for the next two hours until it was time to leave for the airport. By then, the pyramids on her forehead had finally disappeared.

The hotel in Arequipa was very picturesque. It was nestled in the mountains with a beautiful view of an imposing volcano. There were beautiful, white fluffy llamas with long eyelashes loose in the garden where we sipped hot coca tea. About three hours after our arrival, Victor Estrada paid us a visit. He went with Pat to her room and I went to mine to settle in. There, an iridescent green/blue hummingbird, the first one I'd ever seen, hovered over the flower patch outside my French doors. Peru kept revealing its mysteries to me, and I was just taking it all in.

After a while, Victor Estrada and Pat emerged from her room. He claimed to have cleansed the energy in her body and said she was going to be okay. He also said he wanted to talk to me. He thanked me for calling him so he could help my friend who was apparently embarking on a new spiritual path, thus her reaction to Machu Picchu. "You're wrong, Mr. Estrada. She is not my friend. I just met her," I said, clarifying the meaning to a very maligned and overused word.

"No, you are the one who is wrong, Señorita. It is not that you just met her, it is that you have just recognized her. You have actually known each other for many lifetimes. And you are both here today going through these experiences to jolt you out of your complacency and to help you realize that there is more to life and reality than what you have been led to believe. You have a responsibility to Mother Earth, to the Pachamama. And you will need to work together to help heal her. That is why all of this has happened." I thought this guy was crazy.

Stunned, I tried to make polite conversation. I mentioned the beautiful hummingbird I had just tried to snap into a picture, but that it was too quick for my camera. "The hummingbird that visited you this afternoon represents the wisdom of the ancient ones, the grandfathers and the grandmothers, those on whose shoulders you will need to stand for your journey," he offered without my asking.

"Okay, no more small talk," I muttered to myself.

Victor Estrada left us with more questions than answers, so after lunch Pat and I decided to take a walk through the cobblestone streets of Arequipa to digest all this new food for thought. We strolled without really talking much to each other. We had our boots shined by some kids in the plaza, bought knickknacks in old dusty shops, and would occasionally glance at each other as if to discover that elusive kinship we were told we had once shared. We were mesmerized, shocked, and, literally, in disbelief.

That night, I got the call I had been waiting for at the hotel. President Alberto Fujimori had agreed to an interview. He would pick me up upon my arrival at the airport in Lima and fly me in his personal army helicopter back to the Andes where he would be conducting business. I could hang out with him all day. He would deliver me back in time to make my midnight flight home.

I got back to the States filled with an unshakeable need to decipher my new "oraculo." For the first time in my life, I felt I had real evidence that there was more to our reality than meets the eye. Instead of interviewing others about their own life experiences, I was undergoing an epiphany of my own. It was the first time I actually felt the presence of God, as evidenced in the notes I jotted down in a journal I began to keep six months later, upon my first of many returns to the Peruvian Andes.

JOURNAL: TUESDAY, OCTOBER 18, 1994

I'm back in Machu Picchu at the Pachamama stone. I again felt her power. My heart started racing, my legs started shaking, and I had to actually gasp for air. I sat in front of her and asked her to embrace me, to accept me as the daughter who returns to her mother. I thanked her for speaking to my soul. Evening turned into night. I didn't feel afraid of being alone in the vastness of my mountains. I felt I was in the presence of God. I told her, "God, I feel you with me."

I could've slept alone in those ruins tonight. They're mine. I'm theirs. I feel them. They energize me. I need them. I love them. They love me.

I've been back to Peru more than half a dozen times since that first working trip. I've met many wise men and women who have helped me grow spiritually. And I've produced three independent documentaries about shamanism, including one where the Q'ero tribe, who call themselves the true descendants of the Incas, revealed a five-hundred-year-old prophecy for the new millennium in front of my cameras.

It was with the help of some of these wise friends that I believe I helped my father die with dignity and liberate his spirit. They have taught me how to unleash incredible powers to affect quick and resolute conclusions to personal problems and traumas.

They are not what you may want to call dabblers into the occult. They don't believe their knowledge should be kept hidden, and they share it willingly with anyone who seeks it, with an impeccability of intent. They may not be scientific, but it is precisely their alienation from a Western belief system that allows them to modify a reality we are too conditioned to think of as set in stone. It's taken me almost a decade to embrace this new paradigm. But the different manifestations of evidence I've witnessed through my personal research are now too overwhelming to ignore.

As foretold by Victor Estrada, Patricia San Pedro and I have become the best of friends and we continue to learn more about the powerful ancient rituals of the Indian communities we now hold in much higher esteem. We haven't yet figured out how to help the Pachamama on a large scale. But we have become practitioners of some of these old traditions that continue to enrich our lives and feed our souls.

I now pray often and with the true conviction that my prayers will be answered. I have made a 180-degree turn in my belief system and I no longer believe in coincidence but in destiny. Was it my destiny to live through these incredible experiences so that I may one day tell this story to my two beautiful children? It especially warms my heart and brings a twinkle to my eye when, every once in a while, for no apparent reason, they just call me *mamita*.

Knock on Wood

SARA

A light rain falls as we walk up to the synagogue. It is Rosh Hashanah, the Jewish New Year, and we are arriving on Saturday morning at the Miami Beach temple we have been coming to for the past three years.

This year is different. A line of well-dressed people curls around the building as we wait to enter. The security precautions are taking a while. Nobody complains. We just snake the line around like one at a Disney World attraction so everyone will have cover and the old ladies with their High Holiday hairdos won't get *farklempt*.

The rain is strange, since the sun is shining brightly and there are no clouds in the sky. Yet it is oddly appropriate, given the mood. Our bags are searched and we are wanded. No one speaks; just a grateful smile to the security men. I present my identification to show that . . . what? I am who I say I am? I have a Jewish last name? Or to provide an accurate list in case . . . God forbid . . . something happens.

It is not such an unreasonable thought. The Jewish Federation has put ads in the local papers for weeks advertising High Holiday services. They are as good as a target that declares, "Here are the Jews, all in one place, and all dressed up, too." It is days before the first anniversary of September 11, and tensions are high.

Rosh Hashanah is a comforting holiday. It is meant to be joyous, a celebration of the New Year, but it also begins a ten-day period of introspection and repentance. Each year, we do the same things, say the same prayers, and tell the same stories. It is pleasing to hear the words again.

The traditions are so strong they may as well be superstitions. We always eat an apple slice dipped in honey so we will have a sweet new year. We eat challah—the bread usually eaten on the Sabbath— baked round instead of braided, in a wish for the coming year to roll around smoothly. I am superstitious, so I make sure I do these things. Why take a chance?

"On Rosh Hashanah it is written, and on Yom Kippur it is sealed." According to Jewish faith, our faith is determined at the beginning of the year. Who will live, and who will die. Who will prosper, and who will falter. I think back to the people who died on September 11, 2001, and wonder if their fate was already sealed a year before their deaths. I remember Rosh Hashanah last year, just a few days after the tragedy, when everyone asked, "Where was God?" Was he just watching a fate that had been predetermined?

Every year, the rabbi reads the same story from the Torah on Yom Kippur. It is the story of Abraham, who was ready to sacrifice his son Isaac because God told him to. His faith was so strong he asked no questions. An angel stopped him from killing Isaac because Abraham had proved his devotion by his intent.

These people—the terrorists who kill us—do it in the name of their God, just like Abraham. Isn't there some crazy irony in that?

"May you be inscribed in the Book of Life for a year of health, peace, and contentment."

I knock on wood. The old ladies would say "God willing" and spit three times. The rabbi speaks of peace in Israel. I knock again. An end to terror. Knock, knock. I don't know who I think I am that my little knock could change world events, but I bang away. Most people believe the custom of knocking on wood is a Christian custom that comes from banging on the wood of the cross; that irony is not lost on me either.

The fact is I have been knocking on wood much more this past year than ever before. I've developed inconspicuous ways to do my knocking so my husband won't notice. And I'll knock on anything that resembles wood and even things that don't. I am frightened.

The images of 9/11 haunt me. In particular, the photos of people jumping to their deaths rather than being burned alive. What a choice to make. What a way to die. Today, in the temple, I wonder if this is my day, if I will see the explosion coming, if it will be painless. I look around at the people who would go with me. Where is the nearest exit?

The Jews, as a people, have always been persecuted, and this persecution is the genesis for most of our holidays. The Jews escape the Egyptians and call it Passover. The Maccabees win the war against the powerful Greek armies and Hanukah is born. One hundred or one thousand years from today, will there be a holiday celebrating peace in the Middle East?

I visited Israel once, about five years ago. Although I was warned, the sight of the soldiers walking through the city with their automatic weapons sent a shock through my system. The gentleman I had dinner with told me he had fought in the Israeli army so that his son wouldn't have to; it was to no avail. Every time the phone rang, his wife tensed appreciably, afraid it would be bad news of her grown-up baby, now a military man. The guns were everywhere: at the mall, on the street, at the beach. And now, a meal at an outdoor café or a ride on a city bus could be your last.

The rabbi concludes the service, and the congregation proclaims, as it does every year, "Next year in Jerusalem."

Knock on wood.

Death Rituals

MERCEDES

I arrived at the hospice late at night after work. As I walked in, my mother informed me, in hushed tones, that the doctor had made a final prognosis. My father would not make it through the night. Mami had been watching over his light coma for several days now and it seemed that he would not come out of it. I approached the bed and kissed his hollow and blistered cheeks, noticing that he was running a very high fever. The tall, handsome, proud man I had always adored was but a shadow of himself, reduced to an almost skeletal state. We had disconnected him from all life-sustaining machines, and as per our orders, no food or medicine would be administered anymore.

After about a half hour of watching Papi lying in his deathbed, I went home and placed a determined phone call to Peru. The time had come to help my father die and I was determined to turn around the atheist in him and have him embrace the spirit world before crossing over. My life-altering experience while visiting Machu Picchu had thrust me into an exploration of the spiritual. For months I had been training with shamans from the Andes who taught me how to perform healings and death rites. I was now determined to use my newfound knowledge and inspiration to help my dad on his journey to the other side.

The man I reached on the other end of the line was one of these specialists. He was a celebrated anthropologist, a Ph.D. and a professor at the University of Cuzco. He was also an Andean priest, and since he would balk at my calling him a shaman, I guess I could translate what he does as someone who works with the energies of the body to heal while still fiercely practicing the Catholic faith, attending mass almost every day, and earning the nickname "the monk."

Dr. Juan Nuñez del Prado listened gravely to my concerns. He imparted very specific instructions on how to connect with my father and help his spirit transition into the next world. He also gave me a stern warning: "Do not," he insisted, "tell your father to die . . . just teach him the process." I, of course, didn't profess to know the process myself. "Trust your instincts," he assured me. "It's the *intent* that's more important than showing him how."

I returned to the hospital armed with my mesa, a small hand-woven cloth filled with power objects. A teacher or mentor will usually pass these objects on to a shamanism apprentice, or the student can select or create his or her own. I had only collected a few rocks in about six months' worth of research on the subject. Some of them had been given to me by Dr. Nuñez del Prado. They were supposed to be "charged" with his healing powers and those of the other healers who had owned them before him.

When I went back to the hospital, nothing had changed. I told my mom I was about to conduct a sacred ritual for Papi and since she is Catholic, and might consider what I was about to do a pagan ritual, she did not have to be present. Mami insisted on staying, and I went to work. I cleansed my dad's luminous body with my mesa and then I tried to connect with his soul. I spoke to him without words and I told him that for the most part, dying, just as anything in life, was an act of choice and if he chose to die he could do so, on his own terms. I explained to him how his soul could leave his body and I made sure he knew I was not asking him to die. After about an hour or two, his fever subsided and I went home.

The following morning, a Saturday, I went to visit Papi early. I entered his room quietly. And, though my father was nearly deaf, he seemed to hear me and focused his eyes on me. "I was in a very dark place," he said, to my amazement. "I'm so glad to be out," he added. I was flabbergasted! He wasn't just speaking. He was coherent. The cancer in his lungs had spread terminally to his brain and he hadn't uttered a lucid statement in weeks. It was a miracle!

I rushed to his side, hugged and kissed him, and wasted no time in sharing with him my amazing experiences in the *altiplanos* (highlands) of Peru. I told him that I, until recently as staunch an atheist as he, had made an incredible discovery. I hadn't necessarily found God, in the Western sense of the word, but I had found a very benign, giving, and loving spirit world in the rich tradition of the indigenous peoples of South America. This revelation had changed the inner core of my being and I now believed that he was not just about to die in the pure organic sense but he was about to be born into the spirit world. I then begged him to trust me enough to believe that. To my second surprise of the day, he did.

And then we did something I hadn't done since I was a child at the behest of my mother, and certainly something Papi and I had never done together. We prayed. We prayed for him, we prayed for us, we prayed for our family, and we prayed for his eternal journey.

At the end of the day, secure in the knowing that he had genuinely embraced all I had asked him to, I went home relieved.

Much to the doctor's surprise, my father didn't die that day, or the day after that. His ability to reason and understand lasted for several days, and in that time my mother and sisters and I seized this golden window of opportunity to say good-bye, to mend old wounds, and especially to tell our father how much we loved him and to thank him for the many ways in which he had contributed to enriching our lives and shaping our characters.

Almost three months later, having regained full control of his bodily functions, Papi got up one morning, had breakfast, took a shower, went to the window, and according to a nurse, called for my mother, sisters, and me, and then lay down and died. We weren't there to help usher him into his new life. But we know he died with dignity, on his own terms, the way I had prayed that he would.

In those precious weeks we were able to steal him away from death, he told us of the visits his dead relatives had started paying him. He told us how his parents and siblings were waiting for him in a happy place and how they looked healthy and well pressed in white linen.

Before he was cremated I performed an ancient death rite on my father to help his spirit leave his body. We spread his ashes in the waters of Miami's Biscayne Bay, and I felt certain that I had done all within my power to help my father die and attain peace.

A year later, my conviction was confirmed when, on All Saints Day, after repeatedly dreaming of my dad for several days and deciding he was trying to reach me, I felt compelled to perform one last ritual for him.

In the ancient Mexican tradition of preparing a feast to celebrate the life of one's dead family member, I decided to make an offering to my dad, albeit a small one. I went to a local Latin grocery store to buy some supplies, a can of guava shells in syrup and some cream cheese, which make for a traditional Cuban dessert. I also picked up a cigar.

Right at twilight, I went to a deserted stretch of Palm Beach and drew a protective circle in the sand with my foot. I opened the contents of my grocery bag and poured them inside, lit up the cigar, and invited my father's spirit to come and enjoy. I smoked the cigar for a while. I knew it was his favorite, so I let the rich thick smoke permeate my balmy surroundings. The soothing sounds of the crashing waves and the smell of seawater filled me with childhood memories. My father had loved the sea and taught me to revere it as well.

Eventually, I walked away and sat on a seawall, still thinking of my dad and talking to him in a whisper. Without realizing it, I began to feel giddy in a strange way that is easy to recognize but impossible to describe. And then I began spontaneously to sing a tango. It was a familiar tune to me, because my father had composed the melancholy lyrics for a lovesick friend when he was a young man in Cuba. But I had never learned the words. Nevertheless, that night, I sang "La Morochita" as if an invisible TelePrompTer (the electronic script machine that anchors read to deliver the news) was showing me the words. I sang it to the wind, I sang it to the ocean, and I'm convinced I sang it with my father.

And as I sat there, drunk with happiness and song and feeling truly connected to Papi, a couple walked up the beach to inform me they had been watching my strange behavior.

They said that as I left the circle on the sand full of sweet dessert and cigar ashes, a soft sparkling whirlwind seemed to have entered the space and they were wondering what it was. I just laughed and claimed to have no idea. But their observation confirmed what I already knew, that Papi had come to revel and join in my feast and, in a delightful reciprocity, he fed me the nourishing words of his beautiful tango. I thanked my wonderful father for my life, and his, for his guidance, for his company, and I told him how much I love him and miss him and I bade him good-bye again, this time without the tears.

Someone to Watch Over Me

TAMMI

They say that men are from Mars and women are from Venus. For most of my life I believed that, until my very best friend married a guy named Skip. Dana had been my friend since the fourth grade, and though her husband and I never had a "thing" for each other, there was no question we came from the same planet. We were so much alike, cut from the same cloth . . . a little too self-important, not very patient with others, set in our ways, and happiest when we were in control. We had both been competitive athletes and winning was very important to both of us. So, whether it was tennis or poker, or all the other unimportant things we took so seriously, it was always more about the destination than the journey. He was the brother I always wanted, even though I sometimes wanted desperately to bash in his teeth.

Dana and Skip were our closest married friends. Each of our spouses was content to let us chauffeur them through life, and Skip and I always fought about the best ways to get there. I made fun of his temper when his wife wouldn't dare. He'd hassle me when I was late and would piss me off by refusing to take our single friends out with us on Saturday nights ("why don't they get their own lives?" he'd grumble). We'd spend hours playfully at each other's throats, and both would cringe when his wife or my husband would compare us both. If we were a couple, there's no doubt we'd have killed each other, with pleasure. But we were the very best of friends. Not even my own husband understood my quirkiness quite the way Skip did. This guy "got" me, warts and all, and although he didn't often tell me how cool he thought I was, he told everyone else, and that was good enough for me.

Skip and Dana's life was finally where they wanted it to be. They had endured seven painful miscarriages before adopting two kids and although their marriage had had its share of ups and downs, it was settling in just a hair shy of nirvana. That was just about the time mine was falling apart. But Skip became my coach, my cheerleader, and the big brother who was going to help me survive an inevitable divorce. He was more than happy to do all my dirty work, which included trying to map out a financial plan to help me stay afloat in my attempt to fly solo.

It was a lousy time in my life, and even on those desperate days when I felt like I might turn back and stick with my marriage for the kids' sake, my buddy was there pushing me on. I hoped that if I made it out of the divorce in one piece, I'd find someone just like him, though a little less of a pain in the ass.

Skip liked my husband a lot, but he was so sure that my real soul mate was just around the corner waiting to love me, he even pledged to help me find him. He was going to be my matchmaker. That was January 31. I made him promise to try and help locate this mystery man by Valentine's Day, and he did.

And so on February 14, a few hours after Skip called to ask my advice about lingerie for Dana, just as I was feeling sorry for my lonely-ass self, celebrating the Day of Love with my daughters, my parents, and Chinese takeout, I got the call.

Skip had had a massive heart attack and died while cooking dinner for Dana and his daughters. That generous heart of his had just stopped beating. Just like that. On Valentine's Day. My best buddy took so many hearts with him that day. He was only forty-one.

Skip had touched so many people's lives during his short time here, more than a thousand people showed up to honor their friend and pay their final respects. But a couple of weeks after he was laid to rest, all had bailed and life had to go on.

The months that followed are still a blur. Dana was my best friend, and I was doing my best to help her hold down the fort, but I felt useless. They were all in so much pain. I had lost my friend, too, but that didn't seem important in the scheme of things. My children were devastated by Skip's loss, and were still reeling from my breakup with their daddy. Time didn't seem to be healing anything. Reality sucked.

"Let's do something to honor Skip," I muttered to a dazed Dana a few weeks after the funeral. Earlier that year, Skip had presided over a program at our kids' school, and I thought we could memorialize him and raise some money to keep it going. Without Skip, the program was doomed.

I hoped planning the event would fill the black hole growing inside me, and I was puzzled by the enormity of my emptiness. But looking back on that terrible time, I suppose I was mourning the loss of my marriage at the same time I was grieving for my friend.

I had never organized such a big fund-raiser, but because everyone loved Skip, the help came pouring in. And the dollars too. Our first annual Skip-a-Thon was a huge success.

But after all the money was counted and the adrenaline rush dissipated, my body and soul still ached. I had been so busy struggling to keep Dana from crumbling, I had forgotten what a source of strength Skip had been for me during this troubling time in my life. I knew it was time to move on, so the week after the Skip-a-Thon, I hired the divorce lawyer Skip had recommended, and then I called the Cuban massage therapist who'd shown up out of the blue to volunteer his services at our Skip-a-Thon. It was my first step toward healing.

The massage was fabulous. It was my first indulgence in months, but apparently my muscles were so tense, when it was over, Emilio began to interrogate me about the pace of my life. I didn't even know this guy, but he had no problem letting me know that in his professional opinion, if I didn't slow down and relax, I too would drop. He was an interesting character, this Emilio guy, though I couldn't help but wonder why he was rubbing shoulders for a living.

We talked for hours, sitting face-to-face at the edge of the massage table, as he shared his fascinating tales of life as an engineer in the Cuban navy, being a student in Soviet Russia, and pretending to live as a Communist. His story was so fascinating, I got lost in the details as he shared his dreams of freedom and ultimate clandestine escape. When I finally got up from the table, I was a little embarrassed that I was still wrapped in a towel. I hadn't even noticed.

I barely slept that night. I felt Skip's presence everywhere. I don't usually believe in all that woo-woo gibberish, but it was hard to ignore as I stared at the ceiling, not sure if the eerie echoes were real or imagined. I had tragically lost two other young friends the year before Skip died, and as hard as I looked for signs from them, I'd never gotten any messages. In my book, when you're dead, you're dead. That was the extent of my spirituality.

But for days, I kept hearing Skip's voice around me. At night, I would put the girls to bed and sit outside with a glass of wine, trying to make some sense of all this weirdness. I'd gaze at the sky and be transfixed by the clouds. But no matter where I looked, I would see Skip's face. With the beard, and without it. I wasn't sure if I was losing it or becoming an alcoholic.

Then, a few days later, Emilio called. Just to say thanks for listening to his story, and for being a nice person, he told me. It was good to hear his voice, though I hadn't thought of him since the night of my massage. I had been married for fifteen years and had no interest in men at that time. Too much healing to do. But after I hung up, I realized something made me want to talk to this man again. So I scheduled another massage.

Emilio and I connected that night in almost an ethereal way. He asked a lot of questions about my friend Skip, and he spoke about being drawn to me with a peculiar pull that he couldn't quite explain. Funny, I felt it too, and over the next few months, we ran with it, spending more and more time together, as he shared his spiritual beliefs with me, opening my mind up to stuff I would've laughed at before Skip died.

Emilio talked about his childhood, growing up around people who believed in the afterlife. His parents, well-respected pillars of the Havana community, actually held séances in their home in Cuba, and as a boy, Emilio would listen from the other room as strange voices took over and delivered messages through the bodies of those present. As he grew up, he was invited to participate in these gatherings, and when he told me those bizarre stories, I wasn't sure what to make of them. I thought he was a little off, but he was growing on me, and before I knew it, we were falling in love.

Emilio always believed it was Skip who was engineering our love affair from above, and he claims to have felt his presence at some pretty awkward moments. I really tried to give credibility to his thoughts, though clearly I was a skeptic. The real truth: I didn't give a damn who sent this fabulous man to me; I was just thrilled to have him in my life. And because I didn't want Emilio to think I wasn't enlightened, I pretended to believe. Maybe I was even starting to, just a little, though I couldn't be sure.

But timing is a funny thing. Just as I was beginning to question the things we cannot feel or see, I received an assignment to interview a psychic who was taking some grieving families on a week-long cruise to help them get in touch with their deceased loved ones. Apparently, water is supposed to be a conduit of energy, which is why they were doing this on a cruise ship. I was assigned to question this clairvoyant and the passengers before and after their journey, and the story was meant to show that grief knows no bounds.

The morning of our meeting, the psychic called from the airport to tell me she'd be late, refusing to take the port bus with the passengers for some unexplainable reason. Just as we got word that the bus had been in a fender bender on the highway, the psychic's taxi pulled up. She shook her head knowingly as she got out of the cab, muttering something about how her dead friends never fail her.

A few minutes later, as the interview was about to begin, the psychic turned to my videographer and ordered him to shut off the camera, claiming her "energy force" was capable of messing with the complicated circuitry of video cameras. I motioned to the frustrated photographer to do as she asked, and almost immediately, the woman's eyes began to glaze over.

First, she asked me who JD was, and I was instantly taken aback. Skip's real name was Jack David, JD for short. She told me he was talking to her, right then and there, surrounded by seven babies and he wanted me to know something. The hair on my neck stood up when I remembered the seven miscarriages he and Dana had endured. Startled by her comments, I moved in a little closer as this psychic took my hand, pierced me with her gaze, and passed along this message. JD, she said, needed me to know that although he had to go, he'd kept his promise by sending me exactly what I needed. Huh? Could he mean Emilio? Why couldn't I see that? she asked, presumably on Skip's behalf. She finished by saying that JD wanted me to know that he was OK now because someone he loved had pulled him to the other side. His time on earth was over. That's what she told me. And that was it.

Then this psychic threw back her head, as if she was shaking water from her ears. The film that looked like it had covered her eyes immediately cleared up, and she snapped her fingers at the photographer, signaling him to crank up the camera and let our work begin. Just like that.

So, in as professional a manner as I could, I conducted the interview, then hurriedly said good-bye to this woman whose confusing revelations had rocked my foundation. I immediately reached for the cell phone.

Emilio wasn't surprised by any of this, more at my continued skepticism. But in the months that followed, I did take Skip's advice and let my guard down, and Emilio and I are now on the road to happily ever after. And it's nice to know we have an angel watching over us.

I have started to pay more attention to the things we cannot see or hear. I was recently sent to Jamaica on assignment to videotape a haunted golf course for a Halloween-related story. This golf course was built on the grounds of an old sugar plantation where, legend has it, the owner, Annie Palmer, had dabbled in voodoo and killed her three husbands, burying them on the property. There are graveyards all over that golf course, containing the remains of hundreds of slaves who worked on the plantation for centuries. We were there to interview the caddies, who claim that ghosts come out at night, and to shoot pictures of the spooky place.

After we checked it all out and mapped out our plans to videotape the golf course the following day, the entire resort had a power outage, and even the generators couldn't light up the place. The electric company in Montego Bay couldn't figure out why, but the local residents were convinced we had angered Annie Palmer and warned us about waking up the spirits. We laughed. They didn't.

The next morning, sitting by the beach before our work began, a colleague and I chuckled at the apparent absurdity of the Annie Palmer myth, but just in case, I looked to the sky and asked for a sign from above. Out loud, I wondered, "If there's any truth to any of this spirit stuff, send me a message . . . something that could make me believe." Nothing.

The water was calm and peaceful without even a boat dotting the landscape. Nikki and I continued to talk about our plans for the afternoon, when I looked up to see that a boat had sailed into the harbor, seemingly out of nowhere. The name painted on the boat? Skip. Nikki freaked. And so did I.

Maybe my angel was looking the other way later that afternoon when I slipped in the cemetery on the golf course and tore a tendon in my knee. The locals say Annie Palmer pushed me because I didn't believe.

I came home in a wheelchair to the man of my dreams, who didn't even flinch when I told him how it happened. He only wanted to know if I was satisfied yet, or if I still needed more evidence of a Higher Power. This man really was sent from heaven.

Do I really believe that I found true love with the help of my dead friend? That his spirit and eternal love burst through the heavens and delivered me the soul mate I've waited for my whole life? I'm still not sure I fully understand the whole meaning of our existence and what follows, but don't tell Emilio. He thinks I do.

The Miami Bombshells

On *Dish and Tell*

We didn't sign on to "dish and tell" when we first began meeting. The true confessions were served up much later, only after we felt safe enough to spill all our beans. As the stories on our plates became more mouthwatering and the dishing more telling, we instinctively closed ranks to protect and honor one another's stories, before we even thought about putting them on paper.

Our ability to unconditionally trust one another became the icing on the cake. That safety net is what ultimately gave us the purpose to stay together, and justified stealing precious time away from our family and friends, who didn't always understand.

Of course, as you know by now, we are a feisty bunch and, in the beginning, were pretty intolerant of one another's differences.

Because we are all so opinionated, self-absorbed, and set in our convictions, there were times we wanted to kill one another but knew we had come together for our own good (at least that's what Pat kept reminding us). These gatherings were supposed to nurture our souls, but sometimes our egos got in the way.

We dealt with our disparate personalities by breaking into sub-groups to help each other cope with the rest. A few of us even threatened to quit the Bombshells when our differences became unbearable and, in the midst of our already overscheduled lives, the group just didn't seem worth it.

Ultimately, our devotion to the Miami Bombshells, as a vehicle to decompress, transformed itself into an unwavering love for one another. And now that we know how to push one another's buttons and survive the backlash that follows, we admit, in a muggy Miami minute, we'd dish and tell all over again.

Patricia

Friendship has always been one of the most valuable and precious commodities in my life. Bringing five of my best and wittiest friends together to form the Miami Bombshells has turned into one of my grandest blessings. It's hard to believe that our lives are now scattered all over these pages. It's also a little scary, but cathartic at the same time. Our Bombshell Circle has offered support, encouragement, trust for one another, and for some, the courage they've needed to make changes in their lives. I think we're all the better for it. My wish is that, through this book, we've shown you that you're not alone. I hope we've empowered you, at least a little, to find the strength you need to make the changes in your life that will bring you greater peace of mind and happiness.

Sara

Miami Bombshell meetings provide unconditional support and a place to air my most personal thoughts, the ones that frighten and make you wonder if you're crazy. But, because of the open atmosphere, and the fact that often a Bombshell meeting is the only place I'm comfortable talking about some issues, the Bombshells sometimes only get to see my dark side. However, being able to write down and talk about experiences that molded me has been like cheap therapy (that comes with wine and chocolate to boot!). I can't imagine where I'd be without it.

Lydia

Emotionally, this endeavor has caused me to release inner feelings that I had never divulged to anyone in my entire life. The Bombshell setting allowed me to speak to virtual strangers about events in my life that had everlasting impact. Simultaneously, I questioned the integrity of the women with whom I was sharing all my inner secrets and their loyalty to me (a stranger) in keeping these thoughts within the confines of their souls and minds. We have come much further than I had ever expected and I am glad that I stuck through this long, difficult, and, ultimately, joyous process.

Annie

Being a part of the Miami Bombshell group has been a completely new experience for me. It happened at a time when my children are older and all of a sudden I found time for myself, even though it often felt like I had to move mountains to get to the meetings. My family met my involvement with mixed reviews. They were accustomed to having me at their disposal 24/7, and they weren't thrilled that I would get up and go whenever the Bombshells called. Toward the end of the project, I learned to develop more self-confidence. Honestly, at times I didn't feel I was in the other women's league. But now I *love* being a Miami Bombshell!

Tammi

I always dreamed about what it would be like to be a Bombshell. Funny that I had to wait till middle age, when I could barely find my navel, to learn that it all comes from within. We didn't believe our grandmothers when they told us that youth is wasted on the young, and it wasn't until I met my fellow Bombshells that I truly believed this. Each Miami Bombshell—incredible women, brilliant in their own right and as *farklempt* as I am in their personal lives—has taught me to value the wisdom we've worked so hard to build as mothers and career women over the past two decades. And to understand the notion that having it all is merely an oxymoron. That is what being a Bombshell is all about. I only hope that from me they have received a fraction of what they have given.

Mercedes

As a public person I've tried very hard to keep my life private. Opening up to the Miami Bombshells has been an act of trust, something I value deeply. As the resident Miami Bombshell diva, my friends have bestowed on me an undeserved dose of hero worship that consistently keeps me from feeling imperfect, affected, accented, or out of place. In them I've found a sisterhood ready for a catfight or a hug, depending on the rigor that will keep me most honest. Every diva should have such backup singers, because being a Bombshell is the BOMB!

Why Create Your Own Bombshell Circle?

Reduce your stress. OK, we can't really take your stress away—only you can do that—but we can encourage you to spend a couple of hours doing something just for you.

Leave the guilt behind. Your Bombshell sisters will talk you out of feeling guilty, even if it only lasts as long as the chocolate high.

Be more self-assured. There's nothing more confidence-building than finding out you're not the only one crashing and that maybe you're not drowning as fast as everyone around you seems to be. After all, misery loves company.

Learn to say <u>no</u>. They say stress comes when your gut says no and your mouth says "I'll be glad to." Say yes to good friends, good wine, and good chocolate, but practice saying no when it comes to overextending yourself and taking on tasks that aren't really necessary.

Bare your soul. Secrets need airing so they don't eat away at your insides. Your Bombshell sisters will take them to the grave, and you'll be amazed at how you feel when you set them free.

How to Create Your Own Bombshell Circle

1. Invite friends who don't know one another. You are the common denominator, like Pat is for our group. Sometimes it's easier to say things to complete strangers who have no preconceived notions or expectations of you. And you'll have the added benefit of creating a new support system.

2. Wine and chocolate are not required, but are highly recommended. Real food is optional.

3. Set up an initial meeting to get you started. Have some stories ready to share, and ask your invited guests to do the same.

4. Try to meet at least once a month. Block it on your Palm Pilot or BlackBerry as if it is a business meeting.

5. Come with an open mind. If you're really prepared to shed your mask, amazing things will happen.

6. Cell phones off! You deserve a couple of hours without the phone ringing. Take a break.

7. Have fun! It's not always about sharing. Often it's about gossiping, or shopping. Use the time the way you need it, so you can leave the Bombshell meeting feeling better than when you arrived.

Now that you've read all about us, we want to hear about you, your life, your struggles and achievements, and your own circle of friends. Which Bombshell do you identify with the most? What stories did you really relate to? Please, stay in touch with us:

www.miamibombshells.com